# GUIDED BY GOD

## ORDINARY AND CHARISMATIC WAYS OF DISCOVERING GOD'S WILL

PAT COLLINS C.M.

First published in 2015 by
New Life Publishing, Luton
Bedfordshire LU4 9HG

*Imprimatur: Most Reverend Peter Doyle*
*Bishop of Northampton, 23 December 2014*
*Nihil obstat: Monsignor Kevin McGinnell*
*Censor Liborum*
*The Imprimatur and Nihil obstat are declarations that this work is considered to be free from doctrinal or moral error. It is not implied that those who granted the same agree with the contents, opinion, or statements expressed.*



British Library Cataloguing in Publication Data
A catalogue record for this book is available
from the British Library

**ISBN 978 1 903623 87**



Typesetting by Goodnews Books,
Luton, UK www.goodnewsbooks.net
Printed and bound in Great Britain

# Guided by God

## Ordinary and Charismatic Ways of Discovering God's Will

Pat Collins C.M.

'Thy will be done, on earth as it is in heaven.'
*(Mat. 6:10)*

'Those whose steps are guided by the Lord
may stumble, but they will never fall,
for the Lord holds their hand.'
*(Ps. 37: 23)*

'Lead kindly light, amid the encircling gloom;
lead thou me on!
...I do not ask to see the distant scene
- one step enough for me.'
*(Bl. John Henry Newman)*

# CONTENTS

# FOREWORD

One of the questions I am most often asked is 'How do I hear from God? I want to do what he's asking me, but how can I find out what that is?'

In this excellent book, helpfully written in a style somewhere between an academic and a popular approach, Fr. Pat Collins helps the reader to appreciate that God is constantly revealing himself and his purposes to us in a variety of ways, but that in order to hear him clearly we must first die to self and focus more on what God is doing.

Acceptance of a supernatural realm is important for a full understanding of 'Guided by God', as the author looks carefully at both the normal and the more unusual ways in which God speaks to us and guides us. Taking us from the Biblical and Greek world view, through the atheist/agnostic, the liberal Christian, and the non-charismatic to the Charismatic-Pentecostal world-view, the book is informed throughout by a distinctively charismatic perspective. Having said that, those who may not naturally be drawn to this point of view will still find enormous benefits in the wide-ranging insights on God's guidance the author brings to his book.

In encouraging everyone to read 'Guided by God' I can do no better than to quote from the author's Conclusion in these words:

'If I were asked to identify the greatest single cause of the current crisis in the Church I would reply that it is due to the fact that so many of its leaders and members are guided by human thinking rather than the mind and will of God. If we desire to see revival and renewal, e.g. by means of the new evangelisation, it will only come about when people are docile to the guidance of the Spirit in the ordinary and unusual ways which I have tried to describe in this book.'

Fr. Pat Collins has written many books and I am sure I have read all of them, but I can say with confidence that this is the best he has written. His balance between an academic and a popular approach, which he maintains throughout, means that every reader will find benefit and grow in his or her understanding of this important topic. Of everything I have read on divine guidance, this book has been by far the most comprehensive and helpful, packed as it is with a wide range of fascinating quotations and references. I found it difficult to put down and I'm sure you will find the same.

**Charles Whitehead**
**2014**

# INTRODUCTION

In 1971 Ray Stephens had a hit single called, 'Turn your Radio On'. Besides having a catchy tune, it also had meaningful lyrics. At one point they said, 'Don't you know that everyone is a radio receiver... get in touch with God, turn your radio on'. In other words that pop tune was suggesting that just as we can tune in to broadcasts on our radios, so we can tune in to the voice of God in our prayer. Conventional radios usually have three wavelengths, FM, MW, and LW. They are good at picking up stations that are not too far away. However, if a person buys a more sophisticated set with Wi-Fi capacity then he or she can listen to broadcasts from all over the world.

This book will suggest that just as conventional radios can pick up relatively local broadcasts, so in prayer, God has ordinary ways of speaking to us, such as the voice of conscience, the scriptures, inspirations and promptings of various kinds. But just as Wi-Fi can pick up internet broadcasts from all the continents, so too God has exceptional ways of speaking to us, such as visions, dreams, and prophetic messages. In the way radio listeners can augment conventional radio by buying a set that includes internet capacity, Christians can add to the ordinary ways in which God can communicate with them by opening themselves to messages that are received by means of the charisms of revelation. When one reads the Acts of the Apostles and New Testament epistles, it is impressive to see the charismatic ways in which God communicated with the first Christians. In his book, *Surprised by the Voice of God,* scripture scholar Jack Deere asked, 'does the book of Acts represent normal Christianity? He answered in the affirmative while saying, 'The very same thing could happen to you if you gave God a chance to speak to you as he did to those in Acts'. However, N.T. Wright adds a cautionary note when he says in *Paul and the Faithfulness of God,* 'Certainly Luke has made no attempt to portray the Apostolic mission in terms of constant supernatural guidance, though that kind of intervention does happen from time to time.'

British and Irish people have endured famines in 1623 and 1845 respectively. Now in the twenty-first century, like people in many other Western countries, they are suffering again, this time from a famine of 'hearing of the word of God' (Amos 8:11). It is obvious in a number of ways.

Firstly, in 1 Peter 4:11 we read, 'whoever preaches, let it be with the words of God.' St Augustine explained, 'Vainly does the preacher utter the word of God exteriorly unless he prayerfully listens to it interiorly.' Pope Francis echoed that sentiment when he said in par 151 of *Evangelii Gaudium,* 'If the preacher does not devote time to pray with the word, then indeed he will be a false prophet, a fraud, a shallow imposter.' Furthermore, St Ignatius of Antioch wrote, 'Close your ears if anyone preaches to you without speaking of Jesus Christ.' Sad to say, on the basis of that criterion churchgoers would often have to close their ears during homilies.

Secondly, Christian leaders, like Nehemiah of old, need to have a vision that has been revealed to them by God and not discovered by merely human effort. It seems to me that at nearly every level of church life, there has been a failure, with some notable exceptions, to offer effective leadership due to a lack of a God given vision. As the King James version of the Bible puts it, 'Where there is no vision, the people perish' (Prov 29:18) and again, 'For lack of guidance a people falls' (Prov 11:14).

Thirdly, when those who do practice their faith attend Christian meetings they usually begin with a formulaic type of prayer, but all too often there is a failure afterwards, to consciously seek the presence, word and will of God in a discerning and heartfelt way. Instead, the people discuss and decide things in a purely human manner while presuming that God is guiding them. Because, they often fail to hear the voice of the Lord, many Christian individuals and groups make well intentioned decisions and get involved in conscientious pastoral and evangelising efforts which, all too often, bear disappointingly little fruit. This is probably due to the fact, as Ps 127:1 reminds us, 'Unless the Lord builds the house, those who build it labour in vain.'

Fourthly, though still nominally Christian, large numbers of people have drifted away from the Church and its moral teachings. As a result they are less inclined to pray either alone or together. Consequently, they are not as attuned to God. As the Lord said in Jer 2:13, 'My people have committed two sins: They have forsaken me, the spring of living water, and have dug their own cisterns, broken cisterns that cannot hold water.' That seems so obvious in Western countries like Britain and Ireland where many people have wandered from the living God to revere the golden calf of possessions, popularity, and power. Many others have had recourse to New Age spirituality, and occult, Gnostic and superstitious practices such as astrology, palmistry, spiritualism, contacting the dead, consulting mediums, and using a Ouija board or tarot cards in a misguided effort to contact the world of spirits or to gain control over their lives and their futures.

## Dangers of occult guidance

The Judeo-Christian religion has always opposed occult forms of divination. In Ezek 21:21 we get some inkling of how people in Old Testament times engaged in superstitious divination: 'For the king of Babylon will stop at the fork in the road, at the junction of the two roads, to seek an omen: He will cast lots with arrows, he will consult his idols, he will examine the liver.' In Deut 18:10-12, however, these and similar activities are condemned: 'Let no one be found among you who . . . practices divination or sorcery, interprets omens, engages in witchcraft, or casts spells, or who is a medium or spiritualist or who consults the dead. Anyone who does these things is detestable to the Lord.'

Needless to say, the New Testament is equally opposed to the occult. In Acts 16:16-18 we are told how Paul delivered a young fortune teller from an occult spirit. Rev 21:8 warns that: 'those who practice magic arts, the idolaters and all liars - their place will be in the fiery lake of burning sulphur. This is the second death.' These sentiments were echoed in the early Church. For example in par. 3 of the *Didache* (130 A.D.) we read: 'Do not be always looking for omens, my son, for this leads to idolatry. Likewise have nothing to do with witchcraft, astrology, or magic; do not even consent to be a witness of such practices, for they too can all breed idolatry.'

Not surprisingly the contemporary Church is also opposed to any involvement with the occult or divination. As the *Catechism of the Catholic Church* says in pars. 2116-2117, this kind of false religion 'conceals a desire for power over time, history and in the last analysis, other human beings, as well as a wish to conciliate hidden powers. They contradict the honour, respect and loving fear that we owe to God alone.' Clearly, involvement in the occult is sinful because it is opposed to the virtue of religion as complete dependence on the providence and provision of God. Just as Josiah (641–609 BC), a conscientious Jewish king, got rid of mediums, psychics, and household gods (cf. 2 Kings 23:24), so contemporary Christians need to renounce all forms of occult knowledge or guidance.

## Divine Guidance in Prayer

True Christians turn to God for knowledge and guidance, especially in prayer. St. John Damascene (676-749) maintained that, 'Prayer is the raising of one's mind and heart to God or the requesting of good things from God.' While this is a classic description, it could be argued that it is inadequate in so far as it is too one sided. While it describes what the praying person does, it says very little about the all important role of the God who wants to communicate with us. In one of his writings, St Vincent de Paul wrote, 'Prayer is a conversation of the soul with God, a mutual communication in which God interiorly tells the soul what he wishes it to do, and in which the soul tells its God what he himself has taught it to ask for.' Notice how this description sees prayer in relational terms as a conversation, discussion, dialogue, or colloquy. It is true that we raise our minds and hearts to God, but the Lord responds by revealing the divine Self, mind and purposes to us. This book is going to focus, not so much on what the praying person does, as on what God does. I have described what the praying person does in, *Prayer in Practice: A Biblical Approach* and also in *Preparing to Pray: 101 Reflections on Scripture.* Suffice it to say that, the role of the persons who pray is important. Not only do they need to be in touch with the deeper things of their own hearts, they also need to be willing to reveal them to the Lord. There is a preface of the Mass which could be rephrased to read, 'God has no need of our self-revelation, yet our desire to disclose ourselves to the Lord is itself God's gift. Our self-disclosure adds nothing to God's knowledge, but helps us to open our inner selves to receive divine inspirations promptings and revelations.'

## Contemplative attention

Simone Weil (1909-1943), a Jewish mystic, was once asked by a

Dominican priest how he could instruct his pupils to pray. She wrote him a long letter about the importance of fostering the children's ability to pay undivided, self-forgetful attention to whatever they were studying. In her book, *Waiting for God* Weil's thoughts were included in a chapter entitled, 'Reflections on the right use of school studies with a view to the love of God.' Adults can learn to pay sustained attention, of a contemplative kind, by doing concentration exercises. Weil explained, 'Attention consists of suspending our thought, leaving it detached, empty and ready to be penetrated by the object . . . The soul empties itself of all its own contents in order to receive into itself the being it is looking at.' In this connection the words of a Beatles' song come to mind, 'Mother Mary comes to me speaking words of wisdom, 'Let it be'.'

Weil explained that concentration and attention were important where prayer is concerned. 'The quality of attention counts for much in the quality of the prayer,' she wrote because, 'warmth of heart cannot make up for it. It is the highest part of the attention only which makes contact with God, when prayer is intense and pure enough for such a contact to be established; but the whole attention has to be turned towards God.' This kind of attention surrenders wilful control over its awareness of God. Instead, of projecting preconceived ideas and images on to the Lord, it is willing to let God reveal the divine Self and purposes to the receptive person. It is interesting to note that in Greek the word for attention is *epistrophe* which can mean 'conversion.' In other words self-forgetful attention sometimes involves a type of cognitive crucifixion or change, in so far as God can reveal truths that challenge our preconceived ideas, values, beliefs and desires. We need to be willing to die to self in order to listen to God.

## MARY AS OUR MODEL

If there is one person who epitomises the Biblical ideal of contemplative listening, it is Mary the mother of Jesus. She was full of grace from the moment of her conception. Throughout her life, she not only shared the deep things of her heart with God, she was also completely open to receive what God wanted to say to her. On June 1st 2013, Pope Francis said of her, 'Mary knows how to listen to God. But be careful: this is not a simple 'hearing' but a 'listening based on paying attention, a welcoming, an openness toward God. It isn't the distracted manner that we sometimes have when dealing with the Lord or others when we hear their words, but we don't really listen.' The words of Is 50: 4-5 can be applied in a pre-eminent way to her, 'Each morning he wakes me to hear, to listen like a disciple. The Lord Yahweh has opened my ear.'

At the annunciation the angel Gabriel appeared to Mary and brought her the message that she was being invited to become the mother of the promised Messiah through the overshadowing of the Holy Spirit. Mary took that word to heart, believed what it promised, and cooperated by saying, 'be it done to me according to your word' (Lk 1:48). Like any devout Jewish person, she believed what the Lord had promised in Is 55:11, 'my word that goes out from my mouth: It will not return to me empty, but will accomplish what I desire'. No wonder Catholics refer to Mary as their model of faith. In this connection it is worth noting that in par. 51 of his encyclical, *Dominum et Vivificantem,* St. John Paul II could have been describing Mary's prayer of a contemplative kind, when he wrote, 'faith in its deepest essence is the openness of the human heart to the gift: *to God's self-communication in the Holy Spirit.*'

As Jesus grew in age, Mary listened to all he had to say. In doing so she was listening to the very voice of God. As Jesus testified, 'my word is not my own, it is the word of Him who sent me' (Jn 14:24). On one occasion during his public ministry, when Jesus was informed that his mother and his brothers wanted to talk to him, he replied, 'My mother and brothers are those who *hear* God's word and *put it into practice*' (Lk 8:21). On another occasion a woman in the crowd said that the womb that bore Jesus and the breasts that nursed him were blessed. He replied, 'Blessed rather are those who *hear* the word of God and *obey* it!' (Lk 11:28). That being so, we can say with confidence that Mary was *the* model of true discipleship because she was pre-eminent, not only in her desire to listen to the word and will of God, but also in her willingness to carry it out.

## LOVE AS THE CONTEXT FOR DIVINE GUIDANCE

God's will is always loving in nature. Just as the banks of a river channel and direct the flow of water to the ocean, so love channels and directs all forms of divine guidance to the service of God and the neighbour. In Mt 22:37-40, Jesus said, 'Love the Lord your God with all your heart and with all your soul and with all your mind.' This is the first and greatest commandment.

And the second is like it: 'Love your neighbour as yourself.' All the Law and the Prophets hang on these two commandments.' The normal and charismatic forms of divine guidance, which will be discussed in this book are rooted in love, express that love and aim to build up the same love in individuals and the community. So the great commandment provides us with an overall, paradigm or contextual framework for all our reflections.

## GENERAL AIM

Friedrich Heiler (1892-1967) maintained, in his well known book, *Prayer*, that from the beginning Christendom has had a platonic bias which tends to favour an apophatic type faith which goes beyond thought and images. However, there is also a more kataphatic approach of a prophetic kind, which favours images and ideas. Like Heiler, I believe that the latter approach is more authentically Christian. This book will focus on the normal and more unusual ways in which the Lord reveals the divine presence, mysteries and purposes to us. As such, it is an exploration of important aspects of religious experience of a Christian kind. It is also a study, albeit in an implicit way, of topics such as discipleship, holiness, and the belief that God has a providential plan for our lives while providing us with the means of carrying it out.

Following introductory chapters the book will be divided into two main sections which will deal, firstly with the normal, and secondly, with the unusual, charismatic ways in which the Lord can speak to our hearts. This distinction is to be found in official Church documents, e.g., par. 12 of the *Constitution on the Church* where it talks of, 'more outstanding . . . extraordinary,' and 'more simple' gifts. Par. 24 of the *Decree on the Role and Apostolate of the Laity* spoke in a similar way about gifts which are 'exceptional and great' and 'simple and ordinary.' If a person looks for descriptions of the unusual forms of openness to the voice of God they are to be found in books on mysticism. There can be little doubt that there is sometimes a mystical dimension to the spirituality of the Pentecostal Churches and the Charismatic Movement. Often one has to consult books such as R. P. Poulain's classic *The Graces of Interior Prayer* or Jordan Aumann's *Spiritual Theology* in order to find descriptions of phenomena which are fairly commonplace in both. One could refer to it as everyday mysticism.

It is my hope that the content of this exercise in spiritual theology will interest Charismatic and non-Charismatic Christians alike, especially bishops, priests and religious as well as those who want to be true disciples of the Lord such as people who have done an Alpha Course or Life in the Spirit Seminar. I have decided to write for thoughtful readers in a style that is about half way between an academic and a popular style. Because of the constraints of space I have reluctantly omitted footnotes. I am well aware that the autobiographical anecdotes I have included are questionable, especially if they seem to draw favourable attention to myself. However, scripture says, 'it is good to keep the secrets of kings but to make known publicly the glorious works of God' (Tob 12:11). St. Paul added, 'Let him who boasts boast in the Lord' (1 Cor 1:28-31). Anything I have experienced, or shared, is entirely the gift of God's unmerited grace (cf. Eph 2:8-9). I am well aware that this study is far from comprehensive. It is merely one person's limited understanding of the nature of divine guidance. I am also painfully aware that there is quite a gap between what I advocate in these pages and what I actually do in everyday life. In the words of C. S. Lewis (1898-1963), 'my imagination far exceeds my obedience.' Even so, I hope that those who read these pages will find them helpful. I also pray that they will prompt not only imitation, but also thoughtful reflection, fervent prayer and further reading. I've written this book from my own particular standpoint of being Catholic in the charismatic tradition. It expresses my personal and spiritual experiences in that tradition. The scripture quotations in this book are mainly taken from The New International Version, The Revised Standard Version, and the New Jerusalem Bible.

## Conclusion

I would like to thank the many men and women in different countries, who I have had the privilege of meeting over the years, for the encouragement, enlightenment and inspiration they have given me. I also want to say a big thank you to my friends, Vincentian colleagues, and to the members of the New Springtime Community in Dublin. With St. Thomas Aquinas I pray at the beginning of this book, 'O Creator of the universe, who has set the stars in the heavens and causes the sun to rise and set, shed the light of your wisdom into the darkness of my mind. Fill my thoughts with the loving knowledge of you, that

I may bring your light to others. Just as you can make even babies speak your truth, instruct my tongue and guide my pen to convey the wonderful glory of the Gospel. Make my intellect sharp, my memory clear, and my words eloquent, so that I may faithfully interpret the mysteries which you have revealed.'

# SECTION ONE

## FROM SILENCE TO HEARING

# CHAPTER ONE

# THE APPARENT SILENCE OF GOD

In early April 2013, six of us set off from Dublin to Kiev in Ukraine to conduct Global Alpha Training (GAT) for a congregation of Messianic Jews. On the Saturday, we attended the Sabbath service. It lasted for over four hours and included a lot of singing, dancing, a wedding service, and prayer for healing. Just before the service concluded, the pastor Boris Grisenko, surprised us when he unexpectedly mentioned that the six guests from Ireland were willing to pray for members of his congregation. In the event many men and women came forward. When I asked the individuals who approached me, what they would like me to pray for, the majority of them said that they wanted to hear the voice of God and to do the divine will. They reminded me of a verse in Jer 42:3-4 which says, 'Pray that the Lord your God will tell us where we should go and what we should do.' 'I have heard you,' replied Jeremiah the prophet. 'I will certainly pray to the Lord your God as you have requested.'

Afterwards, when I reflected on that memorable experience two points struck me. Firstly, instead of asking what God could do for them, e.g. to give them peace of mind or health, the majority of the messianic Jews asked what they could do for God.

Clearly, in terms of Heb 5:12-14 they had moved from drinking milk to eating more solid food. Secondly, it was clear from their prayer requests that, those who made them believed that God could reveal the divine presence, word and will to their hearts. However, we can ask the all important question, was that expectation a realistic one? The way one answers, depends on one's world view, i.e. the conscious and unconscious beliefs and assumptions that influence one's perception and interpretation of reality. There are many of them.

## THE BIBLICAL AND GREEK WORLD VIEW

The people of the Bible believed that reality was a combination of three interrelated realms. Firstly there was the natural, material world in which we live. Secondly there was the transcendental world of God. Thirdly, there was an intermediate realm of the supernatural which consisted of such things as angels, evil spirits, inspired dreams, visions, prophesies, healings, miracles, discernment of spirits and the like.

When one reads the Old and New Testaments it is obvious that Jews and Christians alike believed that God could, and did communicate with human beings in different ways. The Old Testament abounds with examples of this kind of divine revelation. For example, following his mystical encounter with the living God in the burning bush (cf. Ex 3:2) the Lord spoke to Moses on Mount Sinai. As Sir 45:5 tells us, 'God let him hear his voice and led him into the cloud, where he handed over the commandments, the law of life and understanding.' God also gave instructions to numerous other people in Biblical times, especially the prophets. In Sir 48:22;24 we are told that Isaiah 'saw the truth in visions ... by his powerful spirit he looked into the future.' So it is not surprising that Heb 1:1 attests, 'in the past God spoke to our forefathers through the prophets at many times and in *various ways*.'

There are also many examples of this kind of revelation in the New Testament. It is clear that the believers expected God to reveal the divine presence, word and will in ordinary ways, e.g. through an inspiring word of scripture. As 2 Tim 3:16-17 says, 'All Scripture is God-breathed and is useful for teaching, rebuking, correcting and training in righteousness, so that the man of God may be thoroughly equipped for every good work.' God's will could also be expressed through people who exercised legitimate authority in the Church. As Heb 13:7 says, 'Remember your leaders, *who spoke the word of God to you*. Consider the outcome of their way of life and imitate their faith.' God's will could even be expressed by means of the civil authorities. In 1 Pet 2:13-14 we read, 'Submit yourselves for the Lord's sake to every authority instituted among men: whether to the king, as the supreme authority, or to governors, who are sent by him to punish those who do wrong and to commend those who do right.' But when all was said and done, God's will was encapsulated in the great commandment to love one another as Christ loved us. How do we love? Jesus answered, 'in everything, do to others what you would have them do to you, for this sums up the Law and the Prophets' (Mt 7:12).

God could also speak to the believers in more extraordinary ways by means of the charisms of revelation such as wisdom and knowledge, dreams, visions, prophecy, tongues and discernment of spirits (cf. 1 Cor 12:8-10). For instance, the gospel of Matthew tells us that St Joseph received messages from God in the form of dreams on four occasions (cf. Mt 1:20; 2:13; 2:19; 2:22). The Acts of the Apostles describes the decisive influence of supernatural forms of communication. St. Peter was prompted to take the momentous step of preaching the gospel to the gentiles as a result of a vision (Acts 10:11-33) and St. Paul was led to preach in Europe as a result of a religious dream (cf. Acts 16:6-11). Surely scripture scholar Jack Deere is quite correct when he says in his book, *Surprised by the Voice of God*, 'The people of the Bible heard God speak in a variety of ways. He spoke through an audible voice, through dreams, visions, circumstances, fleeces, inner impressions, prophets, angels and other ways, as well as through Scripture. These things were so common in the New Testament times that Paul had to give detailed instructions to the Corinthians concerning the use of prophecy, tongues, words of wisdom, words of knowledge, and discernment of spirits (1 Cor 12-14).'

In many respects, the Greeks, like other peoples at the time, would have shared the Biblical world view of the three interrelated realms of nature, the transcendent and the supernatural. As a result, they believed that God could communicate with human beings. For example, in the *Phaedrus* Plato wrote, 'There is also a madness which is a divine gift, and the source of the chief blessings granted to people.' In another place he wrote, 'God has given the art of divination not to the wisdom, but to the foolishness of man. No man, when in his wits, attains prophetic truth and inspiration; but when he receives the inspired word, either his intelligence is enthralled in sleep, or he is demented by some distemper or possession.' When he referred to madness he seemed to have been describing a trance-like state which could be the birthplace of prophetic knowledge. A person could be possessed by the divine and thereby enabled to have a glimpse either of the future or the true meaning of the present.

The most important oracles of Greek antiquity were those of Pythia, priestess to Apollo at Delphi in the 8th century B.C. Writing about this in 44 B.C., Roman orator and statesman Cicero said, 'The oracle at Delphi never would have been so much frequented, so famous, and so crowded with offerings from peoples and kings of every land, if all ages had not tested the truth of its prophecies.' So in ancient Greece it was believed that divine inspiration, possession or madness could put a person in touch with the transcendental realm as a result of prophetic messages. By means of supernatural knowing men and women could come to an experiential awareness of the person and purposes of God.

## THE ATHEISTIC/AGNOSTIC WORLD VIEW

It is not surprising to find that because they deny that the transcendental or supernatural realms exist that atheists deny that God can or does communicate with human beings. For example, in Act III of his 1951 play, *The Devil and the Good Lord,* atheist philosopher Jean Paul Sartre wrote these poignant words, 'I prayed, I pleaded for a sign, I sent Heaven messages: no reply. Heaven doesn't even know my name. I kept wondering what I was in God's eyes. Now I know the answer: nothing. God doesn't see me, God doesn't hear me, God doesn't know me. You see the void above our heads? That is God. You see the hole in the ground? That's what God is. You see the crack in the door? That's God too. Silence is God. Absence is God. God is human loneliness.'

Although it sounds like a contradiction in terms, there are some Christian atheists and agnostics. One of them is Don Cupitt, a well known Anglican theologian and author, who used to lecture in Cambridge University. Like Ludwig Feuerbach (1804-1872) he sees God as a projection of human thinking. God is in truth, a word that refers to human potential. All theology, therefore, should be converted into anthropology. Speaking about prayer Cupitt says that he doesn't commune with God. Rather, 'For me,' he explains, 'mostly prayer becomes meditation. One way I pray is simply by attending to natural movements and trying to sense the forthcoming of the world in time. I watch the clouds move, I watch the plants move in the wind. I watch insects. I watch simple natural movements and try to become sensitive to time.' Richard Holloway, a retired Episcopalian bishop of Edinburgh, describes himself as a secular Christian who no longer believes in God. Talking about his type of prayer he says, 'But when I'm out on the hills, I carry people with me in a loving, intercessory, prayerful way. I love walking out there and hope I'll be able to carry on doing it until I snuff it.' It is clear that given their views, neither man believes in an objectively existing God, who can communicate with him. Their notion of prayer is naturalistic, an appreciation of nature and people.

## THE LIBERAL CHRISTIAN WORLD VIEW

Nowadays there are many Christians who, although they believe in the existence of God and the sending of his Son Jesus Christ into the world, do not really believe that God communicates directly with people. It could be argued that this attitude can be traced back to the Enlightenment, and especially to the writings of Rene Descartes, David Hulme, and Immanuel Kant. Kant maintained that due to the inherent limitations of human reason, one cannot prove whether the transcendental realm of God or an afterlife exists. He himself believed in the reality of both. He argued that most people have an intuition that there is a moral order in which justice is of vital importance. However, in this world it is evident that justice does not always prevail. Good people often suffer while those who are evil often prosper at their expense. Kant believed that God and an afterlife would need to exist in order that justice might finally prevail. Otherwise, the intuition of a moral order would prove to be ultimately groundless

Kant's philosophy implied that the world was an autonomous, closed system, governed by its own inexorable physical laws. For all intents and purposes, he believed that it eliminated the intermediate realm of the supernatural, which has already been adverted to. Philosopher of religion, Keith Ward, said in his *The Development of Kant's view of Ethics*, 'any sense of personal fellowship with God, revelation from God or redemption by God is entirely lacking in the Kantian scheme.' So instead of understanding prayer as a spiritual dialogue with God, he saw it solely in this-worldly, moral terms. He wrote, 'A heartfelt wish to be pleasing to God in all our actions, that is, the disposition to transact all our business as though done in God's service, is the spirit of prayer which 'without ceasing' can and ought to be in us.' This is tantamount to saying that to work in a moral way is to pray. It says nothing about prayer as listening to the revealed word and will of God.

Kant's de-supernaturalised perspective has had a big impact, especially on liberal Protestant thinking. For example, in the last century Anglican theologian John Macquarrie wrote an interesting book entitled, *Twentieth Century Religious Thought.* It analysed the writings of more than a hundred influential Christian writers who had published books between 1900 and 1960. Out of all of these, only two, Baron Friedrich von Hugel, a mystical theologian, and Carl Jung, a psychologist who was interested in religious experience, maintained that there could be a direct encounter between God and human beings.

Liberal Christian scripture scholars, such as Rudolf Bultmann, who had been influenced by Kant and other Enlightenment thinkers, believed that the biblical authors often expressed themselves in mythological ways. Bultmann wrote in his book *Jesus Christ and Mythology*, 'The cosmology of the New Testament is essentially mythical in character. The world is viewed as a three storied structure, with the earth in the centre, the heaven above, and the underworld beneath. Heaven is the abode of God and of celestial beings -- the angels. The underworld is hell, the place of torment. Even the earth is more than the scene of natural, everyday events, of the trivial round and common task. It is the scene of the supernatural activity of God and his angels on the one hand, and of Satan and his demons on the other.

These supernatural forces intervene in the course of nature and in all that men think and will and do. Miracles are by no means rare. Man is not in control of his own life. Evil spirits may take possession of him. Satan may inspire him with evil thoughts. Alternatively, God may inspire his thought and guide his purposes. He may grant him heavenly visions. He may allow him to hear his word of succour or demand. He may give him the supernatural power of his Spirit.'

Bultmann contended that in our scientific culture the mythological world view of the Bible had to be rejected and that only faith in the kerygma, or core proclamation, of the New Testament was necessary for Christian belief. As writer Morton Kelsey has pointed out, if one accepts Bultmann's world view, and many contemporary Christians do, then the supernatural realm and the charisms of revelation described by Paul in 1 Cor 12:8-10, must be reinterpreted in a naturalistic way. So for example, the devil would be seen as nothing but a projection of the dark side of the human unconscious, or a metaphor for the systemic injustice implicit in the oppressive structures of society. Exorcism would be explained as a primitive form of magic, psychiatry or psychological suggestion. As for healing, it could be explained in psychosomatic terms. Bultmann has influenced many Christian theologians. For example, in his *Principles of Christian Theology*, John Macquarrie seemed to reject any notion of supernatural intervention in human affairs. He wrote, 'we have a duty to struggle against any mythological explanation and try harder to find an explanation in terms of this-worldly factors.'

Ten years after the conclusion of the Second Vatican Council, Langdon Gilkey, a well known Lutheran theologian in America, wrote a book entitled, *Catholicism Confronts Modernity*. In it he acknowledged that the Catholic Church was experiencing a transitional crisis. He said that one of the main causes was 'the dissolution of the understanding of the supernatural as the central religious category.' Rather than questioning this change, Gilkey proposed that Catholics should engage in a 'reinterpretation of the transcendent, the sacred, the divine – the presence of God to men – into worldly or naturalistic forms of modern experience rather than in the super-naturalistic forms of Hellenic or Medieval experience.' In other words Gilkey felt that Catholicism should travel down the liberal road which had already been traversed by many Protestants. Nowadays there are Catholics whose understanding of prayer is often influenced by a de-supernaturalised world view.

For example, commenting on the practice of asking God's help in difficult situations, in his book *Asking the Father*, Irish theologian Gabriel Daly, O.S.A. said, 'It is theologically and scientifically wrong to think of nature as operating according to its own laws, except where God intervenes in the process as an extrinsic cause, thus producing an effect which would not otherwise have come about . . . I am not looking for a 'miracle' in the pre-critical sense of an unmediated, direct intervention of God in the processes which he himself has created.' I tried to address this problem in an article entitled, 'Towards a Theology of Prayer of Petition,' in *Milltown Studies*, (Winter 2000). Given the tendency toward a de-supernaturalised world view, many Catholics are sceptical about the possibility of God communicating with them in pre-rational ways such as dreams and visions.

## THE NON-CHARISMATIC CHRISTIAN WORLD VIEW

Karl Rahner, a Jesuit, was one of the most eminent Catholic theologians of the 20th century. He was an innovative, progressive, but orthodox thinker. He wrote a number of books on prayer. In one particular chapter entitled, 'Prayer as Dialogue' in his book *The Practice of Faith* he stated, 'Writing about prayer, man today finds it very difficult to discover anything in his prayerful consciousness which he could interpret as an address by God distinct from his own mental processes. Prayer seems to him to be a monologue or at best a talking to himself, but not a dialogue with God, an event which one could seriously and without too many reservations call a conversation or an exchange.' Rahner, who was much influenced by Immanuel Kant, proposed a rather demythologised form of prayer which did not leave much room for any notion of supernatural communication from God. God, he maintained, speaks not many words to us, but rather a single word. The word divinely spoken is nothing less than the life of the one who prays, where the praying person who is loved by God is seen as God's main word or utterance.

Given this rather anthropomorphic understanding of prayer, it is not too surprising that there seems to be very little emphasis on hearing the alive and active word of the Lord in many of his writings. Repeatedly Rahner talked about the silence of God. For instance, he wrote, 'Why are You so silent? Why do You enjoin me to speak with You, when You don't pay any attention to me? Isn't Your silence a sure sign that You're not listening? Or do You really listen quite attentively, do You perhaps listen my whole life long, until I have told you everything, until I have spoken out my entire self to You? Do You remain silent precisely because You are waiting until I am really finished, so that You can then speak Your word to me, the word of Your eternity? Are You silent so that You can one day bring to a close the life-long monologue of a poor human being, burdened by the darkness of this world, by speaking the luminous word of eternal life, in which You will express Your very Self in the depths of my heart?' It is not clear whether Rahner was expressing his own personal sentiments - I suspect he was - or trying to articulate the experience of many of his contemporaries. One way or another, his was a rather bleak view of prayer. God is referred to as being distant and silent, not just during a limited period of desolation of spirit, but for a lifetime. That implies that although God's words can be read and savoured in scripture, God never seems to say anything directly to the believer.

Over the years, I have talked to many lay people and priests about their experience of prayer. Although they might not understand Rahner's complex ideas, many of them have said that although they may have been aware of God's mysterious presence, God had, nevertheless, remained silent. As a result, they would be sceptical if anyone claimed that God had spoken to him or her personally. As Jack Deere observes in *Surprised by the Voice of God,* some of them are like the Pharisees of old who 'had a theoretical belief in the supernatural – they believed in angels and the resurrection of the body – but expected nothing supernatural in their own lives. They did not listen for

God's voice apart from the Scriptures, and they never heard his voice in the scriptures.' As Jesus said of them, 'You diligently study the Scriptures because you think that by them you possess eternal life. These are the Scriptures that testify about me, yet you refuse to come to me to have life' (Jn 5:39-40).

## THE CHARISMATIC-PENTECOSTAL WORLD VIEW

The modern Pentecostal movement came into existence at Azusa Street in Los Angeles in 1906. When those present were baptised in the Holy Spirit they received an outpouring of the charisms mentioned by St. Paul in 1 Cor 12:8-10. I would be inclined to agree with Morton Kelsey when he observed in his book, *Encounter with God* that, 'the only large group who take the idea of a direct divine encounter seriously, aside from certain conservatives, are the Pentecostals, and they have come in for derision from every side since they emerged as a modern movement about 1900. . . The Pentecostal leaders have realised that they cannot stand against the powerful rationalistic and naturalistic thinking of modern society, and so have withdrawn into their own structured subculture.'

That said, Harvey Cox has shown in *Fire from Heaven,* and Philip Jenkins has indicated in *The Next Christendom,* that it would probably be true to say that worldwide Christianity is moving toward supernaturalism, and in many ways toward the ancient world view expressed in the New Testament. That would be particularly true in places like Africa and South America. This perspective was epitomised on one occasion by David Du Plessis (1905-1987), a well known South African Pentecostal. In a tongue in cheek sort of way, he recounted in his book *Simple and Profound* how he was once asked by a disciple of Rudolf Bultmann, 'What is your approach to the Bible?' 'To demythologise it' Du Plessis replied. Surprised by this answer, the questioner asked, 'How will you do this?' 'It is very simple,' Du Plessis responded, 'we Pentecostals take the things in the Bible that you say are myths, and we make them happen today so that they are demythologised!'

A very interesting debate occurred during the Second Vatican Council. It was about the lay apostolate and the charisms of the Holy Spirit. There were two schools of thought. The traditionalists, led by Cardinal Ruffini, adopted a rather cessationist point of view. They argued that the charisms were granted to the early Church in order to get it firmly established. When Christianity took root in the Greco-Roman world the charisms mentioned in 1 Cor 12:8-10 were withdrawn. The progressives, led by Cardinal Suenens argued that there was a spectrum of charisms ranging from the commonplace to the more unusual. Many of these, especially the more ordinary gifts, such as leadership, administration, and teaching, were already widely dispersed among the faithful for the edification of the Church. Suenens argued that God could restore the more extraordinary gifts to the Church at a future date. In the event the second point of view was supported by the majority of the bishops and was expressed in par. 12 of the *Dogmatic Constitution on the Church.* The *Catechism of the Catholic Church* also mentions the charisms in pars. 799-801; 2003.

In 1965, two years after the ending of Vatican II, the Catholic Charismatic Renewal came into existence when students, from

Duquesne University, met for a weekend of prayer and fasting. Speaking about the retreatants Kevin Ranaghan said that, 'There was something lacking in their individual Christian lives. They couldn't quite put their finger on it, but somehow there was an emptiness, a lack of dynamism, a sapping of strength in their lives of prayer and action. It was as if their lives as Christians were too much their own creation, as if they were moving forward under their own power and of their own will. It seemed to them that the Christian life wasn't meant to be a purely human achievement.' Each of the people who attended the retreat read David Wilkerson's *The Cross and the Switchblade,* the first four chapters of the Acts of the Apostles and asked for a new outpouring of the Holy Spirit. Afterwards they claimed to have experienced a release of the Spirit and the charismatic gifts. Kevin Ranaghan said that the blessing they received wasn't a separate grace from the one received in baptism and confirmation, 'It seemed, rather, a kind of adult re-affirmation and renewal of these sacraments, an opening of ourselves to all their sacramental graces.'

Soon, an ever increasing number of American Catholics began to have similar experiences. Prayer groups quickly sprang up all over the country, in universities, parishes, monasteries and convents. Within a relatively short period of time the movement spread to all the five continents. Writing in *L'Osservatore Romano* on Jan 2nd 1975, Prof. Marie-Joseph Le Guillou, went so far as to say that with the 'liberation' of the charisms 'we are certainly at the dawn of a new era in the history of the Church.' It is estimated that at present there are nearly 600 million Pentecostals and Charismatics in the world, over 120 million of whom are Catholic. Not only have they grown rapidly in numbers, and developed a distinctive approach to the Christian life, some of the movement's scripture scholars and theologians have written in a perceptive way about the divine-human encounter and how God can communicate with us in ordinary and charismatic ways. They have rejected the de-supernaturalising tendencies of liberal Christian thought, and the non-charismatic bias of many in the mainline Christian churches. This book will be informed throughout by that charismatic perspective. I was interested to see that, speaking about the charisms, Pope Francis said in par. 130 of *Evangelii Gaudium*, 'They are not an inheritance, safely secured and entrusted to a small group for safekeeping; rather they are gifts of the Spirit integrated into the body of the Church.' Not only is the Holy Father addressing this observation to members of the Charismatic Renewal Movement, he is also addressing it to the whole Church and saying, 'don't dismiss the Charismatic Renewal Movement as if it were just another group in the church, it has recovered, on behalf of all believers, the charismatic dimension of the entire Church.'

## Conclusion

Protestants pray for revival and Catholics pray for renewal. The truth is they are interrelated phenomena. Once revival has taken place, in the form of mass conversions as a result of a Pentecostal outpouring of the Holy Spirit, there is a need for on-going renewal and spiritual transformation in the lives of Christian individuals and communities. I am convinced that neither revival nor renewal will take place unless Christians can reject the excesses of contemporary, materialistic rationalism by embracing a world view that acknowledges, with certain caveats, the existence of a supernatural realm. Secondly, I am also convinced that the revival and renewal which many of us desire, will only become possible when Christians learn to listen to the guidance of God in the ordinary and more unusual ways which will be described in this book. As Pope Benedict XVI said at his weekly audience on September 5th 2012, 'prayer is, above all, a listening to God, who speaks.' In saying this he echoed the words of scripture, 'you do not ask for sacrifice and offerings but an open ear' (Ps 40:6).

CHAPTER TWO

# TO PRAY LIKE JESUS

In 1976 I bought a *Deutsche Grammophon* recording of Herbert von Karajan's rendition of Beethoven's Ninth Symphony. I can remember the first time I played the two discs. I was on my own, so there was no distraction. When I was totally absorbed by the magnificent choral movement, which was sung in German, I can remember seeing a starry plough in my mind's eye. Then I noticed the North Pole Star. As I did so, I heard a voice saying within me, 'I am your Father who lives beyond the stars.' At that moment I experienced a profound sense of connection with God the Father. When the recording ended, and I had returned to my everyday awareness, I found that in the record sleeve there was a copy of Schiller's 'Ode to Joy' which Beethoven had set to music in the fourth movement. I was surprised and moved when I read the following words, 'Brothers, surely a loving Father dwells above the canopy of stars . . . Seek him then beyond the stars!' It is possible that I had read those words sometime in the past and so my mental image and the accompanying words may have been rooted in an unconscious memory. Even so, they came alive in that prayerful moment of grace. The sense of being in touch with God, which I experienced while listening to Beethoven's music, was a key factor in biblical spirituality as we shall see.

Moses, was one of the outstanding people of prayer in the Old Testament. In the book of Exodus we are told how he used to pray in the tent of meeting in the wilderness. 'As Moses entered the tent, the column of cloud, [a symbol of God's presence], would come down and stand at its entrance' (Ex 33:9). Presumably, Moses poured out his heart to the Lord and spoke to him about his struggle to lead the Jewish people. Then we are told that, 'The Lord used to speak to Moses face to face, as a person speaks to a friend' (Ex 33:11). God commented on the unique relationship Moses enjoyed with the divine by saying, 'When a prophet of the Lord is among you, I reveal myself to him in visions, I speak to him in dreams. But this is not true of my servant Moses; he is faithful in all my house. With him I speak face to face, clearly and not in riddles' (Num 12:6-8). There is a poignant passage which describes how Moses made the following petition, 'Please let me see your glory!' And the Lord said, 'I will cause all my goodness to pass in front of you . . . But,' he said, 'you cannot see my face, for no one may see me and live ' (Ex 33:18; 19, 22).

One might wonder why Moses was chosen to enjoy such unprecedented intimacy with God. In 1 Pt 5:5 we are told that, 'God opposes the proud but gives grace to the humble,' and in Num 12:3 we are informed that, 'Moses was a very humble man, more humble than anyone else on the face of the earth.' And yet, in spite of all the graces he received, Moses only had intimations of God's great glory.

## THE PRAYER OF JESUS

In Heb 1:1-2, we are told that, 'In the past God spoke to our forefathers through the prophets at many times and in various ways, but in these last days he has spoken to us by his Son.' I like to think of Jesus as the new Moses, the great prophet Moses had foretold when he said, 'I will raise up for them a prophet like you from among their brothers; I will put my words in his mouth, and he will tell them everything I command him' (Deut 18:18). Although he did not enter the tent of meeting in the same way as Moses, he did so in another symbolic manner. All Jewish men had to wear a cloak with tassels. This was so because in Deut 22:12, they were instructed, 'You shall put tassels on the four corners of the cloak that you wrap around yourself.' In Num 15:37-40 the command was explained, 'When you use these tassels, the sight of the cord will remind you of all the commandments of the Lord and you will do them . . . Thus you will remember to do all my commandments and you will be holy to your God.' As time went by the cloak was also used as a prayer shawl or *tallit*. The word literally means 'little tent.' So devout Jews could enter their own tent of meeting by pulling the prayer shawl over their heads.

It is moving to think of Jesus humbly going off alone to pray. For example, in Lk 6:12 we are told that, 'Jesus went out to a mountainside to pray, and spent the night praying to God. 'It is quite possible that when he did so he pulled his cloak over his head and entered the tabernacle of his heart which was overshadowed by the Holy Spirit. There he would talk to his Father and listen to him. As a person with a divine nature Jesus was completely at one with his Father. As he attested, 'I and the Father are one' (Jn 10:30). On another occasion he said, 'No one knows the Son except the Father, and no one knows the Father except the Son' (Mt 11:27). This implies that unlike Moses, his predecessor, who only enjoyed an indirect awareness of God, Jesus beheld God's glory face to face. Pope Benedict XVI adverted to this fact when he wrote in *Jesus of Nazareth*, 'What was true of Moses only in a fragmentary form has now been fully realised in the person of Jesus: He lives before the face of God, not just as a friend, but as a Son; he lives in the most intimate unity with the Father.'

## THEOLOGICAL CONSIDERATIONS

Whenever Jesus prayed he did so in the context of a vivid awareness of the benevolent, affirming love that the Father had for him. Speaking about that love Pope Paul VI said in his apostolic exhortation *Gaudete in Domino*, 'He knows that He is loved by His Father . . . This certitude is inseparable from the consciousness of Jesus. It is a presence which never leaves Him all alone. It is an intimate knowledge which fills Him: '...the Father knows me and I know the Father' (cf. Jn. 10:15). It is an unceasing and total exchange: 'All I have is yours and all you have is mine' (Jn 17:10).' As a result, Jesus enjoyed the beatific vision in his human nature. Commenting on this mysterious point, Karl Rahner suggested in a book entitled, *Dogmatic Versus Biblical Theology*, that Jesus' human soul always enjoyed the direct vision of the Father and the Father's infinite love for him. The knowledge implicit in that vision was not necessarily reflected upon or objectified in a conceptual way. As a person with a human nature Jesus had to learn. Through his interaction with life and people he had to discover and conceptualise what he already knew in a non-thematic way.

Those who represent the views of high Christology which stresses the divinity of Jesus , as opposed to low Christology which stresses his humanity, would maintain that Jesus knew all the truths which can be revealed by prophecy and so could, in virtue of his own habitual knowledge, prophecy without waiting for any revelation or word from his Father. It seems to me that this view is hard to square with what the scriptures tell us about the *kenosis,* i.e., the voluntary renunciation by Christ, not of his divine identity, but rather of his divine prerogatives and his humble acceptance of human status with all its limitations (cf. Phil 2:7). It is significant that the scriptures clearly attest that, as a person with a human nature, Jesus grew in obedience (Cf. Heb 5:8) and knowledge like the rest of us (Cf. Lk 2:22; Heb 4:15).

At this point it is worth asking whether Jesus the man, was sometimes aided by the charisms of the Spirit in hearing the word and the guidance of his Father. In his *Summa Theologiae,* St Thomas wrote, 'Charisms all serve the proclamation of the faith and spiritual teaching; so Christ as the principal teacher of our faith had these charisms in a surpassing degree. The grace that makes us pleasing to God disposes us to the kind of interior and exterior action that reaps a reward; charisms dispose us to the kind of external actions that proclaim the faith, like the working of miracles. Christ had both of these kinds of grace to the full.'

It is also worth noting that in par. 4 of his encyclical *Divinum Illud Munus* (1897), on the Holy Spirit, Pope Leo XIII endorsed Thomas's view when he wrote: 'In him [Christ]... were all the treasures of wisdom and knowledge, graces, *gratis datae* [i.e. charisms], virtues, and all other gifts foretold in the prophecies of Isaiah.' So if we take Thomas's and Leo's words literally, it would seem that they were implying that Jesus did exercise the charisms of revelation. These gifts would have enabled him, as a man, to receive inspirations and prophetic revelations from the Father.

It can be observed in this context that our English word, 'prophecy' is derived from the Greek *prophetes* which refers to a spokesman or interpreter who announces the word and will of God. Jesus displayed a prophetic awareness on a number of occasions, e.g. when he informed the apostles they would find a coin in a fish's mouth (Mt 17:27), when he instructed the apostles to find a tethered donkey and colt in Jerusalem (Mt 21:2) and when he foretold the destruction of the temple in Jerusalem (Lk 21:20-24) and when he foretold the way in which Peter would die (Jn 21:19). Having told the Samaritan woman that she had five husbands, she said 'Sir I can see that you are a prophet' (Jn 4:19). Then, leaving her water jar, the woman went back to the town and said to the people, 'Come, see a man who told me everything I ever did' (Jn 4:28-29).

## Jesus as Prophetic Guide

No doubt when Jesus prayed he poured out his love, thoughts, feelings and desires to the Father. For example, on one occasion he said with great joy, 'I praise you, Father, Lord of heaven and earth, because you have hidden these things from the wise and learned, and revealed them to little children. Yes, Father, for this was your good pleasure' (Mt 11:25-26). In the course of his prayer, the Father reciprocated by pouring out his love, thoughts and will to Jesus. In this way the Father's presence and desires were experienced directly by him. He testified, 'For the one whom God sent speaks the words of God' (Jn 4:34) and again, 'What I speak, I speak just as the Father has told me' (Jn 12:50), and yet again, 'My word is not my own: it is the word of the one who sent me' (Jn 14:23). With this point in mind, Pope Benedict wrote in *Jesus of Nazareth,* 'Jesus' teaching is not the product of human learning, of whatever kind. It originates from immediate contact with the Father, from 'face-to-face' dialogue – from the vision of the one who rests close to the Father's heart. It is the Son's word. Without this inner grounding, his teaching would be pure presumption.'

The Father also told Jesus what to do. He testified, 'Very truly, I tell you, the Son can do nothing on his own, but only *what-ever the Father does,* the Son does likewise' (Jn 5:19). Later in the same chapter he said, 'By myself I can do *nothing;* I judge only as I hear, and my judgment is just, for I seek not to please myself but him who sent me' (Jn 5:30). Although the apostles acknowledged that Jesus was unusually close to the Father, e.g., when they asked him to teach them to pray, they did not quite grasp just how intimate his union with God the Father really was. You will recall that when Philip said to Jesus, 'Lord, show us the Father and that will be enough for us,' our Lord responded, 'How can you say, 'Show us the Father'? Don't you believe that I am in the Father, and that the Father is in me? The words I say to you are not just my own. Rather, it is the Father, living in me, *who is doing his work*' (Jn 14:10-11).

In Mk 1:32-38 there is an interesting and instructive example of the way in which the prayer of Jesus to his Father influenced his way of acting. It contains three distinct phases. Firstly, we are told that late one evening, Jesus arrived in a village after sunset. News of his coming spread quickly, and many sick and oppressed people were brought to him. We are informed that, 'Jesus healed many who had various diseases. He also drove out many demons.' Secondly, the scene quickly changed. 'Very early in the morning, while it was still dark, Jesus got up, left the house and went off to a solitary place, where he prayed.' We know that as a man of prayer, he often went off on his own to get in touch with God his Father. Presumably, on this particular occasion, Jesus discerned that his Father wanted him to continue to carry out his mission as the Suffering Servant by bringing the Good News to the poor (Cf. Lk 4:18). Thirdly, the scene changed yet again. We are told that: 'Simon and his companions went to look for him, and when they found him, they exclaimed: 'Everyone is looking for you!'

Because of his magnetic personality, his authoritative teaching, and deeds of power, it is not surprising that crowds were always longing to meet Jesus. Presumably, as soon as word spread about the healings and exorcisms he had performed the previous evening, lots more people had gathered in the village square hoping for his therapeutic and liberating touch. Yet in spite of his unquestionable compassion, Jesus unexpectedly replied: 'Let us go somewhere else – to the nearby villages – so I can preach there also. That is why I have come' (Mk 1:38). Commenting on this episode, Pope Francis wrote in par. 21 of *Evangelii Gaudium,* 'Once the seed has been sown in one place, Jesus does not stay behind to explain things or to perform more signs; the Spirit moves him to go forth to other towns.' In other words, he seemed to be saying, 'During my prayer to the Father, I was aware that although there are more pastoral needs, such as the ones in the village square, in the name of the priority God the Father gave me at my baptism I realise that it is his will that I decline your request in order fulfill my mission by proclaiming the coming of the Kingdom in other villages in Israel.' Implicit in this story is the fact that, during his prayer, God the Father helped Jesus to discriminate between pastoral needs and evangelical priorities. Not only is this episode particularly relevant for anyone who is a leader in the Christian church, it also illustrates what Jesus had in mind when he said, 'seek first his kingdom and his righteousness' (Matt 6:33). It is worth remembering that those who focus on the satisfaction of urgent needs to the exclusion of evangelical priorities contribute by default to the decline of the Christian church.

## THE TRANSFIGURATION AND LISTENING

Peter, James and John had an intimation of Jesus' prayerful awareness of the Father's glory when he was transfigured on Mount Tabor. We are told that, 'His face shone like the sun, and his clothes became as white as the light' (Mt 17:2). St. Bede

(673-735) observed that by His loving foresight, Jesus allowed the apostles to taste for a short time the contemplation of eternal joy, so that they might bravely bear the persecution to come. In virtue of the hypostatic union Jesus had a divine nature equal to that of his Father, but as someone with a human nature, like ours, he was subordinate in role. That is why he could say, 'the Father is greater than I' (Jn 14:28). Furthermore, as a man, Jesus was like us in all things except sin (cf. Heb 4:15). When he asked, 'can any of you prove me guilty of sin?' (Jn 8:46), not only was the answer no, it showed that he had a perfectly clear conscience. As a result he was never duped by illusions or false inspirations which originated either in selfish desires or the promptings of the evil one. He epitomised what Prov 4:23 had in mind when it said, 'guard your heart, for it is the wellspring of life.' As Jesus testified, 'Blessed are the pure in heart, for they will see God' (Mt 5:8) and 'He who belongs to God hears what God says' (Jn 8:47). Not only was Jesus the perfect exemplar of these truths, as a result, his words were 'spirit and life' (Jn 6:63).

The theme of listening is prominent in the account of the transfiguration. We are told that Moses, the archetypal lawgiver, and Elijah, an outstanding prophet of the Old Testament, who both had encountered God on mountains, appeared with Jesus. Their differing historical contributions found fulfilment in the person of the Messiah. Then, 'a cloud appeared and enveloped them [the apostles], and they were afraid as they entered the cloud' (Lk 9:34). At first, the apostles could see Jesus. But as the cloud of fog grew denser, a metaphorical cloud of unknowing covered them. As a result, although they could no longer see

Jesus, they knew in faith that he was still present. As Pope Benedict XVI said in *Jesus of Nazareth,* the cloud 'is a sign of God's presence, of God's self-revelation in hiddenness.' Then in the gospels we are told that, 'a voice from the cloud said, 'This is my Son, whom I love. *Listen to him!'* (Mk 9:7). As far as I am aware this is the only recorded instance of the Father giving a direct instruction to humanity in the New Testament. Surely it is highly significant that what he asked us to do was to listen to the words of his divine Son which were his own words.

In this regard there is a line in Lk 5:1 that I particularly like. The evangelist tells us that 'the crowd were *pressing in* on Jesus and *listening* to the word of God.' In Luke 15:1 there is a similar verse. We are told, 'Now the tax collectors and 'sinners' were all *gathering around* to *hear* him.' The Spirit not only attracts us to the person of Jesus, it prompts a desire to know him more intimately and to reach out and touch him. Those desires are fulfilled when we hear him speak. As he said to his Father, 'the words you gave to me I have given to them' (Jn 17:8). It is interesting to note that speaking about Jesus in Acts 3:22-23 Peter said, 'Moses declared, 'The Lord your God will raise up for you a prophet like me from among your own people; *you must listen to everything he tells you.'*

## Christian prayer as hearing God's word

Thanks to baptism, Christians die to sin and are intimately united to Christ. Just as he was one with his Father, so, as a result of justification by grace through faith, Christians are one with Christ. Jesus himself talked about this, e.g. in his discourse on the vine and the branches. He said, 'Remain in me, and I will remain in you. No branch can bear fruit by itself; it must remain in the vine. Neither can you bear fruit unless you remain in me' (Jn 15:4). Sometime later St Paul testified in Gal 2:20, 'I have been crucified with Christ and I no longer live, but Christ lives in me.' This intimate union has profound implications. Just as Jesus was one with the Father, the believer is one with Jesus. Just as Jesus was aware of the incomprehensible love of his Father so believers have, 'power, together with all the saints, to grasp how wide and long and high and deep is the love of Christ, and to know this love that surpasses knowledge' (cf. Eph 3:18).

Once a person is consciously aware of the loving indwelling of Christ's presence in his or her innermost self, he or she understands the Orthodox Church's notion of *theosis*, i.e., divinisation. If a poker is plunged into a fire, it may appear to merge with the flames when it becomes red hot, but nevertheless it retains its own identity and is not literally part of the fire. So it is with the soul. While it may appear to be God like, it retains it's own identity and separateness. Speaking about the nature of this kind of divinisation Thomas Merton explained in his book *What are these Wounds: The Life of a Cistercian Mystic, Saint Lutgarde of Aywieres*, 'The union between the soul and God in love is so close and so complete that the only remaining distinction between them is the fundamental distinction between two separate substances. Otherwise they are identical: that is to say, the soul has 'become God,' and God has 'become the soul,' and the only trace of distinction that remains between them is the fact that what is God's by nature is the soul's by participation and by God's free gift, that is, by love. God is love. The soul has love. But once the soul reaches transforming union its acts are not only Godlike, they become God's own acts.' In the Preface to Book V of *Adversus Haereses,* St. Irenaeus referred to the purpose of divinisation when he wrote, 'Jesus Christ, through His transcendent love, became what we are, that He might bring us to be even what He is Himself.'

That point found an echo in a treatise of St John Eudes (1601-1680), entitled, *The Life and the Kingdom of Jesus in Christian Souls.* He began by quoting a familiar verse from Col 1:24, 'I rejoice in my sufferings for your sake, and in my flesh I complete what is lacking in Christ's afflictions for the sake of his body, that is, the church.' Eudes felt that if Christians seek to continue and complete the suffering of Christ, surely that principle could be applied to all the Saviour's activities. He wrote, 'We ought to imitate and complete in ourselves the various states and mysteries of Christ . . . The Son of God plans to make us sharers in his mysteries, and, in a certain manner, continues them in us and in the Church by the graces which he has decided to communicate to us.' That point is summarised in a succinct way in par. 521 of the *Catechism of the Catholic Church* where it says, 'Christ enables us to live in him *all* that he himself lived, and he lives it in us.' St John Gabriel Perboyre, C.M., (1802-40) composed a prayer which expressed this mystical notion very clearly, 'O my Divine Saviour, transform me into yourself. May my hands be your hands. May my tongue be your tongue. Grant that every faculty of my body may serve only to glorify you. Above all, transform my soul and all its powers, that my memory, my will, and my affections may be your memory, will and affections. I pray you to destroy in me all that is not of you. Grant that I may live but in you and by you and for you and that I may truly say with St. Paul, 'I live now—not I—but Christ lives in me.'

This notion of living in Christ all he himself lived including his capacity to listen to the word of the Father is a vital presupposition of this book. He does so from within the tent of the Christian's heart by the power of the Holy Spirit. As Jesus said in Mt 6:6, 'when you pray, go into your room, close the door and pray to your Father, who is unseen.' Like Jesus we pray, 'Abba, Father,' (Rm 8:15; Gal 4:6). Is it any wonder that par. 2680 of the *Catechism of the Catholic Church* says, 'Prayer is primarily addressed to the Father.' Needless to say there are times when it is also appropriate to pray to Jesus, the Spirit, Mary, angels and the saints. When we pray we can expect, like Jesus, to hear the Father speak to our hearts as he reveals his living word and will to us.

## I WILL PUT MY LAWS IN THEIR MINDS

Some time ago I was so touched by the thought of Jesus pulling his *tallit*, or little tent, over his head, that I ordered a prayer shawl from a shop in Jerusalem. When I am alone in my room I sometimes put it on, pull it over my head and try to pray like Jesus to the Father. For example, about a year ago I was in Malta. On my final day there I spent some time in prayerful meditation. I imagined I had put on my prayer shawl and asked the Lord to speak to my heart. After a relatively short time I vividly saw a bunch of large green grapes in my mind's eye. I prayed, 'that is a good start Lord, but what is the significance of those grapes?' Then inwardly I thought that I heard the Lord saying to me that I should open the Bible at random and that he would speak to me about the grapes. I closed my eyes and cut the scriptures in faith. When I opened my eyes and looked at the verse where my finger was resting I read these words, *'the teeth of everyone who eats sour grapes shall be set on edge!'* Then I read on , . . . 'I will put my laws in their minds, and I will write them on their hearts. I will be their God, and they will be my people' (Jer 31:31-34).

When I finished praying I met a man who was in charge of the retreat centre where I was staying. He was excited about something or other. He said, 'stay where you are, there is a scripture reading I want to share with you, but I have to get a book first.' When he returned he said, 'the Lord really spoke to me this morning. I was reading a passage from Jer 31:31-34 in this book of meditations. I really felt that it was the Lord's word to me.' I expressed my delight in knowing that the Lord had spoken to him and informed him that it was the very same passage that I had been led to read around the same time. I had the distinct feeling that God was confirming, in this providential way, the importance of what God had spoken to me a little earlier.

The passage in Jer 31:31-34, which had moved both of us, has been referred to as 'one of the profoundest and most moving passages in the entire Bible.' So it is not surprising to find that it is referred to in the New Testament, e.g. in Heb 8:8-12. Jeremiah is predicting that a time will come when there will be an internalisation of religion so that the external legal code will no longer be the sole regulator of human behaviour. Instead, people will be motivated by means of inspiration active within the human heart under the influence of the Holy Spirit who will give believers an ability to know God and the divine purposes in an intimate way. As Ps 40:8 says, 'I desire to do your will, O my God; *your law is within my heart.*' Jesus also echoed the prophecy of Jeremiah when he explained that, 'the Counsellor, the Holy Spirit, whom the Father will send in my name, will teach you all things and will remind you of everything I have said to you' (Jn 14:26).

In this regard one is also reminded of two other passages. The first in 1 John 2:27 says, 'the anointing you received from him remains in you, and you do not need anyone to teach you. But as his anointing teaches you about all things.' In 1 Cor 2:9-16 Paul says that what, 'No eye has seen, no ear has heard, no mind has conceived . . . God has revealed it to us by his Spirit. . . The Spirit searches all things, even the deep things of God. . . We have not received the spirit of the world but the Spirit who is from God, that we may understand what God has freely given us. . . 'For who has known the mind of the Lord that he may instruct him?' But *we have the mind of Christ.*' Needless to say, these texts do not mean to imply that religion is an entirely individual, interior affair which no longer requires the mediating role of such things as the commandments, tradition, the Christian community or the teaching authority of the

Church. Surely however, these texts from scripture are assuring Christians that, in virtue of their intimate union with God the Son, they will be capable of receiving inspirations and revelations just as Jesus did. Church teaching, can also be used to test whether the inspirations we do receive are truly from God or not. It is interesting to note that the English word 'dogma' is derived from the Greek *dokein* which means 'that which one thinks is true.' So Christian dogma helps believers to discern true, orthodox inspirations, promptings and revelations from those which are false.

## CONCLUSION

In par. 40 of the *Constitutions of the Congregation of the Mission* we read these succinct and insightful words, 'Christ, the Lord, remaining always in intimate union with the Father, used to seek his will in prayer. That will was the sole aim of his life, mission, and giving of himself for the salvation of the world. He likewise taught his disciples to pray always in the same spirit, and never to loose heart. We too sanctified in Christ and sent into the world, should try to seek out in prayer the sign's of God's will and to imitate the responsiveness of Christ, discerning everything according to his mind.' Surely, those words apply not just to followers of St. Vincent de Paul, but to all committed disciples of the Lord. Just as Jesus listened to the voice of his Father, we have to listen to *his* voice.

# CHAPTER THREE

# WHAT IS NEEDED TO HEAR GOD'S VOICE?

In the late 1970s or the early 80's I attended a Mass in the chapel of Ampleforth Abbey, Yorkshire. The celebrant was Fr. Leonard May, a parish priest from Maltby. I can remember how he preached eloquently about God the Father. As he did so, there were occasional peals of thunder and dramatic flashes of jagged lightning. It appeared as if the heavenly realm was endorsing what he was saying. At communion time he prayed that a number of ailments would be healed, including poor hearing. When the Mass ended, I left the church to walk to a nearby residential block. As I did so I heard a man behind me shouting, 'I can hear, I can hear.' I turned round to see what was happening and noticed a man removing his hearing aids. As he did so he was saying loudly to his wife, 'Because of the thunder and lightning I wasn't quite aware of it at the time, but I can hear, praise God, I can hear perfectly!' Just as God the Father opened that man's ears to the sounds of the world, so he wants to open the inner ears of his sons and daughters to hear him speak in ordinary and extraordinary ways. But this is only made possible when certain conditions are met. As Jesus said, 'He who belongs to God hears what God says. 'The reason you do not hear is that you do not belong to God' (Jn 8:47).

## A Personal relationship with Jesus

I'm fully persuaded that the first thing all Christians need in order to hear the voice of God is a personal encounter and relationship with Jesus Christ. Unfortunately there are many contemporary Christians who are undergoing a faith crisis of head, heart and hands which prevents this from happening.

The faith crisis of the *head* has to do with knowledge. Sad to say, many Catholics and Protestants are unaware of the basic teachings of the Christian faith. They are sometimes referred to as the kerygma. Fr. Raniero Cantalamessa, the papal preacher, stated in *Remember Jesus Christ*, that many baptised people are *de facto* deists rather than Christians. He observed, 'What do those who call themselves 'believers' really believe in? Most often, they believe in the existence of a Supreme Being, a Creator, and in an 'afterlife.' However, this is deist faith but not yet Christian faith. If we take into account Karl Barth's famous distinction, this is *religion* but not yet *faith*. Various sociological surveys highlight this fact even in countries and regions with ancient Christian traditions. In practice, Jesus Christ is absent in this kind of religiosity.'

The faith crisis of the *heart* has to do with experience. Even if some Christians are intellectually aware of the core teachings of Christianity, that doesn't necessarily mean that they are consciously aware of their liberating power in their own lives. Although they may go to church on a regular basis and are, to a certain extent, sacramentalised and catechised, many of them are not yet fully evangelised. To use a phrase of John Paul II, in par. 19 of *Catechesis in Our Time,* they have not yet crossed 'the threshold of faith' to form *'an explicit personal attachment to Jesus Christ.'* Clearly Archbishop Diarmuid Martin, of the Archdiocese of Dublin, had this in mind when he said, 'Everywhere I go . . . I am asking people the same question: 'Do you really know Jesus?' It is a question which surprises people to be asked at Church gatherings. You can see on their faces that they seem to be saying 'we would not be here if we did not know Jesus Christ; that is why we come to Church.' At the same time I can see that people are slightly stopped in their tracks and they begin to ask themselves: 'what is the Archbishop really saying to me? Am I clear in my own mind about who Jesus is and what Jesus Christ really means to me in my life?'

The faith crisis of the *hands* has to do with Christian action. If the truth of the gospel has failed to fall from head to heart, it is not surprising that cultural Catholics and Protestants often fail to act in a way that is consistent with the teachings of Christ, e.g in the realms of sexual and business morality. What is said in Judges 21:25 is often true today, 'In those days Israel had no king; *everyone did as he saw fit.'*

What is needed is a new evangelisation. It was succinctly described by Cardinal Wuerl of Washington in these words, 'At its heart the New Evangelisation is the *re-proposing of the encounter with the Risen Lord,* his Gospel and his Church.' I sometimes try to help people to have such an encounter by saying to them, 'imagine that you are in a magnificent hall in a royal palace. In the centre is the king's impressive throne. Who sits on that throne, you or Jesus the king? If it is you, has Jesus any place in your life? If you say that he has, is he like one of your courtiers or servants? Are you continuously asking him to do acts of service for you? Would you be willing to vacate the throne, so that Jesus might sit there as your king? Are you willing to serve him, and to do what he wants? To accept Jesus Christ into your life in this way means that you allow him to take centre stage from this time forward. As Jesus said in Jn 12:26, 'Whoever serves me must follow me; and where I am, my servant also will be. My Father will honour the one *who serves me.'*

In order to accept Jesus as the centre of their lives, some people say a prayer like this one which is attributed to Fr. Peter Rookey a well known Servite healer, 'Lord Jesus, I come before you, just as I am, I am sorry for my sins, I repent of them, please forgive me. In your Name, I forgive all others for what they have done against me. I renounce Satan, the evil spirits and all their works. I give you my entire self, Lord Jesus, now and forever. I invite you into my life, Jesus. I accept you as my Lord, God and Saviour. Heal me, change me, strengthen me in body, soul, and spirit. Come Lord Jesus, cover me with your Precious Blood, and fill me with your Holy Spirit. I love you Lord Jesus. I praise you Jesus. I thank you Jesus. I shall follow you every day of my life. Amen.' Happily, nowadays an ever increasing number of people are encountering the Lord in this sort of way. It is often the result of being evangelised by a committed Christian or attending such things as an Alpha Course, a Life in the Spirit Seminar, or a Cursillo Weekend. As a result, many Catholics and Protestants experience a spiritual awakening.

It is only when people become true friends of Christ, either as a result of a sudden or gradual conversion experience that they will hear his voice speaking to their innermost selves. As Jesus stated, 'I no longer call you servants, because a servant does not know his master's business [i.e. before conversion]. Instead, I have called you friends [i.e. after conversion], for everything that I learned from my Father *I have made known to you'* (Jn 15:15-16). On another occasion Jesus said in similar vein, 'The sheep that belong to me [i.e. as a result of a personal encounter with Jesus] *listen to my voice*' (Jn 10:27).

## THE INFILLING OF THE HOLY SPIRIT

In Eph 5:18 the inspired writer says, 'Be filled with the Spirit.' Rather than being a word of advice this is a command of God. Not only is such an infilling necessary in order to grow in holiness and to evangelise effectively, I'm also convinced that one cannot hear the voice of God, especially in charismatic ways, unless one experiences what Pentecostals and Charismatics refer to as baptism in, or release of the Holy Spirit. In recent years there has been a lot of writing on this important topic. For instance, in 2012 the Doctrinal Commission of the International, Catholic, Charismatic Renewal Services published a short, but important book entitled, *Baptism in the Holy Spirit.* It argues that a Pentecostal in-filling of the Spirit is *integral* to the sacraments of baptism and confirmation, and *normative* for all Christians. It is both a *release* of the graces we received in a sacramental way when we were baptised and confirmed, and also a *reception* of charisms which are necessary for effective evangelisation. In an important definition the book states that, 'Baptism in the

Spirit is a life-transforming experience of the love of God the Father poured into one's heart by the Holy Spirit, and received through a total surrender to the lordship of Jesus Christ. This grace brings alive sacramental baptism and confirmation, deepens communion with God and with fellow Christians, enkindles evangelistic fervour and equips a person with charisms for service and mission.' To experience baptism in the Spirit does not necessarily mean that the recipient has joined a movement, any movement. Rather it is an appropriation of the fullness of Christian initiation, which belongs to the church. It is also an empowerment for evangelisation. Is it any wonder, therefore, that Pope Benedict XVI said, 'let us rediscover, dear brothers and sisters, the beauty of being baptised in the Holy Spirit; let us recover awareness of our Baptism and our Confirmation, ever timely sources of grace.'

I am convinced that a Spirit given awareness of the love of Christ, as a result of baptism in the Spirit, is a preparation for receiving promptings, inspirations and revelations in prayer. It is worth noting that St Teresa of Avila said in her *Autobiography,* 'prayer is nothing but an intimate friendship, a frequent heart to heart conversation with him *by whom we know ourselves to be loved.'* In other words, she is saying that friendship with Jesus, which is made possible by a religious awakening must be anchored in a conscious awareness of the incomprehensible love of God which is poured into our hearts by the Spirit (cf. Rm 5:5). It is this awareness that creates the atmosphere of intimacy and trust which not only enables us to pour out our deepest thoughts, feelings, and desires to the Lord, it also enables us to sense the presence of the Lord, and to hear the Father's word and will as it is spoken in ordinary and unusual charismatic ways to the heart. As Pope Francis says in par. 280 of his Apostolic Exhortation *Evangelii Gaudium,* 'There is no greater freedom than that of allowing oneself to be guided by the Holy Spirit, renouncing the attempt to plan and control everything to the last detail, and instead letting him enlighten, guide and direct us, leading us wherever he wills. The Holy Spirit knows well what is needed in every time and place.'

## Intimacy with God the Father

In Jn 17:3 we read, 'Father, . . . this is eternal life, that they may know you the one true God.' Sad to say, many Christians have very little sense of the presence and love of God our Father. Recently I listened to a recorded talk by the late Derek Prince, who was a well known evangelist and writer. Commenting on the words of Jesus, 'I am the way, the truth and the life. No one comes to the Father but by Me' (Jn 14: 6), he made the following observation. "This verse speaks about a pathway and a destination. Jesus is the way, the Father is the destination. ' Then he went on to say, 'The problem with most of the church today is that we have become stuck on the way!' However, as soon as the Holy Spirit enables people to get to know Jesus and the power of his love, they can enter an intimate Christ-like relationship with God the Father. As Jesus promised, 'No one knows the Father except Me *and those to whom I choose to reveal Him'* (Lk 10:22). In Rm 8:14, St Paul said, 'For those who are led by the Spirit of God are the children of God.' When believers enjoy a revelation of who the Father is they can pray, 'Abba

Father' (Cf. Rm 8:15; Gal 4:6). As a result they say with heartfelt conviction, 'Blessed be the God and Father of our Lord Jesus Christ' (2 Cor 1:3).

It can be observed in passing that it is significant that St. Paul says in Eph 3:14-16, 'I kneel before the Father, from whom his whole family in heaven and on earth derives its name.' In other words, human fathers, though important, are not primary. God is the primordial Father. No matter how inadequate earthly fathers may be, they cannot totally eclipse that all important fact. Understandably, people who had absent, inadequate or abusive fathers can have difficulties relating to God the Father. Pope Benedict XVI adverted to this problem when he said, 'imagining God as a father becomes problematic, not having had adequate models of reference. For those who have had the experience of an overly authoritarian and inflexible father, or an indifferent father lacking in affection, or even an absent father, it is not easy to think of God as Father and trustingly surrender oneself to Him.' I feel that many of us, men and women alike, need to experience healing if there was anything amiss in our relationship with our own earthly fathers.

The prophet said, 'The hearts of fathers must be returned to the children and the hearts of the children to the fathers' (Mal. 4:6 ). This can come about by sharing one's inner pain with a friend, counsellor or a therapist who can help one to explore the nature and implications of the paternal wound in a context of psychological safety. When the person has gained some emotional insight he or she could tell God about their feelings and ask a competent person for a prayer of inner healing.

Sooner or later, a vital way of overcoming the orphan spirit is by means of heartfelt forgiveness (Col 3:13) and a willingness to thank God in those circumstances (cf Eph 5:20) in the belief that, in God's providence, good will flow from the hurt (cf. 2 Cor 1:4). It is then that the words of Jesus are fulfilled, 'I will not leave you as orphans' (Jn 14:18). On another occasion God added, 'I will receive you and I will be a father to you… and you shall be my sons and daughters' (2 Cor 6:17-18.) So when people develop an intimate relationship with their heavenly Father they know that, he not only has a plan for their lives; in his benevolence he provides for them as his adopted children in natural and supernatural ways. As scripture assures us, 'For I know the plans I have for you,' declares the Lord, 'plans to prosper you and not to harm you, plans to give you hope and a future' (Jer 29:11-12).

When I experienced that kind of healing of the father wound a number of years ago, I can remember reading the parable of the Prodigal Son with fresh insight. When I got to the words the father spoke to the elder brother, 'all I have is yours' (Lk 15:31), they suddenly became radiant with new meaning. I sensed that God the Father was saying to me, and to all his adopted children, that he would not withhold any of his myriad blessings from us. When this truth made it's home in my heart, a number of associated texts came to mind. For instance, Jesus once said, 'If you, then, though you are evil [i.e. sinful], know how to give good gifts to your children, how much more will your Father in heaven *give good gifts to those who ask him!*' (Mt 7:11). St Paul had this same truth in mind when he wrote in Romans 8:32-33,

'He who did not spare his own Son, but gave him up for us all - how will he not also, along with him, *graciously give us all things?'* Finally, the author of Eph 1:3-4 said, 'Praise be to the God and Father of our Lord Jesus Christ, who has *blessed us in the heavenly realms with every spiritual blessing in Christ.'* Ever since hearing those words in my heart I, like many others, have had a much greater sense of the Father's good will and generosity. I am convinced that he really desires to do what is best for me and for others. Foremost among those blessings is the Father's willingness to speak to our hearts, as his adopted sons and daughters, just as he did to Jesus.

## A SINGLE-MINDED DESIRE TO HEAR THE LORD

In the past I formulated the following axiom for myself, 'There is no blessing or growth in the Christian life without preceding desire, the deeper and stronger the desire the greater the openness to blessing and growth.' In the context of this book it means that we are likely to hear the Lord speak to our hearts to the extent that we have a desire for that kind of intimate communication. It has to be rooted in humble poverty of spirit, an awareness that one needs a sense of meaning and direction which only God can satisfy. Sometimes when we are perplexed by suffering, facing a difficult decision, experiencing vulnerability, or some other human need, we can ask God to respond. As the psalmist wrote, 'Out of the depths I cry to you, O Lord; O Lord, hear my voice. Let your ears be attentive to the voice of my pleading' (Ps 130:1-2). For instance, in the New Testament we are told that Sergius Paulus, a Roman pro-consul in Cyprus from 46-48 A.D., 'a man of intelligence, summoned

Barnabas and Saul and *sought to hear the word of God'* (Acts 13:7). Although Elymas the magician tried to oppose Paul and to turn Sergius away from the faith, the Roman official became a believer. So with the psalmist any Christian can say, 'May my cry come before you, O Lord; give me understanding according to your word' (Ps 119:169).

Strange as it may seem, fasting is sometimes relevant where a desire to hear the Lord is concerned. We know that the members of the New Testament church fasted regularly. Among other things, their acts of self-denial expressed, in a symbolic way, a creaturely dependence on God, and a hunger to receive the daily bread of God's word. As Mary said in her *magnificat*, 'He has filled the *hungry* with good things but has sent the rich away empty' (Lk 1:53). In the Acts of the Apostles we are told that the believers sometimes received divine guidance following periods of fasting and prayer. For instance, in Acts 13:2-3 we are told that, 'While they were worshiping the Lord and fasting, *the Holy Spirit said*, 'Set apart for me Barnabas and Saul for the work to which I have called them.' So any individual or group that longs to hear the word of the Lord could engage in prudent fasting, e.g., skipping one or two meals in a day, or taking no solid food at all.

In what is known as 'The Principle and Foundation' at the beginning of the *Spiritual Exercises*, Ignatius of Loyola wrote, 'it is necessary to make ourselves indifferent to all created things in all that is allowed to the choice of our free will and is not prohibited to it; so that, on our part, we want not health rather than sickness, riches rather than poverty, honor rather than dishonor, long rather than short life, and so in all the rest; desiring and choosing only what is most conducive for us to the end for which we are created.' It is important that those who desire to hear the voice of the Lord are as detached as possible from worldly things and open to what God wants to say, and not just to what they want to hear. We all like to stick to our comfort zones and are inclined, albeit in an unconscious way, to edit out anything we don't want to hear from the Lord, such as a need to renounce a sinful habit, end an unhealthy relationship, or to change our priorities, values, beliefs, or way of living.

Speaking about this kind of resistance Pope Francis said in a homily in 2013, 'We have to empty ourselves of the many small or great idols that we have and in which we take refuge, on which we often seek to base our security. They are idols that we sometimes keep well hidden; they can be ambition, careerism, a taste for success, placing ourselves at the Centre, the tendency to dominate others, the claim to be the sole masters of our lives, some sins to which we are bound, and many others. This evening I would like a question to resound in the heart of each one of you, and I would like you to answer it honestly: Have I considered which idol lies hidden in my life, . . . even the most hidden ones, and choosing the Lord as the centre, as the highway of our lives?' All of us tend to hear what we want to hear and to ignore, or reinterpret what we don't want to hear. Perhaps that is why Jesus said insistently, 'He who has ears to hear, let him hear' (Lk 14:35).

## THE IMPORTANCE OF SILENCE

If you look at a mountain lake on a day when the wind is blowing and the rain is falling, its agitated surface will be unable to reflect the sky above. But as the wind ceases to blow and the rain drops stop falling, not only does the surface of the lake get calmer, it also begins to reflect the sky above. So it is in prayer. The calmer the praying person is, the deeper his or her concentration, the greater will be his or her receptivity to the inner voice of God. Unfortunately we live an age of distraction. We are distracted by many things such as the various forms of social media. As Esther de Waal said in *A Life-Giving Way,* 'When God's voice is drowned out by incessant clamour, whether inner or outer, in whatever shape or form, then continuous dialogue with God becomes impossible. An inner monologue with myself, constant chatter with others, the invasion of the spoken word through the press and television are the ever present realities in my daily life over which I need to exercise some sort of discipline if I am to keep any quiet inner peace in which to listen to the Word.'

Silence, has always been highly regarded by Jesus and saintly people (cf. 1 Kings 19:11-13). In par. 124 of the Apostolic Exhortation, *Verbum Domini,* we read, 'Let us be silent in order to hear the Lord's word and to meditate upon it, so that by the working of the Holy Spirit it may remain in our hearts and speak to us all the days of our lives.' So it is important to learn how to be quiet in order to listen to the voice of God. Just as participation in sport involves discipline, so does spirituality (cf. 1 Cor 9:25). An important discipline is the ability to go to a silent place and to quieten the body and mind. When I am praying I try to sit with my back straight and my arms either folded or resting gently on my knees. Once I have assumed my prayer pose I try to remain completely still during my prayer time without moving a muscle. I find that if my body is quiet, my mind also tends to become quiet. I also seek to control my thoughts by focusing in a sustained way on a particular point of meditation. It might be a scripture text, something that occurred to me during the last day or two, or an idea I pondered in a prayerful way on a previous occasion. If perchance my mind wanders, I gently try to bring it back to the topic of my meditation and prayer.

## LACK OF REPENTANCE AS AN OBSTACLE TO HEARING GOD

At the end of 2002, well known Italian journalist Eugenio Scalfari published a thought provoking article in the December 26th edition of *L' Espresso*. It was entitled, 'The Anger of God.' It maintained that as the Holy Father, John Paul II, neared the end of his pontificate, he was becoming increasingly frail, isolated, and disillusioned with a wayward world. Scalfari referred to an address the Pope had delivered on December the 11th. It took the form of a commentary on Jer 14:17-21. The well known Italian journalist stated that John Paul believed, in an apocalyptic sort of way, that, just as God had withdrawn the divine presence from the rebellious Israelites, so the same God was now withdrawing the divine presence from our sinful world and threatening it with retribution. I found that hard to believe so I found and read the Pope's homily on the internet.

As I suspected, Scalfari may have misinterpreted the Holy Father's message. What John Paul actually said was, 'God's silence was provoked by man's rejection. If the people will be converted and return to the Lord, God will also show himself ready to go out to meet and embrace them.' In saying that, the Holy Father seemed to echo a point he had made in his book, *Crossing the Threshold of Hope*. There he wrote, 'It is truly difficult to speak of the silence of God. We must speak, rather, of the *desire to stifle the voice of God.*'

Surely that is true. If there is un-repented sin in people's lives, such as a lack of love or forgiveness, it prevents them hearing God's voice. In Zech 7:11-12 we are told that the Jewish people, 'refused to pay attention; stubbornly they turned their backs and stopped up their ears. They made their hearts as hard as flint and would not listen to the law or to the words that the Lord Almighty had sent by his Spirit through the earlier prophets.' Jesus echoed those words when he said on one occasion, 'In them is fulfilled the prophecy of Isaiah: 'You will be ever hearing but never understanding; you will be ever seeing but never perceiving. For *this people's heart has become calloused;* they hardly hear with their ears, and they have closed their eyes. Otherwise they might see with their eyes, hear with their ears, understand with their hearts and turn' (Mt 13:14-15).' When people turn away from sin they experience the kind of inner peace which enables them to hear God speaking to their hearts. As the Lord says, 'This is the one I esteem: he who is humble and contrite in spirit, and trembles at my word' (Is 66:2).

## THE HEART VEILED BY THE DEVIL

The Bible makes it clear that the devil tries to prevent people hearing the word of God. As soon as Jesus was anointed by the Spirit and received his calling as the Suffering Servant, he was tempted by the devil to abandon his vocation. In Lk 4:5-7 we read, 'The devil led him up to a high place and showed him in an instant all the kingdoms of the world. And he said to him, 'I will give you all their authority and splendour, *for it has been given to me, and I can give it to anyone I want to.* So if you worship me, it will all be yours.' It seems to me that this temptation was much more subtle than it sounds. It is inconceivable that Jesus would have ignored the first commandment in order to worship Satan. But it is plausible to think that the devil might have tempted Jesus, as an angel of light (cf. 2 Cor 11:14), by effectively urging him to abandon his vocation as the suffering servant in order to embrace another which was biblical, namely, to become the political and military messiah of popular expectation. Like king David of old, he could conquer the world for God. What Luke seemed to be saying was that if Jesus had espoused this kind of worldly approach it would have been tantamount to worshipping the devil. As the devil said, the world had been given to him. It is worth noting that Jesus seemed to acknowledge that this was true when he referred to the devil as the 'prince of this world' (cf. Jn 12:30; 14:30; 16:11). In other words, whenever people seek first the kingdom of this world with all its disordered desires, values, beliefs and activities, they play directly into the hands of the evil one who, not only manipulates worldly affairs like a puppeteer, he also deafens people to the word of God.

Bible scholars are generally agreed that Mark's gospel ends at Mk 16:8. The additional verses in Mk 16:9-20, though canonical, were added in the second century. However, I discovered recently that, in an early manuscript, there is an interesting, but non-canonical addition to verse fourteen. It explains why the apostles didn't really hear and understand the word of God. 'They replied saying, this age of lawlessness and unbelief is under the sway of Satan, *and does not allow those under the yoke of unclean spirits to understand God's truth and power.*' In 2 Cor 4:4 St. Paul said something very similar, '*The god of this age* [i.e. Satan] *has blinded the minds of unbelievers,* so that they cannot see the light of the gospel of the glory of Christ, who is the image of God.' It is clear from these scripture texts that the devil, the father of lies (cf. Jn 8:44), can prevent worldly people from hearing the life-giving truth of God's word.

In his *Spiritual Exercises* St Ignatius of Loyola suggested that, typically, the evil One uses three worldly loves or attachments to lead good souls away from God. First, is a love of riches and the things money can buy, such as material goods, pleasures, power, security, and earthly fulfilment. Second is a love of being noticed, an inordinate desire for things such as a good reputation, popularity, success, qualifications, status, and honours. Third, there is a desire for an exaggerated independence, or autonomy, which can lead to such things as moral relativism and subjectivism in the pursuit of personal goals. The devil can tempt us to regard the objects of our desires as absolutes, and therefore as idols which become substitutes for God. St Ignatius says that when we read the Gospels we see that

Jesus was poor, humble/humiliated, and dependent on God. He felt that a true Christian could imitate Jesus by desiring to be like him. When Christians detach themselves from worldly desires, they like Jesus, will have the ability to hear the Father's voice. But wouldn't it be true to say that the lives of many of us are compromised. Unwittingly, we are influenced by a false synthesis of worldly and gospel values. Not surprisingly, therefore, we frequently lack the spiritual purity of heart that is necessary to hear the voice of God and to discern the divine will. As Heb 5:14 says, 'You will never be able to . . . understand the deeper things of God's Word until you become better Christians and learn right from wrong by practicing doing right.'

In Jn 12:31 Jesus predicted that his death and resurrection would overcome the power of Satan. He said, 'now shall the *ruler of this world* be cast out.' Ever since that has been true in *principle,* but how can Satan's power be overcome in *practice?* As far as the praying person is concerned he or she needs to renounce all forms of worldliness. Christians also have the power to counteract the devil's work in the lives of others. As St. Paul said, 'For though we live in the world, we do not wage war as the world does. The weapons we fight with are not the weapons of the world. On the contrary, they have divine power to demolish strongholds [of Satan in the mind]. We demolish arguments and every pretension that sets itself up against the knowledge of God, and we take captive every thought to make it obedient to Christ' (2 Cor 10:4-5). Sometimes we have to intercede for people, such as relatives, friends, acquaintances and even people in designated geographic areas that they may be freed from the spiritual deafness that currently prevents them from hearing and understanding the word of God. Pope Francis has written on this topic in pars. 281-283 of his Apostolic Exhortation, *Evangelii Gaudium*.

## Desolation of spirit

Another reason why God can seem to be distant and silent is the fact that although the Lord may be speaking, we may fail to hear God's voice because we are enduring an extended period of desolation of spirit. In his *Spiritual Exercises* St. Ignatius of Loyola indicated that the Lord will sometimes withdraw consolations from people in order to purify their wills and to invite them to be more fully devoted to the person and will of God. Speaking about desolation, Ignatius said: 'It is the contrary to consolation. Contrary to peace there is conflict; contrary to joy sadness: contrary to hope in higher things, hope in base things; contrary to heavenly love; earthly love; contrary to tears, dryness; contrary to elevation of mind, wandering of mind to contemptible things.'

Like Jesus himself in Gethsemane and on the cross, every Christian has to endure this kind of spiritual dryness and darkness at one time or another. During periods of desolation God seems to be silent, prayer is onerous, the scriptures as dry as sawdust, inspirations notable by their absence, and temptation commonplace. Ignatius argued that even if one seemed to get an inspiration or revelation from God during a time of desolation of spirit, there would be no reliable way of being sure that it was from God or not. This is so because genuine inspirations are normally associated with consolation of spirit, but during periods of desolation there is no consolation. So Ignatius warned Christians not to change major life choices during a time of desolation in case they would have the devil as their spiritual director.

When we endure times of desolation, we are participating in an experience that Jesus himself endured. Speaking of our Lord St. Paul said in 2 Cor 5:21, 'God made him who had no sin to be sin for us,' and in Gal 3:13 we are told that he took the curse of sin upon himself, especially during Holy Week. In effect it meant that Jesus felt abandoned and separated from God. It is moving to see how, in Gethsemane, the Father was silent when Jesus prayed to him. On the cross, he cried out, 'My God, my God why have you forsaken me' (Mt 27:46) but there was no apparent response.

Writing about this experience in his book, *Life in Christ: A Spiritual Commentary on the Letter to the Romans,* Raniero Cantalamessa says, 'On the cross Jesus experienced the ultimate consequence of sin, which is the loss of God. He has become the godless one, the atheist. The word *atheist* can have either an active or a passive connotation. It can indicate someone who *refuses* God, but also someone who is *refused* by God. In the second significance the word applies to Jesus on the cross. His atheism was one of pain not of guilt. It expiated all the culpable atheism that exists in the world and in each one of us under the form of rebellion against God and of indifference to God.' For Jesus the silence of God came to an end with his resurrection.

Fortunately, in God's good time, our periods of desolation also give way to periods of consolation. It is during these times that God not only speaks, but the person has an experiential means of checking whether the inspiration, prompting, or revelation was from God or not. When authentic they are associated inwardly with the consoling fruits of the Spirit such as on-going joy, hope and peace.

## CONCLUSION

Those of us who recite the *Divine Office* each day are aware of the fact that in Morning Prayer we begin with a psalm which includes the words, 'O that today you would *listen to his voice!* Harden not your hearts as at Meribah' (Ps 95:7-9). When I recite those words it is as if God is saying to me, and to all believers, that we should not inure our hearts in any of the ways described in this chapter, such as un-repented sin, worldliness and succumbing to the temptations of the evil one. Rather we are called, on a daily basis, to be open to the voice of God. When I recite the words of the psalm just quoted, I have the conviction that I, like others, will be enabled to hear the living, alive voice of God which will empower me to do God's will on earth as it is done in heaven.

# SECTION TWO

## ORDINARY WAYS OF HEARING THE LORD

## CHAPTER FOUR

# GOD GUIDES BY MEANS OF SPIRIT-PROMPTED DESIRES

I once heard a story about a schoolboy who used to pass a sculptor's studio. Occasionally he would drop in to watch the man at work. When he asked him questions he quickly discovered that they were not welcome because they distracted the artist. So he learned to look rather than to talk. When it was coming close to the summer holidays the boy noticed that a large block of granite had been delivered to the sculptor's workshop. He wondered what he would create from it, but he didn't dare to ask him any questions. When the holidays ended, and he returned to school, the boy visited the sculptor's workplace once again. There in the middle of the floor he saw a magnificent lion. Evidently the sculptor had chiselled him out from the rock during the summer months. The boy was in awe. He spontaneously blurted out the question, 'how did you know that there was a lion in the stone?' 'Good question,' responded the sculptor in a kindly voice. 'I couldn't find him in the stone until I could first find his image in my heart.' Arguably, the image and the subsequent statue embodied a desire that the sculptor had nurtured for some time.

In many ways human desires are the dynamism of life

propelling us to engage in different forms of action. They are rooted in our needs. Abraham Maslow (1908-70), a well known humanistic psychologist, described a hierarchy of such needs, physical, psychological and transcendental. Among our physical needs are food and drink, heat and shelter. Among our psychological needs are self-esteem and a feeling of belonging. Among our transcendental needs are a sense of beauty and of unconditional meaning. Needless to say, well ordered desires, which are God given, motivate and energise us to satisfy our different needs in wholesome and legitimate ways.

However, we are all too well aware that, because of original sin, many of our desires are disordered. St Paul expressed what we experience when he said, 'I have the desire to do what is good, but I cannot carry it out. For what I do is not the good I desire to do; no, the evil I do not desire to do - this I keep on doing' (Rm 7:18-19). St James added, 'each one is tempted when, by his own evil desire, he is dragged away and enticed. Then, after desire has conceived, it gives birth to sin' (Jm 1:14-15). These dynamics are especially evident where money and sex are concerned. While it is good to desire to earn an honest living to support one's family, many people have an inordinate desire for wealth and they can try to acquire it in greedy, dishonest ways. Equally, while it is good for a spouse to desire to give sexual expression to his or her love in the context of marriage, it is not good to desire to have sexual satisfaction in thought or deed in any other way, such as prostitution or adultery.

That said, it is important to assert that well ordered desires, especially transcendental ones, which originate in our spirit and engage our ability to make free choices, can be Spirit prompted expressions of God's guidance and will. They have been variously referred to in spiritual writings as 'God prompted desires,' 'holy desires,' and 'religious desires.' It is interesting to note that our English word, 'desire' leans toward a transcendental understanding because it is derived from the Latin *sidus* which means, 'a star, constellation or heavenly body' i.e. suggesting something ecstatic or otherworldly.

## JESUS AND HOLY DESIRES

Down the centuries, great spiritual writers have agreed that transcendental desires, are of great importance in the Christian life. In doing so, they have pointed to Gospel texts which make it clear that Jesus sometimes focused on such desires in his ministry. For example, echoing the words of Ps 42:1-2, 'As the deer pants for streams of water, so my soul pants for you, O God. My soul thirsts for God, for the living God,' Jesus said, 'If anyone is thirsty, let him come to me and drink' (Jn 7:37). In Jn 1:35-38, John the Baptist told two young men that Jesus was the Lamb of God. 'When the two disciples heard him say this, they followed Jesus. Turning around, Jesus saw them following and asked, '*What do you want?*' They said, 'Rabbi'[which means Teacher], 'where are you staying?' 'Come,' he replied, 'and you will see.' By responding in such a positive way Jesus was indicating that God can reveal his will in and through such desires. Again in Mk 10:49-51 we are told that when Jesus met Bartimaeus the blind man he stopped and said, 'Call him.' So they called to the blind man, 'Cheer up! On your feet! He's calling you.' Throwing his cloak aside, he jumped to his feet and came to Jesus. '*What do you desire me to do for you?*' Jesus asked him. The blind man said, 'Rabbi, I want to see.' There is reason to believe that Bartimaeus was not only asking Jesus to open his physical eyes but also the eyes of his heart so that he might see Jesus by faith. In the event he not only believed in the Lord, Bartimaeus became his disciple. We are told that, 'he followed Jesus along the road' (Mk 10:52).

Why did Jesus focus on people's transcendental desires? He answered the question himself when he said, 'No one can come to me unless the Father who sent me draws him' (Jn 6:44). The word draws here means 'attracts him,' or 'pulls him.' It can also refer to magnetism. So God the Father attracts us to the person and will of Jesus by means of a desire which is prompted in the human spirit by the working of the Holy Spirit. But not all ostensibly religious desires are necessarily graced ones. For instance, when Jesus asked the mother of two sons what she wanted, she said that she desired that Jesus would command that one son might sit at his right and the other on his left in the kingdom of God. Jesus refused to satisfy her desire, presumably because he discerned that it originated in her psyche and was prompted by her worldly ambition rather than a touch of God's grace (cf Mt 20:21-23).

## Spiritual writers on holy desires

St Augustine wrote: 'The whole life of a good Christian is a holy desire.' He went on to add: 'The things you desire you cannot see yet. But the desire gives you the capacity, so that when it does happen that you see, you may be fulfilled…This is our life, to be motivated by holy desire. But we are motivated by holy desire only in so far as we have cut off our longings from the love of the world. I have already pointed out – empty that which is to be filled. You are to be filled with good, pour out the bad.' Pope St Gregory the Great, known as the 'Doctor of Desire' argued that desire and love are related etymologically and in fact signify a longing for an absent person. When someone desires God because he or she perceives God's absence, the very desire is a form of presence: 'Whoever desires God with his or her whole mind already has the one he or she loves.' It can also be said that God is not in the business of frustrating us. As St Therese of Lisieux asserted in her autobiography, 'God would never inspire me with desires which cannot be realised; so in spite of my littleness, I can hope to be a saint.'

Perhaps one of the most instructive examples of God's will being expressed through holy desires is to be found the autobiography of St Ignatius of Loyola. When he was recuperating from a war wound he happened to read two religious books. The first was *The Life of Christ* by Ludolph of Saxony and the second, a collection of saints' lives known as *The Golden Legend* by Jacopo de Voragine. As a result he found himself desiring to imitate the heroic lives and deeds of Jesus and the saints. But he tells us that he also had another more worldly desire. He often thought about a lady, perhaps Princess Catherine, the beautiful sister of King Charles of Spain. He imagined what he would do and say if he visited her. He says that, 'this succession of such diverse thoughts either of the worldly deeds he wished to achieve or of the deeds of God that came to his imagination, lasted for a long time. . . yet there was a difference. When he was thinking about the things of the world, he took much delight in them, but afterwards when he was tired and put them aside, he found he was dry and discontented. But when he thought of going to Jerusalem . . . not only was he consoled when he had these thoughts, but even after putting them aside, he remained content and happy . . . He began to marvel at the difference and to reflect upon it, realising from experience that some desires left him sad and others happy. Little by little he came to recognise the difference between the spirits that agitated him, one from the demon, the other from God.' Ignatius says that God can lead us by means of wholesome desires that are associated with the on-going consolation of the Spirit.

In his *Spiritual Exercises,* St Ignatius describes two types of Christian desire. In the first the main dynamic at work is that the person is motivated by a self-centered need. So if a spiritual director were to ask such a person what grace he or she wanted from the Lord, the man or woman would typically respond, 'I desire to experience the mercy . . . love . . . consolations . . . peace . . . or gifts of God etc.' I may say in passing that there is nothing wrong with these kinds of desire. They are prompted by the Lord and are a necessary preparation for the second stage of spiritual development. A problem arises when individuals and groups get stuck at this point. For some reason or other they fail to move on to the more mature stage where the main dynamic at work in the person is that he or she is motivated by a more God-centered desire, e.g., to be united to Jesus, poor, humble and dependant on God. The person no longer focuses on the gifts or consolations of God, but rather on the God of consolation and the gifts. Inwardly, the person shifts from asking, 'what can God do for me?' to asking 'what can I do for God?' More often than not the man or woman, at this stage, desires to be 'guided by the Spirit' (Gal 5:16; 18; 25) more than to satisfy self-centered needs.

Ignatius was so convinced about the important role of religious desires in the Christian life that it would probably be true to say that the *Spiritual Exercises* are, first and foremost, a method of discovering what it is that the praying person really wants in his or her relationship with God. He firmly believed that in helping people to identify their religious desires, in a discerning way, they were discovering God's guidance for their lives. Scripture promises on a number of occasions that such desires will be satisfied by God, e.g., 'from there you will seek the Lord your God, and you will find him, if you search after him with all your heart and with all your soul' (Deut 4:29).

## How can we get in touch with our transcendental desire?

We get in touch with our transcendental desires by asking and answering the question, 'what is it deep down that I really want?' For example, besides having physical and psychological desires as a boy, I not only had a longing to know God but, as I explained to my mother at the time, I also had a desire to serve the Absolute God in an absolute way as a priest. And although subsequently I sometimes doubted God's existence, and tried to suppress my sense of vocation, both desires persisted. When I was eighteen I had a profound religious experience which left me in no doubt about the fact that God was calling me to be a priest. When I told a trusted cleric about it he said that, he not only thought my desire was prompted by God, I also had the graces and natural gifts needed to fulfil that calling. Many years later in middle-age, I experienced a strong desire to become a writer of Christian books. I felt that it amounted to a specific evangelising vocation within my priestly calling. It was confirmed when my provincial gave me permission to devote time to writing. Twenty years later I felt a persistent desire to get involved in the new evangelisation called for by St John Paul II and Benedict XVI. So, again with my superior's approval, I headed off to Detroit to do a post graduate degree in the subject. In each of these three phases of my life I felt that my inner desire was the voice of God. Of course, on a day to day basis, I still ask myself the question, 'what do you want at this time?' More often than not, rather than pointing me in a new direction, my desires are to do with fulfilling the small print of the vocations I have already received.

In my experience, an inner desire which has been prompted in the heart with accompanying consolation, may be confirmed some time later by outward events, e.g. by a person who exercises legitimate authority, or by providential occurrences. For example, an idealistic young nurse desires to do voluntary service overseas. At about the same time she happens to meet a man who organises such projects in troubled parts of the world. He asks her whether she has ever considered the possibility of offering her expertise to needy people abroad. Some time later she decides to go to Africa for two years as a result of the congruence of her inner desire and the outer invitation. In my experience it is a mistake to make a decision solely on the basis of an external stimulus. I know of one priest who entered a seminary because a trusted adult had told him when he was a young man that God had revealed to him that the youngster had a vocation. Subsequently that priest was laicised on the grounds that his choice to become a priest had not originated in himself. Any external influence needs to be matched by a free, spontaneous and independent inner desire, if it is to be seen as a legitimate expression of divine guidance. As a general rule, the Lord acts first and foremost in and through our own inner desires which may, or may not, be confirmed in an external way.

## BLOCKS TO THE AWARENESS OF TRANSCENDENTAL DESIRE

Sad to say, many people in contemporary society seem to have suppressed their transcendental desires and are apathetic where God and religion are concerned. As the Lord says in Is 65:1-2, 'I was ready to be sought by those who did not ask for me; I was ready to be found by those who did not seek me. I said, 'Here am I, here am I,' to a nation that did not call on my name.' Although there are many people who believe in the Lord they are often vague about what they desire from God. When I trained as a spiritual director in the early 1980's I was told that whenever I met with a person for spiritual direction, one of my first questions should be, 'what grace do you most desire from the Lord at this time?' However, I have found that Christians are often quite unclear about the grace they most desire. There are a number of reasons why this might be so.

Firstly, as a result of excessively extroverted ways of living and a consequent lack of self-awareness, they may have lost touch with their deeper spiritual needs. Secondly, they may have dropped some of their spiritual exercises, e.g. regular bible reading, personal prayer and the examen of consciousness, with the result that their spirituality has become more superficial. Thirdly, having lost touch with their deeper desires they may have replaced them with more worldly ones, sometimes of a sinful nature. As Jesus said: 'the cares of the world and the delight in riches choke the word [in this instance the word of God prompted desire] and it proves unfruitful' (Mt 13:22). As far as lukewarmness like this is concerned, two related texts come to mind. The first says: 'Stand at the crossroads and look; ask for the ancient paths, ask where the good way is, and walk in it' (Jer 6:16). In the second, the Lord says: 'I hold this against you: You have forsaken your first love. Remember the height from which you have fallen! Repent and do the things you did at first' (Rev 2:4-5). You will notice that both verses encourage the backslider to recall the deep and passionate desires that led him or her to form a personal relationship with Christ and to be guided by his Holy Spirit. Fourthly, some people are inhibited by a moralistic attitude. When they are asked what grace they desire, they respond by telling the director what grace they 'ought, must, or should desire,' instead of what they actually desire at a gut level. Furthermore, despite the fact that they may have positive ideas of God at a conscious level of awareness, many of them are unconsciously inhibited by negative images of the Lord as someone who is distant, hard to please and demanding. These images are often associated with negative feelings, such as fear, guilt and anger, which can distance them from their suppressed desires for God. Fifthly, un-acknowledged and unresolved, negative feelings such as grief, hurt, shame, and resentment, which are the result of life's hurts and disappointments, can also inhibit awareness of one's deepest desires.

## GOD HELPS US GET IN TOUCH WITH OUR TRANSCENDENTAL DESIRES

Because our transcendental desires are the primordial way in which God guides us, God can help us, in providential ways, to get in touch with them. Firstly, God can allow a person to suffer as a result of predictable and un-predictable crises in life, such as a woman experiencing the death of one of her children (unpredictable) as she is undergoing the menopause (predictable). Afflictions of this kind attack one's ego defences, thereby releasing the suppressed voice of the deeper, constricted self which can only be satisfied by genuine religious experience. God says in a metaphorical way, 'Remember how I the Lord your God led you all the way in the desert . . . to humble you and to test you in order to know what was in your heart' (Deut 8:2) and likewise in Jer 17:10, we read, 'I the Lord search the heart and examine the mind,' usually by means of the difficult circumstances of life.

Secondly, the Lord can allow a person to experience moral

failure, e.g. as a result of an addiction like alcoholism or infidelity. Typically it leads to an awareness of the gap that exists between one's ideal and one's real self. The consequent sense of disillusionment can uncover a need for God's liberating, mercy, power and guidance. Surely that was St Peter's experience when he denied Jesus three times. Afterwards, the self-knowledge he gained led to a strong desire for the Spirit. That desire was finally satisfied at Pentecost.

Thirdly, desires for transcendence can be evoked by the witness of an admired person who already enjoys a deep sense of union with the Lord e.g. a happy or virtuous man or woman that one has met or heard about. It leads the person to say in a longing way, devoid of envy, 'I wish I had what that other person has.'

Fourthly, as one reads and prays the scriptures one can find that the word of God evokes a deep desire to know the Lord and the divine will. In exercise 44 of *Sadhana : A Way to God*, Anthony de Mello, S.J., suggests a number of imaginative ways of getting in touch with holy desires.

## How can a person know if a desire is prompted by God?

In the introduction to this book I mentioned that all divine guidance expresses, in practical ways, love for God and for the neighbour. So firstly, if a desire is not animated, directly or indirectly, by this kind of Christian love it is not from God. Secondly, spiritual writers such as Pope Gregory the Great have pointed out that God prompted desires for God tend to grow when denied for a time. The Lord does this in order to strengthen, purify and deepen them. Meanwhile those which are not prompted by God, tend to wither through denial. St. Gregory wrote: 'Holy desires grow with delay: if they fade through delay they are no desires at all.' St Augustine said something very similar. Suppose you have some sort of bag. You stretch it because you know that you are going to put something big into it. 'In the same way by delaying the fulfillment of desire, God stretches the soul. By making us desire he expands it, and by this expansion he increases its capacity.' Thirdly, as we saw in the life of St Ignatius of Loyola, genuine desires for God are mainly associated with consolation of spirit e.g. inner peace and joy, whereas, those which are not from God, are mainly associated with desolation of spirit e.g. agitation and sadness of spirit.

## Conclusion

This relatively short chapter has proposed a counter intuitive point, namely that we can receive divine guidance by asking 'what do I deep down really want?' as opposed to asking, 'what does God want of me?' The truth is, the two questions are in effect interchangeable. God wants, what I want, because that desire has been planted within me by means of actual grace. In that sense, the Lord does not stand before me as my Lord and master with a list of demands. Rather, as the Suffering Servant he kneels before me and asks, 'what deep down do you desire, so that I may grant your request. Believe me when I say, I want what you want, not only because I love you, but because your deepest desires have been planted within you by the Spirit of my Father.' Understood in that sense, our truly transcendental desires are a foundational form of divine guidance which, more often than not, accord with the will of God.

# CHAPTER FIVE

# GOD SPEAKS THROUGH THE SCRIPTURES

In 2010 the world held its breath as it waited for daily bulletins from Chile where 33 miners were trapped nearly half a mile underground. During that time mini bibles were lowered to the men by means of a pipe that reached from the surface to where they were entombed. They were also given magnifying glasses to read the small print. Psalm 40 was highlighted in each Bible. Part of it read, 'I waited patiently for the Lord; and he inclined to me, and heard my cry. He also brought me up out of a horrible pit . . . and set my feet upon a rock, and established my steps.' Apparently the men's faith was strengthened by the prayerful reading of this and other scripture verses. After 63 days, millions of people all over the world watched as each of the rescued men was brought to the surface. Many of the waiting helpers, family members and friends at Camp Esperanza wore T-shirts which had the following verse printed on them, 'To Him be the glory and honour. Because in his hands are the depths of the earth, and the heights of the mountains are His' (Ps 95:4). Afterwards the miners explained that the things that sustained their hope during their anxious days underground were mutual support, prayer, and encouraging bible verses.

Like any devout Jew, Jesus believed that the Old Testament was the inspired word of God. As he grew up, he regularly read and prayed the scriptures. In Jn 10:35 he showed his reverence for the inspired word of God when he said, 'the scripture cannot be set aside.' There are clear indications in the Gospels that on a number of occasions the Father responded to his sense of need by bringing inspiring verses to mind. We can look at three of many possible examples. Firstly, when Jesus endured the triple temptations of the devil in the wilderness, he repelled him with the sword of the Spirit, which is the word of God, by quoting three verses from Deut 8:3; 6:13; & 6:16. Secondly, when he went to his local synagogue in Nazareth to make his mission statement, the Spirit prompted him to read a passage from Is 61:1-2. Thirdly, when Jesus met the two disciples on the road to Emmaus we are told that, 'beginning with Moses and all the Prophets, he explained to them what was said in all the Scriptures concerning himself' (Lk 24:27). What an inspiring explanation that would have been! Is it any wonder that their hearts burned within them as they listened. As was noted in chapter two, Jesus maintained that everything he spoke, including scripture quotations, had been inspired by his Father, 'what I have heard from him I tell the world' (Jn 8:26). The saints are those who best reincarnate the life of Jesus. God spoke to their hearts, as he had already spoken to the heart of Jesus, in and through the scriptures.

## THE *LOGOS* AND *RHEMA* WORD OF GOD

The word of God can be viewed as a noun or a verb. As a noun God's word is objectively true upon the page. As such it can be studied and interpreted in an academic way. Good scripture scholars know the biblical languages and the religious, political, cultural, sociological, and economic history of their time. They are also familiar with relevant archaeological discoveries and literary finds such as the Dead Sea Scrolls of Qumran. Scholars can also use contemporary forms of interpretation such the historical critical method and form criticism. By using these and other means of study the authors of commentaries, books and articles on scripture provide believers with information about what the graced writers intended to say. Although knowledge of this kind is interesting and useful, it is not necessarily a form of inspiration to the heart. Indeed, there are some scripture scholars who, in spite of all their study and learning, do not even believe in God.

As a verb that is spoken to the heart, the word of God can become subjectively true, at a particular time, in a particular circumstance, for a particular individual/s. When this happens the person goes beyond knowing the literal meaning of the word with the mind to experience its spiritual significance in the heart. In Pentecostal and Charismatic writings a distinction is sometimes made between the *logos* and the *rhema* word of God. In the Greek language *logos* and *rhema* both mean 'word.' Although they are sometimes used interchangeably, it could be said that at other times they have slightly different nuances of meaning. The authoritative Greek lexicon of Liddell and Scott defines *logos* as '*the power of the mind or reason which is manifested in speech.*' In this sense *logos* refers primarily to the objective, unchanging word of God. On the other hand *rhema* is derived from the verb meaning 'to speak,' and *refers primarily to a word that is uttered* in specific circumstances. Put briefly, *logos* refers to the word that is true in itself, and *rhema* refers to the word that is subjectively true for me as a result of being spoken to the heart. For instance, at the annunciation, Mary said to the angel, 'Let it be to me according to your word [*rhema*]' (Lk 1:38)

There is a story in the first Book of Samuel which illustrates the difference between the *logos* and *rhema* word of God. We are told that the young Samuel was living at a time when, 'the word of the Lord was rare; there were not many visions' (1 Sam 3:1). In other words it was a time when revelations from the Lord had become uncommon. We are informed that Samuel 'did not yet know the Lord: The word of the Lord *had not yet been revealed to him*' (1 Sam 3:7). That comment is a little surprising in view of the fact that Samuel had been dedicated to God at birth, he believed in God, and presumably had heard the scriptures being read on many occasions. What the inspired author seems to be saying is that, while Samuel knew the *logos* word, he had not yet heard the *rhema* word of the Lord. He had the general knowledge of the mind, but not yet the particular awareness of the heart. 'Eli [the priest] realised that the Lord was calling the boy. So he told Samuel, 'Go and lie down, and if he calls you, say, 'Speak, Lord, for your servant is listening' (1 Sam 3:8-9).

It is evident from this passage that Eli believed that Samuel would receive the prophetic spirit from the Lord. And subsequently he did. In 1 Sam 19:20-21, for instance, we are told that Saul's soldiers were sent to capture David, 'But when they saw a group of prophets prophesying, with Samuel standing there as their leader, the Spirit of God came upon Saul's men and they also prophesied. Saul was told about it, and he sent more men, and they prophesied too. Saul sent men a third time, and they also prophesied.' It would appear that the Spirit of the Lord came upon them and they experienced a form of pre-rational, ecstatic frenzy. However, there is no evidence in this incident that the pre-classical prophets uttered intelligible messages. Even so Samuel's fame and influence as a prophet spread far and wide. With the advent of the classical prophets the Bible switched from saying, 'the Spirit of the Lord came on so and so,' to, 'the word of the Lord came to so and so.' Not only were prophets such as Jeremiah and Isaiah inspired by the Spirit like their predecessors, they were able to express their pre-rational experience of God in intelligible speech. As the Lord said in Deut 18:18, 'I will put my words in his mouth, and he will tell them everything I command him.'

The possibility of receiving and sharing revelation in this way is referred to in a number of places in the Old Testament. Here are just two related examples. In Jer 29:12-14 the Lord said, 'you will call upon me and come and pray to me, and I will listen to you. You will seek me and find me when you seek me with all your heart. I will be found by you.' In Jer 33:3 the Lord added, 'Call to me and I will answer you and tell you great and unsearchable things you do not know.' This text is about revelation and clearly referring to the *rhema* rather than the *logos* word of God.

## SAINTS AND THE *RHEMA* WORD IN SCRIPTURE

In his life of St. Anthony of Egypt, St. Athanasius of Alexandria tells us that six months after his parents' death the young man was going to church as usual. As he walked along he was thinking to himself how, on the one hand, he had to care for the family home and his eighteen year old sister, and on the other, how he felt attracted to abandon everything and to follow Jesus. 'Considering these things,' we are told, 'he entered the church, and it happened that just then the Gospel was being read, and he heard the Lord saying to the rich young man, 'If you wish to be perfect, go, sell all your possessions, and give the proceeds to the poor, and come follow me and you will have treasure in heaven' (Mt 19:21). And Anthony, as if the remembrance of the saints had been placed in him by God and the readings had been made on his account, left the church immediately and gave to the villagers the possessions he had received from his ancestors – three hundred *arourae* [about 200 acres] of fertile and very beautiful land – so that they would no longer trouble him or his sister. He sold all his other movable possessions, collecting a suitable sum of money, and gave it to the poor, although he kept a little for his sister's sake.'

St Augustine recounted a similar experience in his *Confessions.* He had been struggling with sexual problems for some time. On the one hand he desired purity of life, but on the other he desired to live with a mistress. Augustine commented, 'Thus I came to understand from my own experience what I had read, how 'the flesh lusts against the Spirit, and the Spirit against the flesh.' He explained, 'Because my will was perverse it changed to lust, and lust yielded to become habit, and habit not resisted became necessity. These were like links hanging on one another – which is why I have called it a chain – and their hard bondage held me bound hand and foot.' Augustine tells us that the conflict between the addictive desires of the flesh and those of the spirit had reached a point of anguished intensity when he heard a child recite a rhyme, 'Take and read, take and read.' Believing this to be a providential instruction of the Lord he randomly opened his Bible at Rm 13:13 and read, 'Let us behave decently, as in the daytime, not in orgies and drunkenness, not in sexual immorality and debauchery, not in dissension and jealousy.' As Augustine explained, 'I had no wish to read any further, and no need. For in that instant, with the very ending of the sentence, it was as though a light of utter confidence shone in all my heart, and all the darkness of uncertainty vanished away.' Augustine became a Christian and led a chaste life from that time onwards. Sometime later he wrote: 'Your prayer is the word you speak to God. When you read the Bible, God speaks to you.'

God also spoke to the founder of the Franciscans, through the scriptures. St Bonaventure tells us in his biography, *The Life of St. Francis of Assisi,* that following his conversion Francis wondered what he should do. Then one day when he was attending the Mass of the Apostles, the gospel was read which recounted what Jesus said to the disciples when he sent them out to preach, 'The harvest is plentiful, but the workers are few. Ask the Lord of the harvest, therefore, to send out workers into his harvest field. Go! I am sending you out like lambs among wolves. Do not take a purse or bag or sandals; and do not greet anyone on the road' (Lk 10:2-4). Now when the true lover of apostolic poverty heard these words, he was filled with inconceivable joy. 'This,' he said within himself, 'is what I above all things desire. That is what my whole heart craves. . . From that day forward the man of God began, by divine inspiration, to strive after evangelical perfection and to invite all men to holy penance.'

In the early 1970's Fr. Rick Thomas, S.J., was the leader of a prayer group in Juarez, a town in New Mexico, USA. The members held regular Bible studies. Apparently one of the members, a religious sister, often uttered a prophecy near the beginning of the meeting. According to Fr Rick, frequently its true meaning only became apparent in the light of the scripture texts and *vice versa*. In 1972 the members looked at the parable which recounts how people were invited to dinner (cf. Lk 14: 7-14). The members of the prayer group were very much impressed by the verses where Jesus said, 'When you give a luncheon or dinner, do not invite your friends, your brothers or relatives, or your rich neighbours; if you do, they may invite you back and so you will be repaid. But when you give a banquet, invite the poor, the crippled, the lame, the blind, and you will be blessed. Although they cannot repay you, you will be repaid at the resurrection of the righteous.' It became a *rhema* word for them. Fr. Rick admitted to the group that he had never acted on that advice. Many of its members also acknowledged that they had never put those words into action either.

Apparently, a distant shanty town was visible from the room where the Bible studies were held. One or two members were aware that there was a large rubbish dump nearby and that a number of people made their living by scavenging there to find and sell scrap, such as bottles, cans and cardboard. The members of the Juarez group made a prayerful decision to visit the dump on Christmas day with members of another prayer group from El Paso. They decided to bring Christmas dinner to the estimated 125 people who lived and worked there. But when they got to the dump they found, to their dismay, that there were two groups of workers with a combined number of 350 people. The members of the prayer groups wondered what they should do because they hadn't brought nearly enough food to feed that many people. In the event, they decided to share what they had. Hadn't Jesus said, 'I tell you, do not worry about your life, what you will eat . . . But seek first the kingdom of God and his righteousness and *all these things will be given you besides'* (Mt 6:25; 33).

The two prayer groups had brought, burritos, a number of oranges, apples, two hams and some tamales i.e. a Mexican food that consists of seasoned ground meat or beans rolled in cornmeal, wrapped in a corn husk, and steamed. Not only did they feed all the people, they were also able to give them lots of food to bring home. Inexplicably, after all that there was still food left over. So the volunteers brought the surplus to two orphanages for distribution. Fr. Rick and his companions were convinced that the food had multiplied as it did when the apostles presented five loaves and two fish to Jesus for blessing (cf. Lk 9:10-17). That modern miracle initiated a successful evangelistic outreach to the people in the rubbish dump which, over the years, was successful in many ways. This remarkable story with its emphasis on a combination of prophecy and Bible study, is relevant for anyone who wants to hear the Lord.

The accounts of these four saintly people are instructive. In each, the protagonists were wrestling in a prayerful way with meaning of life questions and choices. God spoke to their hearts by means of a passage of scripture which seemed to leap off the page into each person's heart with relevance and conviction. As Heb 4:12 attests, 'the word of God is living and active. Sharper than any double-edged sword, it penetrates even to dividing soul and spirit, joints and marrow; it judges the thoughts and attitudes of the heart.' God's word was not only incisive, it also offered divine guidance to Anthony, Augustine, Francis and Rick. Furthermore, it contained the power of its own fulfilment. When these four outstanding Christians acted in accordance with the prompting they had received, their lives and the lives of others were richly blessed.

## Lectio Divina and hearing the rhema word of God

In Par. 25 of the *Dogmatic Constitution on Divine Revelation* we read, 'Payer should accompany the reading of Sacred Scripture, so that God and human beings may talk together; for we speak to him when we pray; *we hear him when we read the divine sayings.*' Pope Benedict XVI echoed and amplified those sentiments in his Apostolic Exhortation *Verbum Domini*. In par.

86 he wrote, 'The word of God is at the basis of all authentic Christian spirituality.' In par. 72 he added, 'I express my heart-felt hope for the flowering of 'a new season of greater love for sacred Scripture on the part of every member of the People of God, so that their prayerful and faith-filled reading of the Bible will, with time, deepen their personal relationship with Jesus.'

The Catholic Church encourages its members to engage in regular *lectio divina,* as a traditional, yet fruitful way of reading and praying the scriptures. For example, in par. 152 of *Evangelii Gaudium* Pope Francis wrote, 'There is one particular way of listening to what the Lord wishes to tell us in his word and of letting ourselves be transformed by the Spirit. It is what we call *lectio divina*. It consists of reading God's word in a moment of prayer and allowing it to enlighten and renew us.' By the Spirit's help, this way of praying enables the *logos* word upon the page, to become the *rhema* word that is spoken to the heart. Here is a brief description of *Lectio Divina*.

**1.** One begins with a **petition** for divine guidance, e.g., 'Lord, open my heart. Grant me a spirit of wisdom and revelation. Let your Spirit speak to me as I read your word.'

**2.** One goes on to **read** a chosen text and seeks to discover what the inspired author intended to say. Without this kind of objective approach, there is always a risk that one interprets the text in terms of one's own preconceived ideas. Speaking about this possibility Pope Francis said in par. 152 of *Evangelii Gaudium*, 'The spiritual reading of a text must start with its literal sense. Otherwise we can easily make the text say what we think is convenient, useful for confirming us in our previous decisions, suited to our own patterns of thought.' To this end many Christians find that it is useful to have either a Bible with lots of explanatory footnotes, e.g. *The New American Bible* or *The New Jerusalem Bible*; or a good commentary, e.g. *The New Jerome Biblical Commentary*, or *The New Collegeville Bible Commentary: New Testament.*

**3.** Next comes **meditation**, which asks: what does the biblical text say to me, and what relevance has it in today's world? In par. 153 of *Evangelii Gaudium* Pope Francis proposes that the praying person ask the following questions, What is it about my life that you want to change by this text? What troubles me about this text? Why am I not interested in this? Or perhaps: What do I find pleasant in this text? What is it about this word that moves me? What attracts me? Why does it attract me?' Here, each person individually, but also as a member of the community, must let himself or herself be moved and challenged.'

**4. Prayer** follows. As the person ponders God's word it evokes all kinds of inner reactions, feelings and desires. It is important to tell God about them in the form of prayers of petition, intercession, thanksgiving etc.

**5.** *Lectio divina* concludes with **contemplation**, during which the word of God as *logos* and therefore, true in itself, leaps alive and active off the page into the heart as the *rhema* word of God which is true for the hearer right now. It can reveal the person, message or will of God.

**6.** Lastly, one does well to remember that the process of *lectio divina* is not fully concluded until it leads the praying person/s to make a practical **resolution** which is single, precise and possible.

Understood and practiced in this way, *Lectio Divina* can have a transforming effect. As St. Paul said in 2 Cor 3:18, 'And we all, with unveiled face, beholding the glory of the Lord, are being changed into his likeness from one degree of glory to another; for this comes from the Lord who is the Spirit.' Scripture scholars say that implicit in the words 'beholding the glory of the Lord,' is the notion of contemplating the Lord in and through the Scriptures. It is God's way of responding to the following prayer in the *Divine Office*, 'In the scriptures by the Spirit, may we see the Saviour's face, hear his word and heed his calling, know his will and grow in grace.' As I have engaged in regular *lectio divina* over the years, like so many others, I have not only grown in knowledge of God in an through the scriptures, I have repeatedly heard the Lord speak to my heart through them. Here are just a few examples that I can recall.

## A WORD OF COMFORT

In the early 1980s I lived in Boston, USA. While I was there I experienced an extended period of desolation of spirit. On one occasion I went to a Jesuit retreat centre in Weston, Massachusetts, to do a directed retreat. It didn't go well and I felt very disheartened. One evening as I lay on my bed I tried to pray. Suddenly, an image came into my mind. I could see a dimly lit cave. There was a rock in the middle upon which rested an open book. Immediately I thought to myself, 'that's the Bible, if I read what it says on its open pages, God will speak to me.' But when I approached the book, I was disappointed and frustrated to find that its pages were blank! I can remember saying to the Lord, 'Why do you refuse to speak to me in this darkness?' A few minutes later I thought I heard an inner voice saying to me, 'I will speak to you. Read Is 41:10.' At first I was sceptical, feeling that this was a false inspiration, an example of wishful thinking on my part. However, I opened the Bible and read these words, 'fear not, for I am with you, be not dismayed, for I am your God; I will strengthen you, I will help you, I will uphold you with my victorious right hand.' Those words of the Lord really ministered to me. They were so relevant at the time. While they didn't console me in an emotional sense, they gave me the strength to keep going. As Ps 23:4 puts it, 'Even though I walk through the valley of the shadow of death, I will fear no evil, for you are with me; your rod and your staff [the words and Spirit of God], they comfort me.'

## A COMMAND NOT TO BE AFRAID

In 1987 I had a related experience when I travelled to Italy to speak at a conference in Assisi. When I got to Rome I was like a wound-up spring, full of stress. The prospect of having to cope with the language, currency, travel, and the talks filled me with apprehension and dread. I remember praying to God for help. In spite of my many petitions nothing seemed to happen. I can recall that, at one point I felt an inner voice was saying, 'cut the scriptures at random and I will speak to you.' Typically, I doubted that this was a genuine inspiration. But eventually I said, 'Okay', uttered a prayer for guidance, closed my eyes, opened the bible, and put my finger on the page. When I read the verse I was pointing at, I discovered that it was Is 41:10, the same one I had read in Boston years before! I said to the Lord, 'Thanks, that verse is relevant once again, and means a lot to me. Now, please take away my fear.' Nothing happened. Having voiced my feelings of letdown and anger to the Lord, I took another look at the verse. It began, 'Fear not.' Suddenly, I realised that, rather than being a word of advice, it was in fact a word of command. So in obedience to God's word I summoned up all my reserves of courage and said, 'Okay Lord, I will not be afraid, I will take on the whole of Italy if necessary, but I can't do it on my own, you will have to help me.' As soon as I uttered those heartfelt words, a great calm came over me. Tension left my body as I realised that, with God's help, I would be well able to cope. And so I did. When I got to Assisi my ministry was richly blessed in a number of ways.

## FREEDOM FROM CONDEMNATION AND MINISTERIAL AUTHORITY

On another occasion I was asked to attend the fifth night of a Life in the Spirit Seminar in Northern Ireland. I was due to give a talk and afterwards to pray with those attending that they might be filled with the Holy Spirit. While I was convinced that I could give the talk without much bother, I felt very nervous about praying for the people. I suspected that I would be exposed as a phoney, one who was able to speak about the Spirit but not able to pray effectively that it might come upon those who were present. As St. Paul said in 1 Cor 4:20, 'the kingdom of God is not a matter of talk but of power.' When I reflected in a prayerful way on the situation, I came across a verse in Phil 2:13 which really leaped out at me. It read, 'it is God who works in you to will and to act according to his good purpose.' I could see that this short verse made three important assertions. Firstly, Christ was at work within me by his Spirit. Secondly, he would reveal his will and enable me to embrace it. Thirdly, he would empower me to carry it out. Although this verse really spoke to me, I couldn't claim it's power because I was suffering from exaggerated feelings of unworthiness. I felt that, while God was at work in other people, surely he would not be at work in me, a sinner.

Around this time I happened to read Paul's letter to the Romans and had reached chapter eight. It begins with the words, 'There is now no condemnation for those who are in Christ Jesus, because through Christ Jesus the law of the Spirit of life set me free from the law of sin and death' (Romans 8:1-2). As soon as I read those words, I can remember hitting the desk with my fist, and saying out loud, 'that is so true!' I could see Paul was saying that if we believe in Jesus, even though we deserve condemnation on account of our sins, there is no condemnation, we are declared not guilty and acquitted by the grace of God. Once the Lord spoke through that liberating *rhema* verse, I was able to affirm that God would be at work within me when I laid hands on people and prayed that they be filled with the Holy Spirit. In the event, many people did experience a personal Pentecost.

In each of these cases I was facing a dilemma and addressing prayerful questions and petitions to the Lord. God responded when he spoke to me by means of inspired and inspiring words of scripture. God did so in different ways such as, regular reading of the bible, hearing an inner voice directing me to a specific text, or being directed to cut the scriptures at random. In each instance the *logos* word on the page became God's *rhema* word to my heart. I found that in some cases it was only a *rhema* word in the specific circumstances in which I received it. On other occasions, the inspiring word of God remained a *rhema* word ever afterwards, e.g. the conviction that through my faith in Christ I am no longer under condemnation. Whenever God speaks to us through the scriptures, his word requires that we respond appropriately either by means of prayer, and/or faith-filled action.

Over the years I have come to recognise that St. Paul was correct when he highlighted different functions of God's word. For example, in 2 Tim 3:16-17 we read, 'All Scripture is inspired and is useful for teaching, rebuking, correcting and training in righteousness, so that the man of God may be thoroughly equipped for every good work.' It could be added that the word of God is can also be an utterly reliable word of promise and empowerment.

## THE WORD OF TEACHING

St. Paul says that God can teach us about himself and the mysteries of our faith by means of scripture. The Fathers of the

Church stressed the fact that besides having a literal meaning, scripture also has a three part spiritual meaning. While one can access the literal meaning by means of scripture study, the soul is only illumined when the spiritual meaning of the texts is revealed to the heart in the course of prayerful reflection. For example, a few years ago I was walking along the street near my home in a prayerful attitude of mind, when suddenly some words of Jesus drifted into my mind, 'give and it will be given to you . . . for the measure you give is the measure you will get back' (Lk 6:38). While I was quite familiar with those verses, on that graced occasion it was as if God had spoken them directly to me from heaven. The Holy Spirit seemed to unveil their importance in such a way that, ever since then, they have come to assume a central role in my spirituality. I began to appreciate that the principle of reciprocity is important in every aspect of the Christian life. If Christians want to grow in grace they need, to express grace already received in an appropriate way, either spiritually, e.g., by devoting time to prayer, or practically, e.g., by works of mercy such as working for the St. Vincent de Paul Society.

It is a striking fact that in the Holy Land, the Jordan river flows in at one end of the Sea of Galilee and outwards at the other. As a result it teems with life. The same river flows in at one end of the Dead Sea, but fails to flow out at the other. As a result it is lifeless! There is a Gaelic folk tale which illustrates this point. It describes how, in the Autumn, a farmer stored seed potatoes in a large bin with a view to planting them in the Spring. He warned his wife not to use any of them. But when poor people came to the door during the cold Winter months, she felt sorry for them and gave each one a few potatoes from the bin. In the Spring, when the time for sowing arrived, the woman was on tenterhooks because she knew that the bin was nearly empty. But when her husband opened it, surprise, surprise, it was full to the brim with first class seed potatoes! The message is obvious, in giving we receive, even to the point of miracles. Surely C. S. Lewis was correct when he observed: 'Nothing that you have not given away will ever be really yours.'

## THE WORD OF REBUKE

When the word of God comes alive in the life of a believer, it can be a word of correction and discipline. In Jer 17:9-10 the Lord says, 'The heart is deceitful above all things and beyond cure. Who can understand it? 'I the Lord search the heart and examine the mind.' Knowing this to be true David prayed, 'Search me, O God, and know my heart! Try me and know my thoughts! And see if there be any wicked way in me, and lead me in the way everlasting!' (Ps 139:23-24). The scriptures assure us that God answers this prayer. In Wis 12:1-2 we read, 'by degrees you correct those who sin, you admonish them, reminding them how they have strayed so that turning away from evil they may trust in you, Lord.' God will often use a *rhema* word from scripture, 'to judge the secret thoughts and emotions of our hearts' (Heb 4:12). Let me give an example.

When I was newly ordained I was conscientious and idealistic. I intended to preach well and to help the poor. As time passed I got disillusioned. Although people admired how articulate my sermons were, no one seemed to be converted by them. When I met with the poor, all I had to offer was good advice, whereas they needed good news and the power of God. Over a period of time I became disillusioned and restless. One day when I was reading the scriptures a particular verse really struck me. It said, 'You say, 'I am rich; I have acquired wealth and do not need a thing.' But you do not realise that you are wretched, pitiful, poor, blind and naked. I counsel you to buy from me gold refined in the fire, so you can become rich; and white clothes to wear, so you can cover your shameful nakedness; and salve to put on your eyes, so you can see' (Rev 3:17). For some mysterious reason those words hit me in the emotional solar plexus. It was as if a blindfold had been removed from the eyes of my heart and I could see that my self-sufficiency, complacency and presumption were a block in my life. I had been refusing to acknowledge my neediness, vulnerability and poverty of Spirit. Now the Lord was urging me to turn to him for blessing. Instead of being like the Good Samaritan, I was more like the man beaten up on the roadside of life. I needed Jesus to minister to me by pouring the wine of his mercy and the oil of his love into my inner wounds. It was that scripture prompted sense of need which proved to be the prelude to my spiritual awakening. Sometime later, by the grace of God, I experienced a life changing infilling of the Holy Spirit when I was twenty nine years of age.

## THE WORD OF CORRECTION AND TRAINING

The living word of God, 'is a lamp to my feet and a light for my path' (Ps 119:105). In spite of their good intentions, many Christians are unwittingly motivated by worldly ideas, values, attitudes and beliefs. Sometimes when they read and pray the scriptures, they are stopped in their tracks by an arresting verse. Not only does it expose worldliness it invites the believer to live in a more Christ-like way.

I can remember being involved in an ecumenical dialogue in the late 1990s. When we started discussing the contentious, but vital, topic of justification there were differences and misunderstandings between the Catholics and Protestants. At times feelings were running high. At one point during that period of dialogue I came across the following passage, 'make my joy complete by being like-minded, having the same love, being one in spirit and purpose. Do nothing out of selfish ambition or vain conceit, but in humility consider others better than yourselves. Each of you should look not only to your own interests, but also to the interests of others' (Phil 2:1-4). Clearly the Lord wanted us to be united. But what really struck me were the words, 'Do nothing out of selfish ambition or vain conceit, but in humility consider others better than yourselves.' I could see that, as a member of the Catholic contingent, I was in danger of being conceited in so far as I rejoiced in the fact that I belonged to the one true Church founded by Christ and that it was the largest Christian church in Ireland and the world. I felt the Lord was saying, 'you don't have to believe that Protestant doctrine is better than your own, but your attitude to your Protestant brothers and sisters needs to change. You should put a towel of service around your waist and humbly treat them with the deference, honour and respect you yourself would like to receive.' I found that word of guidance from the Lord very challenging. Afterwards I tried, with God's help, to put it into action. As a result of a good deal of mutual goodwill we eventually produced an agreed statement on the topic of justification.

## THE WORD OF PROMISE

Anyone who reads the scriptures on a regular basis will be aware that they abound in divine promises. They seem to cover every exigency of human life. There are at least three kinds, some to do with salvation, others to do with assistance in living the Christian life, and yet others about resurrection and eternal life. Abraham is our father in faith because he took God at his word when he promised that, although he and his wife were senior citizens, they would have a son. St. Paul said of him, 'he did not waver through unbelief regarding the promise of God, but was strengthened in his faith and gave glory to God, being fully persuaded that God had power to do what he had promised' (Romans 4:20-22). The Virgin Mary was much the same. She believed the angel Gabriel when he told her she would be the mother of Jesus. Later when Mary visited her cousin, Elizabeth proclaimed, 'blessed are you because you believed that the promise of God would be fulfilled' (Lk 1:45). Clearly, anyone who wants to live a life of faith, needs to focus on God's promises.

When we face challenges in a prayerful way, the Lord will often speak a scripture promise to our hearts. I can recall an occasion when I went to Dublin airport with the intention of flying to Southern Italy via Frankfurt. I had been invited to speak at a conference in Scalea, Calabria and my hosts had done the booking. When I went to the check-in I was told that the flight to Frankfurt had been booked, but not the second leg to Lamezia Terme. I walked away from the desk wondering what I should do. I sat down and began to pray for guidance. As I did so a scripture text came to mind, one in which Jesus said, 'seek first the kingdom of God and his righteousness, and all these things shall be yours as well' (Matt 6:33). I felt that the Lord was saying, 'you are seeking first my kingdom when you desire to evangelise. So trust me, go to Frankfurt, and I will look after you there.' Then another two scriptures came to mind. The first was from Prov 3:5, 'Trust in the Lord with all your heart and *do not rely on your understanding.*' The second was from Ps 37:5, 'Trust in the Lord, commit your life to him and *he will act*.' Having heard from the Lord I went back to the desk and checked-in for the flight to Germany.

When I got to Frankfurt I went to the transfer desk. The young woman who was in attendance asked me where I was from. I said I was from Ireland. With that she became animated and said, 'I was in your country two weeks ago, I loved it.' Then she recounted some of her adventures. By now a sense of connection had developed between us. I told the German woman about my dilemma. She got working on her computer and made a few phone calls. After a time she said, to my great relief, 'Actually, you are booked on the flight to Italy, there was some complication but I have sorted it out.' I thanked her and when I left the desk I thanked my heavenly Father, not only for his word of promise, but also for fulfilling it to the letter.

## THE WORD OF EMPOWERMENT

Whenever the Lord speaks to a believer's heart by means of a *rhema* word from scripture, it evokes faith in what it promises. As St. Paul said in Romans 10:17, 'faith comes from what is heard' i.e. God's living, alive, and active *rhema* word. It could be saving faith or the kind of faith that is necessary to move mountains (cf. Mk 11:23). There is a good example in the incident where Peter walked on water. In Mt 14:25-29 we read, 'During the fourth watch of the night Jesus went out to them, walking on the lake. When the disciples saw him walking on the lake, they were terrified. 'It's a ghost,' they said, and cried out in fear. But Jesus immediately said to them: 'Take courage! It is I. Don't be afraid.' 'Lord, if it's you,' Peter replied, 'tell me to come to you on the water.' '*Come,*' he said. Having heard the *rhema* word Peter got down out of the boat, walked on the water and came toward Jesus. But when he felt the wind, he was afraid and, beginning to sink, cried out, 'Lord, save me!'

When Peter experienced a desire to walk on water, he knew that, from a human point of view, it was quite impossible. But he also knew that if Jesus invited him to come to him, not only would the *rhema* word evoke unhesitating faith in his heart, it would also empower him to carry it out (cf. Is 55:11). In the event Jesus uttered the all important word, 'come.' Like Mary at the annunciation, Peter's attitude was, 'be it done unto me according to your word' (Lk 1:38). Trusting in Jesus and the *rhema* word he had spoken to his heart, he got out of the boat and did what no mere human had ever done before, he walked on water! But when his attention began to shift from Jesus and his empowering word to wind, wave and gravity, he began to sink. When Peter cried out to Jesus for help, we are told that, 'Immediately Jesus reached out his hand and caught him. 'You of little faith,' he said, 'why did you doubt?' (Mt 14:31).

This is an important point. If we are to claim the mighty promises of scripture, we need to hear God speak his *rhema* word to our hearts. It will evoke expectant faith while providing us with the power to do what it says, even to the point of healings and miracles. As Jesus promised in Jn 14:12, 'I tell you the truth, anyone who has faith in me will do what I have been doing. He will do even greater things than these, because I am going to the Father. And I will do whatever you ask in my name, so that the Son may bring glory to the Father. You may ask me for anything in my name, and I will do it.' Could it be that, more often than not, the contemporary Church fails to claim this mighty promise of God because so few believers seem to be really listening to the word of God in their hearts? That topic will be explored at greater length in chapter eleven.

## Conclusion

There are five principles that committed Christians need to maintain.

- First, read the word of God on a regular basis.

- Second, listen to the word of God with the inner ear of the heart.
- Third, consume the word of God by means of prayerful meditation until it consumes you. (cf. Ezech 2: 8-10)
- Fourth believe the word of God.
- Fifth, act on the word even to the point of healings and miracles.

It is my belief that if Christians followed these steps, not only would their personal lives be transformed, so would the church. The assistance of the Holy Spirit is vital at all five stages. Saint John Chrysostom stated that Scripture, 'needs the revelation of the Spirit, so that by discovering the true meaning of the things enclosed therein, we can reap abundant benefits.' Saint Jerome was likewise firmly convinced that, 'we cannot come to an understanding of Scripture without the assistance of the Holy Spirit who inspired it.' Speaking of the Spirit St. Gregory the Great wrote, 'He himself created the words of the holy Testaments, he himself reveals their meaning.'

# CHAPTER SIX

# GOD SPEAKS THROUGH CONSCIENCE

I am fascinated by mechanical gadgets. My current favourite is a satellite navigation system, known as a GPS. This computerised technology is mostly used by people who travel by road. They enter their departure point and destination. It works out the best way of getting there with the aid of satellites orbiting above the earth. The Sat Nav has a twofold ability to offer guidance. Firstly, an arrow offers precise visual directions on a coloured map which is displayed on a screen. Secondly, a voice gives specific instructions. If perchance the driver makes a mistake, the mellifluous voice graciously suggests an alternative way of getting to the destination, without a hint of criticism. Since purchasing a GPS, I have rarely consulted a map for directions.

It has struck me on a number of occasions that conscience is a bit like a spiritual GPS. It can give those who are tuned into its inspirations the guidance needed for the journey to God. If perchance we make a mistake or ignore its promptings, conscience condemns the action but not the person who performed it. Rather it suggests an alternative way of reaching our destination. What a Sat Nav is to a traveller, conscience is to anyone who wishes to lead a good Christian life. It is an inner voice, so to speak, that gives us a sense of moral direction. It urges us to do what we believe to be right, and dissuades us from doing what we believe to be wrong. If perchance we disobey our conscience we suffer from a sense of healthy moral guilt.

When one looks up par. 16 of *The Church in the Modern World* it describes the function of conscience in these words, 'In the depths of his conscience, man detects a law which he does not impose upon himself, but which holds him to obedience. Always summoning him to love good and avoid evil, the voice of conscience when necessary speaks to his heart: do this, shun that. For man has in his heart a law written by God; to obey it is the very dignity of man; according to it he will be judged.' Some writers make a distinction between the *habitual conscience,* i.e., the person's innate disposition toward the good, and the *actual conscience,* i.e., a process whereby the person comes to an evaluation of what is right or wrong in a particular situation.

## CONSCIENCE IN THE SCRIPTURES

In the Old Testament there is no Hebrew word for conscience. However, the Jewish people were well aware of the concept which they associated with the heart *(leb)*. It was the place in which the law of God is written. Job had a good conscience. He stated, 'my heart shall not reproach me as long as I live' (Job 27:6). On the contrary king David had a bad conscience. We are told that, 'David's heart smote him' (2 Sam 24:10) because of his infidelity. It sounds as if Is 30:21 is referring to the voice of conscience when it says, 'Whether you turn to the right or to the left, your ears will hear a voice behind you, saying, 'This is the way; walk in it.' There is a single reference to conscience in Wis 17:11. which was written in Greek, 'Wickedness is confessedly very cowardly, and it condemns itself; under pressure from conscience it always assumes the worst.'

For me, the real heroes of conscience in the Old Testament are the seven Maccabee brothers and their mother. Their heroic martyrdom is recounted in 2 Macc 7:1-42. In conscience they chose to suffer a painful death rather than eat pork in violation of God's law. Having seen his six brothers cruelly put to death before him, the seventh said, 'Our brothers, after enduring brief pain, have drunk of never-failing life, under God's covenant. But you, by the judgment of God, shall receive just punishments for your arrogance. Like my brothers, I offer up my body and my life for our ancestral laws, imploring God to show mercy soon to our nation, and by afflictions and blows to make you confess that he alone is God. Through me and my brothers, may there be an end to the wrath of the Almighty that has justly fallen on our whole nation.' . . . Thus he too died undefiled, putting all his trust in the Lord' (2 Macc 7:37-40). After this the mother was also killed.

In the Greek of the New Testament the word for conscience is *syneidesis*. Paul borrowed it from the religious language of his time. It was similar in meaning to the Hebrew notion of the heart as the origin of thought, feeling and will. The transition from heart to conscience is evident in 1 Tim 1:5, 'The only purpose of this instruction is that there should be love, coming out of a *pure heart*, a *clear conscience* and a sincere faith.' Paul believed that everyone, whether a believer or not, had a conscience. In Rm 2:14-15, he stated, 'Indeed, when Gentiles, who do not have the law, do by nature things required by the law, they are a law for themselves, even though they do not have the law, since they show that the requirements of the law are written on their hearts, their consciences also bearing witness.' It does not follow that in Paul's mind conscience is autonomous. Its graced activity has to be influenced by one's relationship with the Person and will of God. He wrote, 'True my conscience does not reproach me at all, but that does not prove that I am acquitted; the Lord alone is my judge' (1 Cor 4:4). Again in Heb 10:22 believers are encouraged to, 'draw near to God with a sincere heart in full assurance of faith, having our hearts sprinkled to cleanse us from a guilty conscience.' In 1 Jn 3:19-21 we read words which are equally reassuring, 'Dear friends, if our conscience does not condemn us, we have confidence in the presence of God.'

There is a very interesting passage in 1 Cor 8:1-13 which talks about the role of conscience in the lives of believers. It has to do with the question, could Christians buy and eat food that had been sacrificed to idols? In Corinth pagan services were religious activities that involved the whole family. Animals were brought to the priests for sacrifice to the gods. Some portions were burned, others were given to the priests and the rest was returned to the families. Afterwards they could invite relatives and friends, including Christians to join them. At other times some of the consecrated meat was sold in the market and could be bought by Christians. They wanted to know if it was okay to eat food sacrificed to idols. Paul said that, in view of the fact that there is no God other than the one true God, it was quite irrelevant that food had been offered to false, non-existent gods, so it was permissible to eat it. Yet pastorally, Paul was concerned about weak, poorly instructed converts whose understanding of the issues involved was imperfect. As a result they might think that sitting and eating in the temple of a false god would involve idolatrous worship of that god. Therefore, mature, well informed believers had to be careful not to scandalise the consciences of weak believers. As Paul pointed out, love builds up other people and therefore has sometimes to impose constraints on personal freedom.

In par. 1789 of the *Catechism of the Catholic Church* we read, 'charity always proceeds by way of respect for one's neighbour and his conscience, 'thus sinning against your brethren and wounding their conscience . . . you sin against Christ' (1 Cor 8:12). Therefore 'it is right not . . . to do anything that makes your brother stumble' (Rm 14:21). As Raymond Brown pointed out in his *An Introduction to the New Testament,* this Pauline notion of pastoral limitations on one's rights can be an important challenge to a generation that constantly speaks of rights but not of responsibilities. Paul is saying that it is not enough to say that such and such an action is right in itself and does not trouble one's conscience, one needs to calculate the way in which the action will influence others. For instance, as a celibate priest I might have a good, honourable friendship with a woman. While

I have no problem in my conscience about visiting her, that is not sufficient. I have to exercise prayerful prudence by asking myself, 'if I visit my friend, could neighbours with suspicious minds be scandalised?' A charitable conscience has to take circumstances like these into consideration when making a conscientious decision. To do so, says St. Paul, is to listen to the voice of God.

## Conscience in Church teaching

Catholic theology maintains that conscience is the voice of God within us. Down the centuries this notion has been expressed in a number of important Catholic writings. St. Bonaventure stated that: 'conscience is like God's herald and messenger, it does not command things on its own authority, but commands them as coming from God's authority, like a herald when he proclaims the edict of the king. This is why conscience has binding force.' Writing centuries later to the Duke of Norfolk, Bl. John Henry Newman said that, 'Conscience is the aboriginal Vicar of Christ.' Par, 16 of *The Church in the Modern World* pointed out that, 'Conscience is the most secret core and sanctuary of a man. There he is alone with God, whose voice echoes in his depths. In a wonderful manner conscience reveals that law which is fulfilled by love of God and neighbour.'

Saint John Paul II echoed those sentiments in par. 43 of his encyclical *Veritatis Splendor*. He wrote, 'Conscience is the secret sanctuary in which God's voice echoes. The conscience is the voice of God, even when man recognises in it nothing more than the principle of the moral order which it is not humanly possible to doubt, even without any direct reference to the Creator. It is precisely in reference to this that the conscience always finds its foundation and justification.' In par. 58 the Holy Father added, 'conscience is the witness of God himself, whose voice and judgment penetrate the depths of man's soul, calling him to obedience. Moral conscience does not close man within an insurmountable and impenetrable solitude, but opens him to the call, to the voice of God. In this, and not in anything else, lies the entire mystery and the dignity of the moral conscience: in being the place, the sacred place where God speaks to man.' Those impressive and important quotations, taken from the *magisterium* of the Church, make it abundantly clear that God seeks to speak to all people in and through their consciences.

At this point we will focus on those aspects of church teaching which help us to appreciate what conditions need to be present in order for conscience to be the voice of God. According to par. 1778 of the *Catechism of the Catholic Church*, 'Conscience is a judgment of reason whereby the human person recognises the moral quality of a concrete act that he is going to perform, is in the process of performing, or has already completed.' That being so, conscience is not a mere feeling of subjective sincerity or authenticity apart from notions of objective right and wrong. As I pointed out in a book entitled, *Finding Faith in Troubled Times*, conscience is not the overbearing superego which says, 'do what you ought to do or you will be unable to accept or love yourself.'

Catholic theology insists that besides needing to have self-knowledge and an awareness of one's motivation, believers need to have an *informed* conscience. They have a responsibility to learn what it is that the Scriptures and the Church have to say about different moral issues. It is only when a person has good will, self-awareness and a knowledge of objective norms that his or her conscience is likely to be the voice of God. However, many people suffer from culpable ignorance. Let us take an example. Nowadays a majority of Christian couples live together before getting married. Most of them justify their behaviour for a variety of reasons, e.g., 'we need to live together to see if we are emotionally and sexually compatible,' or 'we love one another and intend getting married so it is okay,' or 'surely whatever nature demands of people cannot be sinful,' or 'there can't be anything wrong with living together before marriage, everyone is doing so' etc. Perhaps couples like these do not know what the Bible and the Church have to say about sex before marriage. But surely they have an obligation to find out. It would not take much effort to discover that the Bible considers sexual relationships between unmarried people to be immoral.

For example, in Acts 15:1-29 we read about the Council of Jerusalem. It decreed that there was no need for the Gentiles to be circumcised. However, the leaders did say that the Gentile converts were to avoid fornication (cf. Acts, 15:27). The word for fornication in the Greek is *porneia* which refers to unchastity, i.e. illicit sexual intercourse in general including sex between unmarried people. In his *Summa Theologica* St. Thomas Aquinas wrote, 'Without any doubt we must hold simple fornication to be a mortal sin' (Q 154, art., 2). Not surprisingly, modern Church teaching endorses this point in par. 2353 of *The Catechism of the Catholic Church*. It says, 'Fornication is carnal union between an unmarried man and an unmarried woman. *It is gravely contrary to the dignity of persons and of human sexuality.'* As such, sex between unmarried people, is seriously sinful from an objective point of view. I suspect that couples don't seek out knowledge like this either because it is not important to them, because of a lack of Christian commitment, or because they fear it might challenge their self-serving assumptions. So if a couple, who were living together, claimed that their decision was made with a good conscience, they would be quite wrong to assume, that, therefore, it was the voice of God. Although I have highlighted the moral issue of sex outside marriage, which is a common one in contemporary society, the principles involved in it are relevant where other moral decisions are concerned.

Three more points. Firstly, there is a clear link between prayerfulness and listening to one's conscience. Authors James F. Keating and Dennis J. Billy make that very clear in their book *Conscience and Prayer: The Spirit of Catholic Moral Theology*. They argue that the act of praying is a profound act of morality in itself, because it gives to God what God is due, that is, a listening heart. Arguably the most profound meeting of morality and prayer occurs in the workings of conscience as we put on the mind of Christ. As *The Philokalia* says, 'A good conscience is found through prayer, and pure prayer through conscience. Each by nature needs the other.'

Secondly, The Catholic Church teaches, and lived experience

confirms the fact, that if a person chooses to repeatedly engage in immoral conduct, his or her conscience becomes blunted like a knife that has not been sharpened for some time. In other words, because of repeated sin, the person is less likely to hear the Lord speak by means of the voice of conscience because it has been willfully muted, to a greater or lesser extent.

Thirdly, when all is said and done, conscience is the final arbiter when it comes to making moral choices. Long before he became Pope, Benedict XVI wrote, 'Over the pope as the expression of the binding claim of ecclesiastical authority, there still stands one's own conscience, which *must be obeyed before all else,* even if necessary against the requirement of ecclesiastical authority. This emphasis on the individual, whose conscience confronts him with a supreme and ultimate tribunal, and one which in the last resort is beyond the claim of external social groups, even of the official Church, also establishes a principle in opposition to increasing totalitarianism.' Although, one should obey one's conscience, as Joseph Ratzinger said so emphatically, that does not necessarily imply that it is always infallible, or necessarily the voice of God.

More recently, Pope Francis responded to a question of non-believing journalist Eugenio Scalfari who had asked him whether God forgave those 'who do not believe and do not seek to believe.' Francis responded, 'Given – and this is the fundamental thing – that God's mercy has no limits, if He is approached with a sincere and repentant heart, the question for those who do not believe in God is to abide by their own conscience. There is sin, also for those who have no faith, in going against one's conscience. Listening to it and abiding by it means making up one's mind about what is good and evil.' Clearly the Pope is saying that while the unbeliever may not consciously acknowledge the fact, his or her conscience is in reality the voice of God.

## CONNATURAL KNOWLEDGE AND CONSCIENCE

At the other extreme, people, who are closely united to God by means of faith and an experience of divine love can grow to have an intuitive or instinctive sense of God's purposes. It is interesting to note that St Thomas Aquinas says: 'To judge well about the things of God....through a certain oneness in nature with God is an act of the Spirit's gift of wisdom. Such sympathy or connaturality with divine things is an effect of the love of charity uniting us to God, so that wisdom's cause is love in the will, even if in essence wisdom is a disposition of the mind to judge well. The gift of understanding guides the mind's perceptions, but the gifts of wisdom and knowledge form its judgements....Wisdom first contemplates divine things, then plans human actions according to God's plan.' Thomist scholar Garrigou Lagrange has written by way of explanation, 'As a bee or carrier pigeon is directed by instinct, and acts with a wonderful certainty revealing the Intelligence which directs it, just so, says St Thomas Aquinas, the spiritual person is inclined to act, not principally through the movement of his own will, but by the instinct of the Holy Spirit.'

Pope John Paul II spoke about this aspect of conscience in par.

64 of *Veritatis Splendor*, 'It is the heart converted to the Lord and to the love of what is good which is really the source of true judgements of conscience. Indeed, in order to 'prove what is the will of God, what is good and acceptable and perfect' (Rm 12:2), knowledge of God's law in general is necessary, but it is not sufficient: what is essential is a sort of 'connaturality' between man and the true good. Such connaturality is rooted in and develops through the virtuous attitudes of the individual himself: prudence and the other cardinal virtues, and even before these the theological virtues of faith, hope and charity. This is the meaning of Christ's saying: 'He who does what is true comes into the light' (Jn 3:21).'

What John Paul is getting at is the fact that a chaste woman will have an instinctive sense of what is sexually appropriate and inappropriate, a just man will have an instinctive sense of what is fair or unfair behaviour etc. People who are endowed with connatural wisdom, have an uncanny ability to work out whether inspirations, - their own or those of other people - have come from the Lord, or not. They are like people who, having heard one syllable spoken on the phone by a person they know well, can distinguish his or her voice from every other voice in the world. People with the gift of wisdom, may not be able to explain why they made the choice they did, but they will usually be correct nevertheless. In this context one is reminded of two texts. In Ps 119:100 we read, 'I have more understanding than the elders, for I obey your precepts,' and in Mt 11:25, Jesus said, 'I praise you, Father, Lord of heaven and earth, because you have hidden these things from the wise and learned, and revealed them to little children.' Commenting on this verse *The New American Bible* says in a footnote that childlike wisdom, 'depends upon the Father's revelation, but it is granted to those who are open to receive it and refused to the arrogant.' Both texts seem to refer to connatural knowledge as an intuitive sense of right and wrong.

The Church also teaches that healthy moral guilt, as opposed to unhealthy or neurotic guilt, is a gift in the sense that we only experience it when we know that we have ignored the urgings of conscience in order to do something sinful. But in the words of the psalmist, the pangs of guilt not only lead one to come to one's senses like the prodigal son, we can also say, 'I know my transgressions, and my sin is always before me. Against you, you only, have I sinned and *done what is evil in your sight*' (Ps 51:3-4). Guilt, though painful, is tinged with hope, and a longing for forgiveness and restoration by a merciful and loving God. As David prayed, 'Hide your face from my sins and blot out all my iniquity' (Ps 51:9).

## Saintly Witnesses to Conscience as the Voice of God

Over the years I have been inspired by the sacrifices that people of conscience were prepared to make in order to remain faithful to the will of God. I have always admired the integrity of St Thomas More (1478-1535), who in the name of conscience, refused to support King Henry VIII's divorce from Catherine of Aragon or to take the oath of supremacy. In Robert Bolt's play, *A Man for All Seasons* Thomas More was urged by his long time friend, the Duke of Norfolk, to change his mind. He pointed out that all of the nobility and bishops, apart from Bishop John Fisher, had signed the oath of supremacy. 'Look at these names, Thomas,' Norfolk pleaded. 'Won't you come with us, for fellowship?' More replied, 'And when you have gone to Heaven for following your conscience,' and I have gone to Hell for not following mine, will you come with me — for fellowship?' As a result of his principled stance More was eventually executed.

Another person who has impressed me greatly is Bl. Franz Jagerstatter (1907-1943). He refused to fight in Hitler's army because he believed that the Fűhrer was waging an unjust war. A religious dream was responsible for informing his conscience. It is worth quoting excerpts from his account. 'Let me begin be describing a dream I had on a Summer night in 1938 . . . All of a sudden I saw a beautiful shining railroad train that circled around a mountain. Streams of children – and adults as well – rushed toward the train and could not be held back . . . I heard a voice say to me: 'This train is going to hell. . . . At first the travelling train was something of a riddle to me. . . Today it seems to me that it was a symbol of nothing but National Socialism . . . Thus I believe that God has shown me most clearly through this dream, or revelation, and has convinced me in my heart how I must answer the question: should I be National Socialist – or Catholic? I would like to call out to everyone who is riding on this train: 'Jump out before the train reaches its destination, even if it costs you your life!' Subsequently, in spite of the pleading of his local priest, diocesan bishop and others, he refused to go against his conscience. He stated at the time: 'Again and again, people stress the obligations of conscience as they concern my wife and children but cannot believe that, just because one has a wife and children, he is free to offend God by lying. Did not Christ himself say, 'He who loves father, mother, or children more than me is not deserving of my love? Or, 'fear not those who can kill the body but not the soul; rather fear much more those who try to destroy body and soul in hell.' Jagerstatter was executed in 1943 at the age of 37. In 2007 he was beatified. Present was his 94 year old wife Franziska, his daughter Hildegard who was born out of wedlock, and Maria, Aloisia and Rosalia the daughters of his marriage to Franziska. She died in 2013.

## CONCLUSION

In the case of the martyrs it is not hard to see how their informed consciences were the voice of God, a voice they heeded and obeyed at the cost of their lives. They provide an example for all of us in today's secular world where Christians are constantly tempted, like Jesus in the desert, to turn away from the will of God in order to gain some temporal advantage. Surely, Cardinal Newman was correct when he said, 'Let us beware of trifling with conscience. It is often said that second thoughts are best; so they are in matters of judgment, but not in matters of conscience. In matters of duty first thoughts are commonly the best – *they have more in them of the voice of God.'*

# CHAPTER SEVEN

# GOD SPEAKS THROUGH INSPIRATIONS AND PROMPTINGS

When I was still a clerical student in the mid 60s I went to London during the summer holidays to work in a biscuit factory. While I was there my mother wrote to tell me that my youngest brother would be coming to London *en route* to the United States. She asked if I would be able to meet him. I replied to say that, much as I would like to, I didn't think it would be possible, for reasons I cannot now remember. When my brother did come to the city he attended Mass in Southwark Cathedral. By chance, he met two friends of mine. They knew where I was staying and brought him to meet me. I was delighted to see him and accompanied him to a terminus where he could get a bus to Heathrow airport. When we got there, I looked around and saw a group of young men standing nearby. I approached one of them and asked, 'do you know where the bus for Heathrow leaves from?' He said that he did, and that he was going there himself. I called my brother over and introduced him. 'This is my brother Peter' to which the young Englishman replied, 'Hi, my name is Stewart.' 'Stewart is going to Heathrow,' I said to my brother, 'stay with him because he knows where to go.' Then I said, 'do you mind me asking, where are you flying to?' 'The United States,' Stewart replied. 'Where exactly?' 'To Birmingham Alabama via New York,' he replied. I said, 'That's a remarkable coincidence because that's where my brother is going. Just for interest sake, where are you going to stay in Birmingham?' I gasped when he said that he was going to be resident in the very same building as my brother. Later we discovered that Stewart was in the room next to my brother's. As it turned out, the two of them spent the whole Summer together. Was that just an extraordinary coincidence or was it an example of divine providence? I myself believe that the Lord inspired me that summer's day to talk to the only person in London who was going to exactly the same place as my brother. My mother's solicitude for his welfare was but a pale reflection of the care of God the Father.

God can speak to us by means of inspirations and promptings like the one I have just described. The word inspiration in English is derived from the Latin *'inspiro'* which means 'to breathe into.' It refers to the breath of the Holy Spirit which can manifest some truth about God or the divine mysteries. Understood in this way, inspirations are a fruit of the gift of knowledge mentioned in Is 11:2 and 1 Cor 12:8. The word prompting in English is derived from the Latin *promptus* which means 'ready or quick.' It is a kind of Spirit given guidance about something that a person should be ready to do, with alacrity, as the will of God. Understood in this way promptings are also fruit of the gift of wisdom mentioned in Is 11:2 and 1 Cor 12:8. Although there is an overlap between these two words, for clarity's sake we will understand them as they have been described here, and look briefly at each.

## Divine inspirations

St. Paul prayed in Eph 1:16-18, 'I keep asking that the God of our Lord Jesus Christ, the glorious Father, may give you the Spirit of wisdom and revelation, so that you may know him better.' I have heard speakers at Charismatic Renewal meetings quote this verse in the belief that it refers to charismatic forms of revelation. Rudolf Schnackenburg says in his *The Epistle to the Ephesians: A Commentary,* 'we are not concerned here with the spirit of prophecy with special 'revelations' (cf. 1 Cor 1:5, 7) but with a spiritual experience possible for all believers.' The well known prayer of St Richard of Chichester (1197-1253) asks for this ordinary kind of revelation, 'Three things I pray, *to see thee more clearly,* to love thee more dearly, and to follow thee more nearly, day by day.' When we pray in this way, we may receive an inspiration that enables us to understand some scriptural truth. Praying Christians will testify how, when they reflected on God's word, there were *eureka* moments when it's meaning and implications became suddenly apparent as their minds were illumined by the light of grace.

This can happen as we reflect on the great mysteries of religion such as the Blessed Trinity, the incarnation, the, resurrection and ascension of Jesus, etc. There is a good example of this in *The Autobiography of St Ignatius of Loyola.* In chapter three he tells us in the third person singular that, 'In the first place, he had a great devotion to the Blessed Trinity. Every day he prayed to the divine Persons individually and in union. While thus praying to the Blessed Trinity, the thought came of how to offer prayers to the Divinity. . . He seemed to behold the Blessed Trinity in the form of a lyre or harp; this vision affected him so much that he could not refrain from tears and sighs. On the same day he accompanied the procession from the church, but even up to the time of dinner he could not withhold his tears, and after dinner his joy and consolation were so great that he could speak of no subject except the Blessed Trinity. In these conversations he made use of many different comparisons to illustrate his thoughts. Such an impression was made on him on that occasion that during his life after that, whenever he prayed to the Blessed Trinity, he experienced great devotion.' Admittedly, Ignatius's inspiration went beyond the ordinary by means of an exceptional vision which enabled him to sense the spiritual meaning of the doctrine of the Trinity, so much so that it exercised an influence on him for the rest of his life.

The mystery of God can also be made known by means of more mundane inspirations, e.g., while watching T.V., listening to uplifting music, talking to another person or contemplating the beauties of the natural world. Speaking about the latter, St. Paul attested in Rm 1:20, 'For since the creation of the world God's invisible qualities-his eternal power and divine nature-have been clearly seen, being understood from what has been made.' Elizabeth Barrett echoed those sentiments when she wrote in her poem *Aurora Leigh,* 'Earth's crammed with heaven, and every common bush afire with God; but only he who sees takes off his shoes; the rest sit round and pluck blackberries.' Christian spirituality abounds with examples of how divine inspiration occurred when believers sensed God's presence in and through created things. For instance, there is the testimony of St.

Augustine in his *Confessions* about the way in which he and his mother Monica, touched the hem of heaven at Ostia, when they discussed what the next life would be like. That experience was referred to by St Therese of Lisieux in her autobiography when she recounted how, like Augustine and Monica, she and her sister Celine had a profound religious experience as they contemplated a beautiful, evening sky.

When I studied to become a qualified teacher I can remember one of our lecturers talking about sociologist Basil Bernstein's notion of restricted and elaborated codes of language. If I recall rightly, the former was concrete and imaginative, whereas the latter was more conceptual and abstract. People tend to relate to God in one or other of those two ways. I suspect, as the Myers- Briggs Test points out, that one's predilection is partly determined by personality type. I have found that people who are imaginative tend to have lots of images come into their minds during prayer, e.g. the picture of the bunch of grapes which I mentioned in chapter two, whereas those with a more intellectual orientation tend to favour abstract ideas. Grace builds on nature. As an old saying puts it, *Quidquid recipitur ad modum recipientis recipitus,* i.e., whatever is received is received in the manner of the receiver. Whether a person experiences God in an imaginative or more intellectual way, he or she can ask three important questions.

- Firstly, what did you feel when you had the experience of God? Was it joy, peace, fear, hope, awe, wonder etc?

- Secondly, what did you notice about the Person of the Lord which would account for the feelings evoked within you? For example, was God compassionate, accepting, understanding, mysterious, fascinating, loving, merciful etc? What word or words would describe the God of your actual experience?
- Thirdly, how did you decide to respond to the inspiration of the Lord? Did you express it in a prayerful way, e.g., in gratitude, praise, sorrow, worship etc? Did it find any practical expression in your everyday life? Guidance is implicit whenever a person is aware of the Lord. The Spirit prompts him or her to, 'be for others what God is for you.' If God was compassionate, accepting or understanding, be compassionate, accepting, and understanding in your dealings with others. These inner imperatives, which are the result of genuine religious experience, are expressions of the will of God.

## Divine promptings

In Eph 5:10 Paul said that it is important to 'find out what pleases the Lord.' He also hoped that believers 'may abound more and more in knowledge and depth of insight, so that they may be able to discern what is best' (Phil 1:9). Paul added: 'since the day we heard about you, we have not stopped praying for you and asking God to fill you with the knowledge of his will through all spiritual wisdom and understanding. And we pray this in order that you may live a life worthy of the Lord and may please him in every way: bearing fruit in every good work, growing in the knowledge of God' (Col 1:9-12). Finally, in Rm 12:2 Paul described a key prerequisite for discerning the will of God, 'Do not conform any longer to the pattern of this world, but be transformed by the renewing of your mind. Then you will be able to test and approve what God's will is - his good, pleasing and perfect will.' Paul was familiar with the fact that molten bronze which is poured into a mould assumes its shape to become a statue. He is saying to Christians that when their attitudes and values are moulded by the mind of the Lord rather than the standards of the world they will be able to discern the will of God.

In Gal 5:18; 25, St. Paul got to the core of the matter when he said that Christians should 'be guided by the Spirit.' Arguably this verse lies at the heart of his ethics. Commenting on this command George Montague has written in his wonderful book *The Holy Spirit: Growth of a Biblical Tradition,* 'The Christian life is not a list of things to do and things to avoid. It is not virtue acquired by practice. It is the gift of being moved by the Spirit of God, and the key to life is to allow the Spirit to lead. Paul clearly speaks here of an inspired ethic and of inspired action ... A crucial point: When confronted with any moral decision, great or small, the Christian's first question should be 'where does the Spirit lead me in this?' Raniero Cantalamessa has echoed that point in *Come Creator Spirit.* As Christians, he says, 'we ought to entrust ourselves in every way and for everything to the inner guidance of the Holy Spirit: to allow the Spirit, so to say, to be our spiritual director . . . Nor should we start anything or do anything at all unless we have first consulted the Holy

Spirit.' Cardinal Jean Verdier (1864-1940) a former Archbishop of Paris gave expression to those sentiments in the following prayer, 'O holy Spirit, love of the Father and the Son, inspire in me always what I should think, what I should say, how I should say it, when I should keep silent, what I should write, how I should act, and what I should do, in order to contribute to God's glory, the good of souls and my own sanctification.'

## Practical examples

A few years ago, I was sitting at my desk thinking of nothing in particular. Suddenly the thought came spontaneously into my mind, 'why not write a prayer which would ask God for daily guidance.' My immediate reaction was to say yes. I felt it would be a relatively easy thing to do and wouldn't take long. So I set to work, thinking I'd complete the task in a day or two. In the event it proved much more difficult than I had ever anticipated. I wrote one draft after another. But none of them satisfied me. Pages were repeatedly scrunched into a ball and thrown into the wastepaper basket. Many was the time I thought to myself, 'why am I putting myself through all this hassle? After all no one asked me to do this!' Then I'd abandon the project for a while. But I would have no peace. So I'd have to take it up again. This went on for months. I lost count of all the versions of the prayer I wrote. None of them really satisfied me. At one point I published a provisional version, in the now defunct *New Creation* magazine, and asked the readers for their feedback. Having taken their replies into consideration I wrote yet another version. I wasn't entirely satisfied with it either. But believing that G. K. Chesterton was correct when he said that, 'if a thing is worth doing, it is worth doing badly!' I brought it to a local printer intending to get 500 copies. I was shocked when he told me how much each one would cost. But he added. 'if you got 5,000, the price for each one would be proportionately less.' Although I thought it would take years to sell the 5000 copies, I decided to think big, and ordered the larger number.

A few days later I collected the box of new prayer cards and returned to All Hallows College where I was living at the time. As soon as I came through the front door I was greeted by a priest and a lay woman, who were standing in the foyer. They asked, 'Are you Fr. Collins?' I said that I was. 'We heard you were writing a daily prayer to the Holy Spirit,' they explained, 'and we have come to see if we could buy some.' I said that, by a remarkable coincidence, I was returning from the printers and that the box in my arms was full of the prayer cards. 'How many copies would you like?' I asked. 'Well, to start with we would like 1,000 copies' replied the priest. I nearly dropped the box with surprise. He wanted exactly twice the number of cards I had originally intended getting printed. That was many years ago. Since then I have sold well over 300,000 copies. Thank God, they're still in demand. As Jesus said: 'No branch can bear fruit by itself; it must remain in the vine. Neither can you bear fruit unless you remain in me' (Jn 15:4). If the Holy Spirit prompts a person to do something and he or she obeys the prompting it will be fruitful. By the way, the daily prayer for guidance reads as follows, 'Father in heaven, yours is a Spirit of truth and love. Pour that same Holy Spirit into my body, my mind and my soul. Preserve me today, from all illusions and false inspirations.

Reveal your Presence, your word and your will to me in a way that I can understand, and I thank you that you will do this, while giving me the ability to respond, through Jesus Christ our Lord. Amen.'

Just to give an example of how God can give a person a prompting. A few years ago I was about to say mass in a small oratory in my community house. When I stood at the altar I happened to look out the window. Directly across the road I saw a neighbour working in his garden. I didn't know him well, but had noticed that he didn't seem to go to church. As I looked at him a strong prompting came to me. It was as if an inner voice were saying, 'you have to talk to that man about Me.' My immediate reaction was one of resistance and confusion. I thought to myself that I couldn't envision how an opportunity to do so would arise. In any case I would be too embarrassed to talk to him about God. Nevertheless, I strongly felt that the Lord was urging me to do so. Later that same day I went to the Milltown Institute where I was due to give the first of a series of lectures on contemporary spirituality. I arrived in good time in order to make some practical preparations. When I went to the lecture room I had been assigned, there was only one person there. It was my neighbour! I was amazed to see him. I greeted him and asked what had motivated him to come. He explained that while he wasn't a church goer he was a spiritual seeker and interested in the topics listed in the course description. The Spirit had given me the prompting to speak to him about God, and then went on to provide me with a providential opportunity to do so.

As was noted in previous chapters, the Lord can reveal the divine will through conscience or a word of scripture. Over the years I have noticed that when I engage in my daily prayer time, I often get ideas floating into my mind when I'm truly at peace in the Lord's presence. They prompt me to do many unremarkable, mundane things, e.g., to pray for someone, to send an email, to take an evangelistic initiative, to write an article, to modify what I had already written in this book, to accept an invitation to speak etc. Nonetheless they are important in the eyes of God. St. Vincent de Paul once wrote, 'There is another way of knowing God's will, and it's by a divine urging; for often God enlightens our understanding and gives promptings to our heart; but we need to test such inspirations in order not to be deceived.'

## Discernment of Spirits

You will have noticed that the prayer for guidance, quoted above, asks, 'Preserve me today, from all illusions and false inspirations.' This petition echoes the words of Jesus in the Our Father where we ask to be delivered from evil, i.e., from the malign influence of Satan. St. Vincent de Paul, like other saints, felt that discernment of inspirations and promptings was necessary in order to establish whether they were the genuine voice of the Lord or not. He said that, 'a supernatural enlightenment from God is necessary in order to discern true insights from false ones.' It is simply naïve to think, as some Christians seem to do, that every pious thought or scripture text that crosses their minds was inspired by God rather than their own imperfect human nature or even the evil one, who can appear as an angel of light (cf. 2 Cor 11:14). As William Shakespeare reminded us in Act 1, Scene 3 of the *Merchant of Venice*, 'The devil can quote Scripture for his purpose.'

St. Vincent said, 'Among the multitude of thoughts and inspirations that come to us, some are apparently good and yet they don't come from God and are not according to his pleasure.' He proposed four main guidelines which he mentioned in a talk entitled 'True Inspirations and Illusions' on October 17th 1659.

> **Firstly:** is the prompting contrary to the commandments of God, the Church or State law? Is it contrary to one's solemn obligations e.g. marriage or priestly vows?
>
> **Secondly:** is there an element of superstition present? e.g., that an action has to be performed so often in such and such a way?
>
> **Thirdly:** is the prompting persistent and troublesome in such a way that it makes one uneasy? 'The Spirit of God,' observed St. Vincent, 'is a Spirit of peace, a gentle light which infuses itself into the soul without doing it any violence. Its action is sweet and agreeable.' We will know an inspiration is from God 'if it instils itself gently into our souls and inclines us to seek whatever concerns the greater glory of God.' St. Ignatius of Loyola said something similar in par. 315 of his *Spiritual Exercises*, those 'who go on earnestly striving to cleanse their souls from sin and who seek to rise in the service of God . . . it is characteristic of the good spirit . . . to give courage and strength, consolations, tears, inspirations, and peace. This

> He does by making all easy, by removing all obstacles so that the soul goes forward in doing good.'
>
> **Fourthly:** Vincent said, 'we should take advice. If a person is graciously, peacefully and quietly receptive to the advice given to him e.g. by a confessor, spiritual director, or a person exercising legitimate authority, and takes account of it, that is a sign that there is no illusion whatever in what he does.' But if a person receives a prompting which he or she is unwilling to share with anyone for discernment it is a bad sign. St. Vincent says, 'The Spirit of God inclines those it animates to submission. The Spirit of the gospel is a spirit of obedience.'

Vincent concluded his talk by saying that he had spoken to experts who knew a lot about the rules for the discernment of spirits. Others could be added he admitted, but he thought that these four would suffice. 'All the others,' he said, 'were connected with those I have mentioned.' He felt that if a person used a more elaborate method, he or she might be tempted to become overly introspective. St. Vincent practiced what he preached. In 1653 one of his priests wrote to him to say that he wanted to leave the Vincentian Congregation in order to join the Capuchins. In a letter dated the 4th of June Vincent discerned that his desire had not been prompted by the Lord. To begin, Vincent thought that having put his hand to the plough in the Vincentians, it was unlikely that the Lord was directing the priest to join another religious community, no matter how good it was. 'Another sign,' he added, 'which makes me think that God has not called you to the Capuchins, is that the desires which have come to you about this matter, trouble and disturb you by their insistence, as those suggested by the evil spirit generally do; while on the contrary the inspirations of God are gentle and peaceful, inclining us in a loving way to the good he desires of us.'

## Conclusion

In this chapter we have noted the fact that God can speak to us by means of inspirations and promptings. Having heard the Lord we need to do whatever he tells us, no matter what the cost. As the psalmist says in Ps 40:6. 'Sacrifice and offering you do not desire; but you have given me an open ear.' Jm 1:23-25 reminds us, 'For if someone merely listens to the message and does not live it out, he is like someone who gazes at his own face in a mirror. For he gazes at himself and then goes out and immediately forgets what sort of person he was. But the one who peers into the perfect law of liberty and fixes his attention there, and does not become a forgetful listener but one who lives it out - he will be blessed in what he does.'

CHAPTER EIGHT

# GOD SPEAKS THROUGH PEOPLE AND EVENTS

I heard a mildly amusing story many years ago about a nun who was praying in her convent chapel. 'Dear Lord,' said Sr. Joan, 'I have two things to ask of you. Firstly, please reveal your divine presence to me. Secondly, speak to my heart that I may hear your word.' As she prayed she was disturbed by the sound of the doorbell. Knowing that she was the only person in the house at the time, Sr. Joan reluctantly headed off down the stairs and opened the door. A Romanian gypsy was there with a baby in her arms. In broken English she said that she had to visit a hospital for an appointment and wondered if the nun could help her with the bus fare of five euro. The sister, said in an abrupt sort of way that she was busy and had no small change. When she closed the door she returned to the chapel and continued her prayer. However, ten minutes later the doorbell rang again. 'My God,' exclaimed Sr. Joan, 'I can get no peace in this house.' Once again she opened the door. This time there was a man from the Electricity Board standing there. He wanted to read the meter. The nun showed him where it was, he took note of the relevant numbers and tried to engage her in some small talk, but Sr. Joan didn't really respond. The man left and the irritated nun returned to the chapel. She couldn't believe it when the phone rang. When she answered it she found that a boy of five, who lived next door, was calling her. 'Hello Sr. Joan,' he said, 'I was playing football in my back garden and the ball went over the wall into the convent. Could you get it for me.' 'I can't get it now,' she said rather coldly, 'but when I have the time, I'll look for it and throw it over the wall. You really need to be more careful when you are playing football.' When she put down the receiver, Sr. Joan returned to the chapel. 'Lord,' she prayed, 'Why have you not revealed yourself to me or spoken to my heart?' Then she thought she heard an inner voice reply, 'I have already appeared to you on three separate occasions in the last hour but you took no notice of me and didn't listen to a word I said!

There is a very interesting verse in Heb 13:2-3, which reads, 'Do not forget to entertain strangers, for by so doing some people have entertained angels without knowing it.' The supreme example of hospitality of this kind in early Jewish literature was the warm welcome which Abraham extended to his heavenly visitors (Gen. 18:2–15). It was they who brought him the prophetic message that he and his wife Sarah would bear a son. It is probably this incident which the author of Heb 13:2 was alluding to. The word 'angel' in English, literally means 'a messenger' in the Greek of the New Testament. The author of Hebrews seems to be saying that when we show hospitality to strangers we may be welcoming the messengers of God. Let us look at a few examples of how this can happen.

## THE LORD SPEAKS THROUGH THE LITURGY OF THE WORD

Those who read the scriptures in church are like angels of the Lord. Speaking about the readings at Mass, par. 7 of the *Constitution on the Liturgy* says that Christ himself, 'is present in his word, since it is he who speaks when Scripture is read in Church.' That point was reiterated in par. 29 of the *General Instruction of the Missal,* where it says, that when the Scriptures are read in church, *'God himself is speaking to his people,* and Christ, present in his word, is proclaiming the Gospel.' It is Christ, too, who speaks through the priest when he gives a homily based on prayerful reflection on the readings. The preacher therefore, 'should be the first to hear the word of God which he proclaims.' If the priest or deacon, has truly listened to the Lord in the course of his homily preparation, the hearts of the listeners may burn within them as they hear that word proclaimed.

Years ago this truth came alive for me when I met a group of travelling people behind St. James' Brewery, in the heart of Dublin. When I arrived by car all the children ran to welcome me with affection and noisy excitement. Then I was led to a small room in one of the caravans. 'You will be hearing confessions here Father,' the owner said. For nearly an hour I administered the sacrament of reconciliation. I was surprised to find that among the Travellers were a few local people from the nearby apartments. As I absolved the people in the name of Christ I had a powerful sense that a canopy of mercy was not only being extended above them as penitents, but also above me as the confessor. We were all the recipients of God's amazing grace. Afterwards I said Mass in that same caravan. It was filled to capacity with about fifteen people. There was a little blond girl sitting beside me.

When the gospel was read I gave a short homily and invited the people to share stories of faith, accounts of how God had helped them when they trusted in the divine promises. Many moving testimonies were recounted. A social worker shared how God had helped her grandchild to recover from a riding accident when she had injured her head as a result of a fall on concrete. A man from the nearby apartments recalled, in an amusing way, how he had asked Mary to help him to avoid going to prison, and the way the prayer had been answered. Finally, the man who owned the caravan told us how, three years before, his daughter had been standing beside the stove when her nylon dress had caught fire. Besides being badly burnt, the fabric had melted into her skin. When she was brought to hospital, the doctors said that there was very little hope that she would recover. The family trusted in God, and prayed fervently for the little girl. Against all the odds she recovered. The father completed his testimony by saying, 'Thanks be to God, that is my daughter, alive and well, sitting beside you, Father.' What a memorable evening that turned out to be. From beginning to end I had a strong sense that the Lord was in our midst and speaking through the people present about the marvellous works of God.

By extension, the Lord can speak through anyone who gives a

talk, e.g., at a prayer meeting, retreat, or conference. Sometimes there can be a real anointing of the Spirit upon the speaker. I can remember many such an occasion. For instance, some years ago I attended an ecumenical conference in Malines in Belgium. At one point Cardinal Suenens, our host, invited an Episcopal priest called Graham Pulkingham of the Church of the Redeemer in Houston, Texas to speak to the gathering. He reflected on the meaning and implications of Acts 4:32-36 and told us about the way the passage had influenced his congregation. His insights about the connection between loving community and effective evangelisation made a big and lasting impression on me. I felt as if I had been listening to the living word of God. I'm sure that many of us have had that kind of experience, on different occasions, over the years, e.g., paying attention to a well known evangelist speaking on T.V. or listening to a CD in the car.

## God can speak through people we meet

We can have a similar experience in the course of person-to-person relationships. We may be seeking God's perspective on some personal problem. We pray to the Lord for guidance but none seems to come. Then we get into a spontaneous conversation with another person, it could be a friend or a stranger. As we share, the other person may speak about a scripture text, or share a personal experience, or give us a book or article to read, which, in the circumstances, seems to be God's answer to the prayer of our heart.

I know from personal experience that there have been times, when I have asked other people to pray for me, that God spoke a word of prophecy through them to me. For example, on one occasion a Protestant woman I knew spoke these words, 'My son, too long you have remained imprisoned by the thoughts and traditions of men and your fear of them, but I am calling you forth into a new place with me. The training I have given you, the dark places through which I have led you, have been but a preparation for far greater things yet. You praise me because of the blessings I have already given you, but this has been but a paddling in the shallows compared with what I wish to do through you, as I call you out to walk on the water with me. It will not be an easy walk my son, but I know your commitment to me and your desire to serve me, so all I ask of you is that you trust me.' Many years later, I can see in retrospect, how, by the grace of God, many of those words have been fulfilled in my life. One could say, therefore, that incidents like the ones I have described are part of God's providential provision for our lives. The Father in heaven uses other people as messengers to speak His inspiring word to our hearts.

Early in 2013 I visited Sicily. While there, a woman told me a very interesting story. When her son was born it became evident that he was very disturbed. When he was assessed by doctors they said that he was psychotic and probably autistic as well. They warned, more than once, that his condition was incurable. Needless to say, the boy's parents were heartbroken and at their wit's end. Neither of them practiced their religion. However, they believed in God and prayed on a fairly regular basis. When the boy was five, his mother was so upset about his worsening condition that she decided to go to Mass for the first time in years. When she got to the church she felt isolated because no one knew anything about her sorrows. During the Eucharist she was so upset that she wept most of the time. Apparently a man who was attending the Mass noticed her distress. Afterwards he approached her and said he wanted to share some scripture verses with her. They were from Jer 31:3; 16; and 31 respectively. They read, 'I have loved you with an everlasting love; I have drawn you with loving-kindness . . . Restrain your voice from weeping and your eyes from tears, for your work will be rewarded,' declares the Lord. . . The time is coming, declares the Lord, when I will make a new covenant with the house of Israel and with the house of Judah.' These words made a big impression on the grieving woman. She was reassured that, in spite of everything, God loved her, and that he didn't want her to weep any longer because a new chapter was about to begin in her life.

When she spoke to her partner about what had happened they both agreed that they would start going to church. Furthermore they made a very difficult decision in their personal lives. As a result of advice from a local priest they agreed to fast from sexual relations until the man got an annulment in order to be married in Church. They stuck to their decision for the ten years it took to sort things out. All the while their love for one another grew. Finally, they were married in church. During their time of sexual abstinence, the couple's son began to heal to such a point that all his mental problems melted away. When I met him I could see for myself that he was perfectly normal. Surely, the man who shared the verses from scripture was God's angel. He spoke a *rhema* word which was God's living message addressed to the woman's heart. When she and her partner listened and responded in faith, it had the power to effect what it said. It led to a transformation of the parent's lives and a miraculous healing for their son.

In a cautionary way I should say in passing that if another person claims to have a word from the Lord for you, two things are necessary before you take it to heart and act on it. Firstly, discern whether what was said really was from the Lord. As St Paul advised in 1 Thess 5:20-21, 'do not treat prophecies with contempt. *Test everything*. Hold on to the good.' Secondly, as I mentioned in chapter four, God's word of direction would need to be confirmed by a touch of divine grace within your heart so that, if you choose to follow it, you do so in a spirit of freedom and conviction rather than a spirit of servile submission to an external authority.

## GOD CAN SPEAK THROUGH PEOPLE WITH LEGITIMATE AUTHORITY

God also speaks through people who exercise legitimate authority. For example in religious life many priests, nuns and brothers would believe that the voice of their superior is the voice of God in things that are not sinful. In the *Autobiography of Ignatius of Loyola*, we are told that following his conversion at Manresa, the founder of the Jesuits felt that God had instructed him interiorly to go to Jerusalem to assist pilgrims there. However, he tells us that when he arrived in the holy city he met a Franciscan who told him to go home. It was probably because there was a strong chance he would be kidnapped. If he was, the Franciscans would probably have to redeem him by paying an expensive ransom. Ignatius, the former soldier, said that he wasn't afraid, had letters of recommendation, and was determined to remain. Then the Franciscan Provincial, 'said he had authority from the Holy See to detain those he thought fit, and to even excommunicate those who would not obey when instructed by him, and he thought in this case it was better for him not to remain. When he wished to show the pontifical papers giving him power to excommunicate, Ignatius said there was no need, as he believed his word. If the Franciscan priest had ecclesiastical authority, he would obey.' As a result of listening to what the friar had to say, Ignatius returned to Europe. In retrospect he felt that the provincial's arbitrary directions were the providential voice of God. As a result of returning to Europe Ignatius was led to found the Society of Jesus. As Romans 8:28 assures us, 'in all things God works for the good of those who love him.'

I have felt for many years that I should listen carefully to what those with legitimate authority have to say to me, e.g., a confessor in the sacrament of reconciliation. Because he is acting in the person of Christ I believe that his voice could well be the voice of God speaking to me. For instance, having heard my confession many years ago, a Vincentian colleague suggested that I read Ps 144:1-2 which says, 'Praise be to the Lord my Rock, He is my loving God and my fortress, my stronghold and my deliverer, my shield, in whom I take refuge, who subdues peoples under me.' Those words made a big impression on me.

I felt they were about spiritual warfare and my need to nestle by faith in the Lord's protection rather than wrestling with temptation and evil. The inspired and inspiring words of the psalmist reminded me of Eph 6:16 which says, 'take up the shield of faith, with which you can extinguish *all* the flaming arrows of the evil one.'

## God can speak through spiritual reading

Edith Stein (1891-1942), a Jewish unbeliever, received a doctorate of philosophy from the University of Göttingen for a dissertation entitled, *On the Problem of Empathy*. On one occasion during her summer holidays in 1921 she visited Bergzabern. While there, she read the autobiography of St. Teresa of Ávila. Edith was so impressed by its contents that she regarded the book as the voice of God. Soon afterwards she became a Catholic. Later on she joined the Carmelites where she was known as sister Teresa Benedicta of the Cross. She was martyred in Auschwitz in 1942, and canonised in 1998.

I have found on many occasions that the Lord may use something which an author has written in a book or article as a way of speaking to me. My religious awakening was indirectly triggered by two Protestant books I read, Merlin Carother's *Power in Praise*, and David Wilkerson's *The Cross and the Switchblade*. Some years afterwards, I can remember reading a book entitled *Compassion* which was jointly written by Catholic writers Nouwen, McNeil and Morrison. At one point I came across a wonderful line which reads, 'When Jesus was moved to compassion, the source of all life trembled, the ground of all love burst open, and the abyss of God's immense, inexhaustible and unfathomable tenderness revealed itself.' Those poetic words touched me very deeply. I have meditated on them many times and they have come to encapsulate my sense of the God who has been revealed in and through the loving life and ministry of Jesus Christ. Sometime later I was equally impressed by these words in the *Summa Theologica* of St Thomas Aquinas, 'As far as outward activity is concerned, compassion is the Christian's whole rule of life.' As a result, I feel that God is constantly saying, 'be compassionate as I am compassionate' (cf. Lk 6:36).

Needless to say, God can also speak to us through other means of communication such as radio, recorded talks and movies. For example, there are wonderful movies such as *Amazing Grace, Padre Pio Miracle Man,* and the superb Visual Bible version of the *Gospel of John* which can be viewed on YouTube. I have watched John's Gospel about twenty times. On every occasion I have felt that God has used that dramatisation to speak to me.

## GOD CAN SPEAK THROUGH EVENTS

To be a Christian is to have a strong sense of the providence of God, i.e. that God has a benevolent plan for our individual and collective lives and that he provides for us internally by natural talents and grace, and externally in many ways, mainly through secondary causes e.g., the help of other people. There is a striking example in the Book of Genesis where Joseph said to his heartless brothers, who had sold him into slavery years before, 'I am your brother Joseph, the one you sold into Egypt! And now, do not be distressed and do not be angry with yourselves for selling me here, because *it was to save lives that God sent me ahead of you'* (Gen 45:4-5). This was not only an example of a *felix culpa*, i.e., a happy fault, it was also an instance of a person discerning that God's will was being revealed in and through events. What was surprising and paradoxical in that instance was the fact that the treachery of the brothers became a springboard to *their* blessing. As St. Paul observed centuries later, 'Where sin abounds, grace abounds much more' (Rm 5:20).

There is a similar notion of God's will being expressed through providential events in the Book of Esther where we are told about a plan to kill all the Jews in the Persian empire. It so happened that king Xerxes's second wife, Esther, was Jewish. Her relative Mordecai said to her *'And who knows but that you have come to a royal position for such a time as this?'* (Est 4:14). In other words, Mordecai discerned in faith that God was speaking through providential events because Esther happened to be the right person, in the right place at the right time. After much prayer and fasting, she was able to intercede with the king on behalf of the Jewish people. As a result, Xerxes relented and authorised Esther to issue a decree, in his name, which spared the Jewish people.

St Vincent de Paul had a strong sense that people should seek God's will in all things. He said, 'Whoever conforms to the will of God and takes his pleasure in it leads a truly angelic life upon earth. He can even be said to be living the very life of Jesus Christ.' Needless to say, he maintained that God could reveal the divine purposes in an inward way by means of inspirations and promptings. However, he also believed, as the Bible illustrates, that they could be revealed by means of providential events. Writing about him, his first biographer, bishop Louis Abelly (1603–1691), said that, 'he closed his eyes to all human considerations, abandoned himself to the designs of his divine master, said in his heart, 'Lord what would you have me do?' In this spirit of dependence, he never undertook an enterprise of his own accord. He waited instead for divine providence to show the work to be undertaken, either by the orders of those he regarded as his superiors, by the advice and persuasion of those he recognised as virtuous persons, or lastly by the contemporary conditions and needs that manifested the will of God to him, which he always followed but never anticipated.' Speaking about Vincent, Abelly added, 'The will of God is known in two ways : either in those events we have no control over, those which depend solely on God's good pleasure, such as sickness, losses, or other accidents of life, or those which his commandments or his counsels reveal to us.'

Let me give two examples of the kind of thing Vincent may have had in mind. Some time ago I was invited to go to an Alpha meeting in London which was going to be attended by leaders from all over the world. Unfortunately, I had written the wrong date in my diary and was disappointed to find that the meeting was taking place much sooner than I had expected. Nevertheless, my Irish colleagues encouraged me to make every effort to book a flight to England in order to attend the meeting. I did try, but nothing suitable was available. I was disappointed, but accepted these events as part of God's purposeful providence. Then I heard that a member of my community, who had been resident in a nursing home for some time, had died suddenly. I was informed that his funeral was taking place on the very day I had planned to be in London. Surely, God had spoken through events and was saying, 'I wanted you to attend the funeral of your confrere with whom you lived for many years in community.' When I saw God's benevolent plan unfold in this way I was full of gratitude.

Some time after that event I went to Liverpool to preach. The morning I was due to return to Dublin I went to a small oratory where the blessed sacrament was exposed. As soon as I took my seat and gazed at the host, the following words drifted into my mind. 'I am present in the host because I give my people their daily bread which is the food of life. I am present in the host, because in sharing it, you become a fellowship. I am present in the host so as to live in your midst. When you meet with one another you meet with my real presence in your brothers and sisters.' I was surprised and touched by how quickly and clearly these inspiring words had come into my mind. When I left the oratory, I had a cup of coffee and headed for the ferry port on my motor scooter. I was guided by my Sat-Nav.

At one point on the journey I suspected I was going in the wrong direction. So I stopped to check if my GPS was receiving a signal. As I did so, I noticed a man on the other side of the road. He was on his hands and knees. He gestured weakly for my help. At first I thought he might be drunk or luring me into a trap.

Nevertheless, I walked over to him, a little cautiously I must admit, and asked what I could do to help. He said, 'I think I may have had a heart attack. I suffer from angina and low blood pressure. I was feeling dizzy and collapsed. I have been on the ground for about ten minutes unable to stand up again. Are you Irish?' I said that I was. 'So you are a Catholic?' 'Yes' I replied. 'Good,' he responded, 'I am a Catholic also.' At first I didn't really know what to do. Then I noticed a phone box nearby and went over to it, only to find that the phone had been vandalised and wasn't working. Although I had a mobile phone I remembered that it had run out of credit. I went back to the man and assisted him to his feet and led him to a nearby bus shelter where there was a seat. I said to him, 'I am going to travel to the port now. When I get there I will phone for an ambulance. It won't take long. You wait here until it comes. Before I leave you, I have one thing to say, trust in the Lord, he will help you.' I was quite moved when the man replied with great sincerity, 'I do trust in the Lord.' Then I headed off on my scooter.

When I got to the port check-in booth I told the official about the man on the roadside. He rang the police. I talked to them and gave information about the man's precise location. They told me they were getting an ambulance to pick him up straightaway. As I returned to my scooter a pretty female official approached me and asked if she could shake my hand. 'My colleague told me what you did for the man in distress,' she explained, ' I just wanted to express my appreciation.' I was taken aback and reminded of some words of a John Lennon song, 'Life is what happens to you, while you're busy making other plans.' To the eyes of faith, however, those kind of unpredictable events are often points of encounter with God and God's providential purposes.

Subsequently, when I reflected on that incident I had a strong impression that God had revealed the divine presence and purposes to me by means of unplanned events. Firstly, there was the prophetic word in the chapel. It seemed to prepare me for what was about to occur. Then, providentially, I just happened to stop at the very place where the afflicted man was on the ground. It was fortuitous, because there was no other traffic on the road at the time, and not another person to be seen. Cardinal Newman once wrote, 'God's presence is not discerned at the time when it is upon us, but afterwards, when we look back upon what is gone and over. The world seems to go on as usual. There is nothing of heaven in the face of society, in the news of the day. And yet the ever-blessed Spirit of God is there, ten times more glorious, more powerful than when He trod the earth in our flesh.' When I looked back on what had happened I had a distinct impression that, not only had I met with Jesus in the person of the man on the roadside, I had also met with him in the kindness of the port official who made the phone call, and in the affirmation expressed by his female colleague. I realised that there was also a contemplative and Eucharistic dimension to those events. I was interested to see that a 1981 document entitled, *The Contemplative Dimension of the Christian Life,* which was published by the Sacred Congregation for Religious and Secular Institutes, stated in par. 30, 'The contemplative dimension is the real secret of renewal for every religious life. It vitally renews the following of Christ because it leads to an experiential knowledge of him. . . The more open a person is to the contemplative dimension, the more attentive they will be to the demands of the Kingdom, . . . because they will look on events with the eyes of faith. *This will help them to discover the divine will everywhere* (my italics).'

## DIVINE APPOINTMENTS

As far as Christians are concerned there are no coincidences, but only God incidents. The late John Wimber maintained in his book *Power Evangelism* that apparently chance meetings between people, like the one I just described, can in fact be divine appointments. 'A divine appointment,' he explained, 'is an appointed time in which God reveals himself to an individual or group through spiritual gifts or other supernatural phenomena...they are meetings he has ordained to demonstrate his kingdom (Eph 2:10).' He cited the story of the encounter between Philip and the Ethiopian eunuch in Acts 8:26-40 as a good example of what he had in mind. Throughout that meeting in the wilderness, Philip was guided by means of the Spirit and his gifts. John Wimber also maintained that when any Christian relies on the fact that God is at work within his or her heart, 'a power encounter' can take place in such a way that there is an in-breaking of the liberating presence of God's grace, e.g., when the person is filled with the Spirit or healed as a result of the laying on of hands. That was true for the eunuch when he was baptised by Philip.

Let me give an example of a divine appointment. A few days

ago I had a chat with a man from County Monaghan, in Ireland. He told me that, following a rather Godless period in his life, he had experienced a spiritual awakening. Since that blessing he has devoted a lot of time to prayer and is open to the voice and leading of the Holy Spirit. He told me that, recently he felt an urge to go to Armagh city to attend Eucharistic adoration which was being held in a church there. He had intended heading off at midday but his son asked him to do something for him at that time. So he put off the trip until three o' clock. But shortly before he intended setting off, his wife asked him to go shopping with her, so he postponed his trip until five o' clock. Finally he drove to the church. When he was praying in the presence of the Blessed Sacrament he noticed a young woman coming into the church. He not only sensed that she was weighed down by troubles, he also felt an inner impulse to talk to her. He went over to the woman and said quietly, 'I felt that the Holy Spirit told me to approach you and to give you a booklet I have with me. It is called *Will You Help Me?* and is about the divine mercy. I hope that you will find it helpful.' Then he returned to his seat.

A short time afterwards the woman came over to him and thanked him for the booklet. She explained, 'I have been going through a really bad time lately. I intended coming to the church at twelve but couldn't bring myself to leave the house. The same thing happened at three. But at five o clock I finally summoned up the courage to come here. The booklet you gave me will be a great help.' 'Wasn't it striking,' said the man, 'that I was prevented from coming to the adoration at the same times that the woman couldn't come. But I was able to get away at the same time that she finally came to the church. It was as if the Lord where orchestrating events so that I could meet her and give her the booklet.' That is a good example of how to listen to God. On the first two occasions the man listened to the Lord through events by listening in a loving way to the needs of his son and his wife respectively. He was willing to sacrifice his own agenda in order to respond to them. When he got to the church he listened to a prompting of the Spirit and acted upon it to good effect. It was an example of the kind of divine appointment that John Wimber had in mind.

## GOD CAN SPEAK THROUGH SUPERNATURAL MANIFESTATIONS

God can also speak through miraculous events. In 1 Cor 12:7 Paul refers to them as *phanerosis,* i.e. manifestations or epiphanies of the Lord's supernatural presence and power. Thankfully, I have had many such experiences of the numinous over the years, such as seeing people falling under the power of the Spirit, being healed, and also delivered from evil spirits. Often a message is implicit in these occurrences. Here is an example of a supernatural manifestation that has spoken to a lot of people including me.

At 7 p.m. on August 18th 1996, Fr. Alejandro Pezet had said Mass in central Buenos Aires. As he was finishing distributing Holy Communion, a woman told him that she had found a discarded host at the back of the church. When Fr. Alejandro saw the soiled host he was unable to consume it, so he placed it in a container of water and put it away in the tabernacle.

When it dissolved he intended pouring the contents down the sacrarium in the sacristy, i.e., a shallow basin used for washing the sacred vessels. When he opened the tabernacle, on Monday, August 26, he saw to his amazement that the host had turned into a bloody substance. He informed Jorge Bergoglio, who was the auxiliary Bishop at that time. He gave instructions that the Host should be photographed in a professional way. Afterwards the Host was returned to the tabernacle, and nothing was said about it. When it was discovered that the Host suffered no visible decomposition, Bishop Bergoglio, who was now the Archbishop, decided to have it scientifically analysed.

On October 5, 1999, Dr. Ricardo Castanon-Gomez, a Bolivian scientist, took a sample of the bloody fragment and sent it to New York for analysis. Since he did not wish to influence the investigation one way or another, he did not inform the team of scientists about its origin. One of these was Dr. Frederic Zugiba, a well-known cardiologist and forensic pathologist. He determined that the analysed substance was real flesh and blood containing human DNA. Zugiba testified that, 'the analysed material is a fragment of the heart muscle found in the wall of the left ventricle close to the valves. This muscle is responsible for the contraction of the heart. It should be borne in mind that the left cardiac ventricle pumps blood to all parts of the body. The heart muscle is in an inflammatory condition and contains a large number of white blood cells. This indicates that the heart was alive at the time the sample was taken, since white blood cells die outside a living organism. What is more, these white blood cells had penetrated the tissue, which further indicates that the heart had been under severe stress, as if the owner had been beaten severely about the chest.'

Two Australians, journalist Mike Willesee and lawyer Ron Tesoriero, witnessed these tests. Knowing where the sample had come from, they were dumbfounded by Dr. Zugiba's findings. Mike Willesee asked the scientist how long the white blood cells would have remained alive if they had come from a piece of human tissue, which had been kept in water. Dr. Zugiba responded by saying that they would have ceased to exist in a matter of minutes. Then the journalist told the doctor that the sample had first been kept in ordinary water for a month and then for another three years in a container of distilled water; only then had it been taken for analysis. Dr. Zugiba was at a loss to account for this fact. He stated that there was no way of explaining the phenomenon scientifically. Only then did Mike Willesee inform the doctor that the analysed sample had in fact come from a consecrated host which had mysteriously turned into bloody human flesh. Amazed by this information, Dr. Zugiba replied, 'How and why a consecrated Host would change its character and become living human flesh and blood, will remain an inexplicable mystery to science—a mystery totally beyond her competence.'

While our belief in the real presence is not based on a miracle of this kind, it is supported and strengthened by it. It seems as if the Lord is saying, 'believe that I am truly present in the consecrated bread and wine. At the heart of the Eucharist is my beating heart of love. That love flows out from me to you in holy communion. Receive it with faith and reverence.' In general terms, heaven touches earth whenever miracles occur. They are testimonies to the supernatural presence of God. The first Vatican Council taught that miracles render divine revelation 'credible though external signs' (Denzinger's *Handbook of Creeds and Definitions* 3033).

## Conclusion: An examen of consciousness

As this chapter comes to a conclusion the issue of discernment is relevant once again. A good way of engaging in it is to do a regular examen of consciousness. It is best done at the end of the day or week. It enables a person to become aware of how the Lord has been revealing the divine presence, word and purposes to the heart, e.g., in and through people and events. Rather than being an examination of conscience, i.e., an itemised assessment of wrongdoing from a Christian point of view; an examen of consciousness aims to focus attention on God-given inspirations, promptings, divine appointments, and providential events, as well as how one did or did not respond to them. In the words of 1 Jn.4:1, it develops the ability to 'test the spirits to see whether they are of God.' St. Ignatius of Loyola wrote in par. 32 of his *Spiritual Exercises*: 'There are three kinds of thought in the mind, namely: one which is strictly my own, and arises wholly from my own free will; two others which come from without, the one from the good Spirit, the other from the Evil One.' In order to engage in an examen of consciousness one begins by asking the Holy Spirit for help, e.g., 'Lord, you enlighten every heart. Enlighten mine to recognise how you have been drawing me to yourself. Help me to appreciate your

Presence and to distinguish those inspirations and promptings that came from You, and those that came from either myself or from the Evil One. Amen.' Then prayerfully consider these two points.

1. 'Lord help me to become aware of the inspirations and promptings you have given me today and to recognise whether I responded to them or not.'
2. 'Lord enlighten my heart to recognise any unloving feeling, mood, attitude, desire, thought, word or deed that saddened your Holy Spirit within me today.'

One could conclude with something like the following prayer. 'Father in heaven, thank you for the gift of your Spirit. Today it enabled me to see and to hear you more clearly, and to follow you more nearly. As for my shortcomings, please forgive them. Amen.'

## CHAPTER NINE

# MAKING CHOICES WHEN THERE ARE LEGITIMATE OPTIONS

I live in Dublin. Driving through its streets can be a real headache. Whenever I have to travel any distance I usually have more than one route I can take. So before I set off I spend some time trying to work out what might be the best one to choose. Many factors have to be taken into account, such as the time of day, toll booths, road works, big sporting or entertainment events which could increase traffic congestion etc. Then I make an informed choice, pick a route and hope that I don't run into unpredictable trouble such as a bad traffic accident. As you will recognize my choice is based on an assessment of the relevant facts in order to come to a prudent decision. In instances like this I have often relied on my own unaided efforts while forgetting to ask for God's help. Evidently, St Peter made a similar mistake. In Luke 5:4-6 we are told that Jesus said to him, 'Put out into the deep and let down your nets for a catch.' And Simon answered, 'Master, we toiled all night and took nothing! But at your word I will let down the nets.' And when they had done this, they enclosed a great shoal of fish.' Among other things, the evangelist was pointing out that when Peter relied on his own considerable natural knowledge, experience and expertise he caught nothing, but when he listened to the Lord and followed his instructions, he was richly blessed. As Ps 127:1 warned him and us, 'Unless the Lord watches over the city, the watchman stays awake in vain.'

In Acts 1:23-26 there is an interesting incident which shows how Peter and the apostles had learned their lesson well. Following the suicide of Judas, the disciples had to replace him. Any prospective candidate needed to have known Jesus throughout his public ministry as well as being able to witness to his resurrection. In the event there were two equally good choices. We are told that the eleven apostles, 'proposed two men: Joseph called Barsabbas (also known as Justus) and Matthias. Then they prayed, 'Lord, you know everyone's heart. Show us which of these two you have chosen to take over this apostolic ministry, which Judas left to go where he belongs.' Then they cast lots, and the lot fell to Matthias; so he was added to the eleven apostles.' Commenting on this verse, Joseph Fitzmyer, S.J., says that what is first and foremost is that Matthias was not democratically elected. Following a time of fervent prayer, he was chosen by lot by the assembled community. The implication is clear: God had selected Matthias as the replacement for Judas. The form of selection was unusual. Instead of being chosen as the result of an angelic intervention, a vision or a prophetic utterance, Matthias was chosen by lot.

In chapter two of his autobiography, St Ignatius of Loyola recounts a similar kind of situation. On one occasion he met a Moslem. They got into conversation about Mary the mother of Jesus. The Moslem said he could not believe that she was still a virgin after the conception of her Son. When Ignatius parted company with the man, he reflected on what he had said and became very angry with him and himself. He felt that the Moslem was in grave error, while he himself hadn't asserted his beliefs in a forceful and persuasive way. Because the stranger had mentioned where he was intending to go, Ignatius decided to follow and kill him. But he did invite the Lord to help him make the right choice. He tells us that he 'resolved to settle all his doubts in the following novel way: he would give free rein to his horse, and if, on coming to the cross-road, his animal should turn into the path that led to the destination of the Moslem, he would pursue him and kill him; but if his horse kept to the highroad he would allow the wretch to escape. Having done as he had decided, it happened through the Providence of God that his horse kept to the highroad.' Prescinding from the fact that the sixth commandment forbids murder - obviously Ignatius thought that if he killed the Moslem it would be justifiable homicide - his method of decision making was interesting. Occasionally in the modern world, a similar method can be used to make a God directed choice.

A few years ago a number of us were led to form a new lay community. In the early days we wondered what name we would give it. Following a good deal of discussion we narrowed down the possibilities to two: The Friends of Jesus and The New Springtime Community. At one point all the community members boarded a Christian ship which was visiting Dublin port at the time. The crew kindly gave us the use of a cabin where we held a community meeting. Its chief aim was to choose, with God's help, a meaningful name for the nascent community. We were inspired by the story in Acts 1:23-26 and decided that, following a time of prayer for God's guidance, we would draw lots. In the event, the New Springtime Community was chosen as our name. We all believed that it was the one given to us by the providence of God. I may say in passing that from that time onward we agreed to conclude any emails we sent to one another with the Gaelic words *Cairde Iosa*, which means, 'Friend of Jesus,' followed by our signature. It would have to be admitted that, although the two examples cited are valid ways of discovering God's will, they are exceptional.

## Discernment and Individual Choices

Ignatius of Loyola has already been mentioned. He had sage advice to offer to those who are faced with a choice between two apparently good options. Let me begin to describe his approach by citing a contemporary example of a choice between two good possibilities. A umber of years ago a woman sought my advice when I was living in Boston, Massachusetts. She said that when she was young her father had died unexpectedly. Her mother was left with the daunting task of raising her three children on her own. She made heroic efforts to do so. At a certain point she sat down her teenage daughter and her younger siblings and asked them to promise that in the years to come they would never send her to a nursing home. Apparently the children, who owed so much to their mother, agreed to her request.

The woman said that now that her mother had grown old, she was looking after her in her home. She explained that as her mother's health deteriorated, her caring task got more onerous. She said that recently, her husband had approached her and expressed his concern about two related points. Firstly, he said he was quite worried about her health. He could see that the task of caring for her mother was increasingly stressful and tiring for his wife. Secondly, he stated that she was so preoccupied with looking after her mother that she had less time and emotional energy to devote to her children or to him. He said that, despite the fact that he loved his mother in law, he thought that the time had come to send her to a good nursing home where she would get the around the clock medical care she increasingly needed. The woman said to me, 'Father Pat I am confused. On the one hand I owe so much to my mother and feel bound by the promise I made her. By the way, my husband thinks it was unreasonable on my mother's part to ask me to take on such an difficult task at such an early age. He says I shouldn't feel bound by it. On the other hand, I love my husband and children, I know I owe my first allegiance to them. What should I do? How can I discover what God's will is for me in these challenging circumstances? Ignatian spirituality would propose the following three steps.

**1] Pray for inner freedom and guidance**

The person prays to God that the Holy Spirit will enable him or her to make the right choice. Here is a suggested prayer. 'Heavenly Father, I thank you that I have been granted a spirit of wisdom and knowledge, and I can have insight into your ways of doing things. I yield to the direction of the Holy Spirit for every decision I must make. I acknowledge You before making any decisions, and I seek Your direction at all times. I am willing to stop if You tell me to stop or go when You tell me to go. Because I acknowledge You, You direct my choices, and in this way I will remain in the perfect will of God the Father for my life. Your word is my final authority, and want every choice I make to line up with it. I will not disregard the peace of God in helping me to make decisions. In Jesus' name, I pray. Amen.'

The person making the choice cannot load the dice so that the more attractive option gets the upper hand. There has to be a genuine desire to do God's will together with a spirit of detachment from self-centred human preferences. For Ignatius the indispensible condition for making a proper choice is a fundamental orientation toward God. This will usually involve elements such as the following. What is my God given vocation in life, whether married or single? Is one of the choices facing me more consistent with that vocation? That was a difficult question for the woman to answer. However, she was helped by recalling the scripture which says, 'a man will leave his father and mother and be united to his wife, and the two will become one flesh' (Mt 19:5-6). This implies that a wife's first obligation is to her husband, and only after that to her parents. I stated in chapter one that the great command to love, by keeping the golden rule, is the context within which any choice has to be made. So the question arises, in this instance which choice would be the most loving of the two?

**2] Assessing relevant facts**

One way of answering those questions is to talk to a trusted person such as a friend or spiritual director about the impending decision, much as the woman spoke to me about her aged mother. A confidant is more detached than the person who has to make the choice. As a result he or she can draw attention to relevant considerations that might have been overlooked by the person who has to make a challenging choice. For instance, I asked the woman whether she was inclined to look after her mother because of a cheerless sense of obligation or a sense of willing love? I also made it clear that I agreed with what her husband had said about the promise her mother had asked her to make. I said that it was unfair of her to have placed such an obligation on young and immature shoulders. I said that in making her decision she shouldn't feel bound by it.

Having shared with a confidant, an individual with a difficult choice to make would be well advised to get a pen and paper in order to write down the pros and cons involved in the decision. Firstly, St Ignatius suggested that one should consider all the reasons against an option. For example, it was clear to me when talking to the woman that she wanted to go on caring for her mother. In that case I urged her to begin by really thinking about what her husband had said concerning her health and her relationship with him and their children. It can be good to imagine whatever possibilities are involved and to let one's feelings about them to surface and to be acknowledged in a prayerful way. Secondly, one goes on to consider the reasons for choosing the more attractive option. The woman could try to imagine how she would cope with her ailing mother in the years to come and possibly the difficulties she would experience in her family due to the neglect of her relationship with her husband and children. In this instance too, she would need to sense and name her feelings and their causes in a prayerful way.

**3] Discernment of spirits**

As has been mentioned elsewhere in this book, discernment is facilitated by noticing which option evokes on-going consolation of spirit, especially inner peace, from the one that fails to do so and therefore ends in desolation of spirit. Some time ago I came across the following helpful criteria for discernment of spirits in the writings of St John Eudes.

- The spirit of Jesus is a spirit of light, truth, devotion, love, trust, zeal and reverence toward God and the things of God. The spirit of the world is a spirit of error, disbelief, darkness, blindness, mistrust, grumbling, impiety, irreverence and hardness of heart toward God and the things of God.
- The spirit of Jesus is a spirit of humility, modesty, distrust of self, mortification, self-denial, reliability and firmness among those who live with this spirit. On the contrary, the spirit of the world is a spirit of pride, presumption, disordered self-love, frivolousness and irresponsibility .
- The spirit of Jesus is a spirit of mercy, charity, patience, gentleness and of unity toward our neighbour. The spirit of the world is a spirit of vengeance, envy, impatience, anger, calumny and division.
- Finally, the spirit of Jesus is the spirit of God, a holy and divine spirit, a spirit of every type of grace, virtue and

> blessing. It is a spirit of peace and tranquillity, a spirit that only seeks the interests of God and his glory. On the contrary, the spirit of the world is the spirit of Satan. For Satan is the prince and leader of the world. Thus it follows necessarily that the world is animated and governed by his spirit; an earthly, carnal and animal spirit, a spirit of every sort of sin and malediction, a spirit of unrest and anxiety, of storm and tempest, *a spirit of devastation* (Ps 10:7). It is a spirit that seeks only its own ease, satisfaction and interest.

Because Ignatius of Loyola was familiar with these spirits his spiritual knowledge helped him to discern God's will when making difficult choices. For instance, he was opposed to any of the first Jesuits becoming bishops or cardinals. In the year 1552, Emperor Charles V requested Pope Julius III to make Jesuit Francis Borgia a Cardinal. When Ignatius heard about this his spontaneous reaction was one of opposition. However, he decided to discern which course of action would be in accord with God's will. Subsequently in an illuminating letter to Francis he described how he had come to a decision. 'Pondering on the matter and discussing it from time to time during this three day span, I perceived that certain fears came to me or at least that there was no liberty of spirit to speak against and prevent the project. I asked myself, 'How do I know what God our Lord wishes to do?' Consequently, I did not feel entirely secure in the thought of obstructing it i.e. the emperor's project. At other times, during my customary prayers, I recognized that these fears had departed from me. Going on with prayer at various times, sometimes with this fear and sometimes with the contrary. I finally found myself during my customary prayer on the third day, and always ever since, with a fully settled judgment that, as much as I could, I should turn the pope and the cardinals from their purpose.' This is a good example of discernment of spirits in action. By the way, although Ignatius didn't receive any form of charismatic guidance, it would have been possible. The letter ended with Ignatius saying that he felt ongoing consolation when he renewed his decision to discourage his priests from becoming bishops or cardinals.

Rightly, it has been pointed out that it rare for inner peace to be pure and completely undisturbed. Any choice we make will have its down side. For example, I discovered to my surprise, that the woman I talked to about her mother, finally chose to go on nursing her at home. Not only was this a demanding task in itself, she was upset by the awareness that she hadn't as much time to spend with her husband and children as she would like. But I think it is true to say that while there was a certain disturbance at the surface of her mind, deep down there was a Godly peace as a result of choosing the divine will no matter what the cost.

## Group Decision Making

Needless to say, while all of us have to make individual choices, Christian communities of different kinds also have to make choices between options that are often good in themselves. In many ways, group decision making is not all that different from individual discernment.

**1] Mission statement/vocation**

If the group has a mission statement they should recall and ponder it in a prayerful way. Such a statement is a brief, written description of the purpose of a group. It includes a vision statement which describes the aim of the group, a list of values that inform its vision, followed by a brief description of the action steps that will give expression to the vision and values of the group. Hopefully such a mission statement is an articulation of God's will for the people involved. Jesus voiced his mission statement was when he said that he had been anointed to bring the Good News to the poor (cf. Lk 4:18). As I mentioned in chapter two, on one occasion Jesus spent the night in prayer. Afterwards he was able to decline a request to respond to an urgent pastoral *need* because he wanted to dedicate himself to his God given *priority* of preaching to the poor. Aware of what they are about, contemporary groups will also be better able to recognize those choices, which though worthy in themselves, are nevertheless not in accord with their God given mission.

2] If possible, especially if a big, important choice has to be made, it is helpful when a skilled and experienced facilitator, e.g. a trained spiritual director, is appointed to help the group to go through the various stages of the discernment process. Because this person is detached and uninvolved in the decision to be made, he or she can help the members of the group to go through the various steps in a peaceful and prayerful way.

**3] State clearly what choice the group is considering**

In his book *Discernment: Seeking God in Every Situation*, Fr. Chris

Aridas says that the group should state clearly what choice they are considering. For example, a Parish Pastoral Council might meet to discuss the following proposition, 'That the number of weekend Masses should be reduced by two, and that the Mass times should be changed.'

**4] Gather relevant information/data**

The Parish Council might design a questionnaire which would explain how, due to the shortage of priests, the parish would no longer be able to have as many weekend masses as before. Hence the need to reduce their number and times at the weekend. The questionnaire would aim to canvass the views and opinions of the parishioners. The Parish council might also try to get information about what other parishes had done in similar circumstances. It is also good to see whether scripture and church teaching have anything relevant to say about the issues involved. For example, in par. 27 of his pastoral exhortation, *Evangelli Gaudium,* Pope Francis says, 'I dream of a 'missionary option', that is, a missionary impulse capable of transforming everything, so that the Church's customs, ways of doing things, times and schedules, language and structures can be suitably channeled for the evangelization of today's world rather than for her self-preservation.'

**5] List and share the pros and cons involved**

Each individual should be familiar with the data collected and having read it, they should prayerfully consider the pros and cons involved in the prospective changes. All this should be done without consulting with the other members of the Parish

Council. When each person's reflection and list is complete, the results are disclosed, e.g. each person shares one con, then another until all the cons are shared. Then the same is done with the pros. Argument about the pros or cons should be avoided. This process is time consuming. If the group is very large it might be a good idea to divide it into smaller groups. When they have concluded their work, they could share their conclusions with the other groups.

**6] Consider the results of the sharing in a prayerful way**
Finally, the group should pray about the proposition/choice that they are considering in a discerning way. It is also possible that one or more of the people involved in the discernment process would receive guidance in one or more of the more ordinary and charismatic ways described in this book. When the time comes for making a decision, each member says something like, 'I feel that the Lord is asking us to follow, or not follow the proposition.' As Fr. Aridas says, there should be no discussion at this stage. No reasons are given other than each person's sense of where the Lord is leading. Usually, a peaceful consensus will tend to emerge as a result of this prayerful process of discernment.

## CONCLUSION

You may remember that in the introduction I said that, 'when those who do practice their faith attend Christian meetings they usually begin with a formulaic type of prayer, but all too often there is a failure afterwards, to consciously seek the presence, word and will of God in a discerning and heartfelt way. Instead, the people discuss and decide things in a purely human manner while presuming that God is guiding.' The individual and group methods that are proposed here, try to overcome these shortcomings. Needless to say, the process may be informed by one or more of the other ordinary and charismatic ways of discerning God's will considered elsewhere in this book.

# Section Three

## Unusual Ways of Hearing the Lord

# CHAPTER TEN

# PRIVATE REVELATION

When Pope Benedict the XVI's successor was elected in March 2013, there were articles in the papers which asked the question, will Francis be the last of the Popes? This speculation was prompted by the fact that St. Malachy (1094-1148), a former Archbishop of Armagh, had allegedly drawn up a list of 112 future popes as a result of a revelatory vision. His prophecies were discovered and published by Benedictine Arnold de Wyon in 1590. Whereas the latter's document was fairly clear about the popes who had lived before that date, it was surprisingly vague about the ones that were to follow. Pope Francis is the 112th pontiff mentioned in the prophecies. Speaking about his papacy it predicted, 'In the final persecution of the Holy Roman Church there will reign *Petrus Romanus,* who will feed his flock amid many tribulations; after which the seven-hilled city will be destroyed and the dreadful Judge will judge the people. The end.' Is this an inspired revelation from God? The question can be answered on two levels. Firstly, if perchance the document is genuine, was Malachy accurate in his predictions? They are so vague and lacking in specific details that it is very hard to say. If Francis is the last Pope, the appellation, *Petrus Romanus,* makes no sense.

He is neither named Peter nor a Roman. Secondly, it is possible that the prophecies were a forgery which was created in the 16th century for political reasons of an ecclesiastical kind. On both counts the prophecies do not seem to contain inspired revelation. This raises the question, what is private revelation and how does it relate to public revelation?

In the previous section on ordinary forms of inspiration, we examined how God can speak to the heart in different ways such as religious desires, rhema words, conscience, inspirations, inner promptings, messages from other people etc. Every Christian can expect to hear from God in these ways. In this second section we are moving on to look at the more unusual, charismatic ways in which God can speak to us by means of such things as dreams, visions, apparitions, words of knowledge, locutions, prophecy etc. These are what are referred to in theology as means of private revelation. Because it is a controversial topic, we will look at its nature, and its relationship to public revelation.

The word revelation in English is derived from Latin and means, 'to unveil.' It is worth noting in this connection that it is similar in meaning to the Greek word for truth, i.e., *aletheia,* which literally means 'the state of not being hidden; the state of being evident.' In a Christian sense, therefore, revelation refers to the fact that God can manifest or disclose some truth by supernatural means. The Lord seemed to promise such revelation in Is 48:6-8, 'From now on I will tell you of new things, of hidden things unknown to you. They are created now, and not long ago; you have not heard of them before today. So you cannot say, 'Yes, I knew of them. You have neither heard nor understood; from of old your ear has not been open.' Again in Sir 42:19 we read that the Lord, 'makes known the past and the future, and reveals the deepest secrets.' The notion of supernatural revelation may also be implicit in 1 Jn 2:27, 'As for you, the anointing you received from him remains in you, and you do not need anyone to teach you. But as his anointing teaches you about all things.'

## PUBLIC REVELATION

The term public revelation refers to the supernatural manifestation of God's wisdom and will for the human race in order to lead humanity to its heavenly destiny. It is contained in Sacred Scripture and tradition and has been entrusted directly to the Church for preservation, interpretation and instruction. Public or official revelation ended with the life, death and glorious resurrection of Jesus Christ and the completion of the New Testament. As John of the Cross wrote, 'Since God the Father has given us his Son, his only word - for he possesses no other - he spoke everything at once in this sole word – and he has no more to say . . . because what he spoke before to the prophets in parts, he has spoken all at once by giving us this All who is his Son.' Bl. John Henry Newman suggested that although public revelation remains constant there is a development of doctrine in the sense that, over time, the Church better understands the deposit of faith. As par. 66 of the *Catechism of the Catholic Church* says, 'Yet even if Revelation is already complete, it has not been made completely explicit;

it remains for Christian faith *gradually to grasp* its full significance over the course of the centuries.'

## Private Revelation

That said, it is obvious that down the centuries many Christians have claimed to have received what are variously referred to as 'private,' 'particular,' 'special' or 'prophetic revelations.' One could argue that Jesus promised that this would be the case in John 16:12-14 when he said, 'I have much more to say to you, more than you can now bear. But when he, the Spirit of truth, comes, he will guide you into all truth. He will not speak on his own; he will speak only what he hears, and he will tell you what is yet to come.' What does Jesus mean here? Although the disciples heard the truth from the lips of Jesus during his public ministry they only appropriated its true meaning with the sending of the Holy Spirit. Besides understanding all that Jesus had said, they received new revelation during their lifetimes through the power of the same Spirit. That is why the Church teaches that public revelation was complete with the death of the last apostle.

Do the words of Jesus in Jn 16:12-14 refer to the possibility of private revelation, e.g., prophetic knowledge of forthcoming events which spell out the implications of public revelation without adding to it? St. Jean-Jacques Olier (1608-1657), founder of the Sulpicians was a sort of cessationist, in the sense that he seemed to believe that revelation was a thing of the past. He wrote, 'Revelations are the aberration of faith; they are an amusement that spoils simplicity in relation to God, that embarrasses the soul and makes it swerve from its directness in relation to God . . . Special illuminations, auditions, prophecies and the rest are marks of weakness in a soul.' Surprisingly, Karl Rahner, S.J. who, as we noted in chapter one, spoke about the silence of God, did not agree. He wrote, 'By no means should we admit too hastily that the charism of prophecy is a privilege, now lapsed, of the primitive Church. The social and psychological forms of the prophetic charism and its intervention in the course of the Church's history can vary. But besides the official power transmitted by the imposition of hands, there should always be in the Church the humanly un-transmittable vocation of the prophet. Neither of the two gifts can replace the other. Wherever in the Church, after Christ, the prophet exercises his or her specific action and communicates a Divine imperative in view of a determined situation, one has 'private revelation.'

It seems to me that there are two main forms of private revelation, which can be referred to as *personal* and *ecclesial*. In personal forms, a believer who is open to the voice of God, may hear a supernatural, revelatory word which is for the person him or herself, for someone being ministered to, or for a local community. This kind of private revelation is common in the Pentecostal Churches and the Charismatic Renewal Movement. In ecclesial forms of private revelation a believer may receive a prophetic message from God which is addressed to the whole Church. In this section of the book we will focus mainly on personal forms of private revelation.

Danish scholar Niels Christian Hvidt has pointed out in his book *Christian Prophecy: The Post Biblical Tradition* that private revelation has been granted to individuals down the centuries. May I say in passing that although his book is excellent in many ways, it is quite unsatisfactory in so far as it virtually ignores the charism of prophecy as experienced in the Pentecostal Churches and the Charismatic Renewal Movement. In the light of the points already made, it was particularly interesting to read what St. John XXIII stated at the close of the Marian Year on February 18, 1959. He said, 'the supreme pontiffs also have the duty, when after mature examination, they deem it necessary for the common good of bringing to the attention of the faithful those supernatural lights which it pleases God to dispense freely to certain privileged souls, not for the purpose of presenting new doctrines, but rather to guide us in our conduct.' Pope Benedict XVI developed that point in par. 14 of his post-synodal Apostolic exhortation *Verbum Domini*. His words are worth quoting at length because this authoritative teaching of the Church's *Magisterium* seems to support Karl Rahner's point of view and to contradict that of Jean-Jacques Olier.

'The value of private revelations,' the Pope wrote, 'is essentially different from that of the one public revelation: the latter demands faith; in it God himself speaks to us through human words and the mediation of the living community of the Church. The criterion for judging the truth of a private revelation is its orientation to Christ himself. If it leads us away from him, then it certainly does not come from the Holy Spirit, who guides us more deeply into the Gospel, and not away from it. Private revelation is an aid to this faith, and it demonstrates its credibility precisely because it refers back to the one public revelation. Ecclesiastical approval of a private revelation essentially means that its message contains nothing contrary to faith and morals; it is licit to make it public and the faithful are authorised to give to it their prudent adhesion. A private revelation can introduce new emphases, give rise to new forms of piety, or deepen older ones. It can have a certain prophetic character (cf. 1 Thess 5:19-21) and can be a valuable aid for better understanding and living the Gospel at a certain time; consequently it should not be treated lightly. It is a help which is proffered, but its use is not obligatory. In any event, it must be a matter of nourishing faith, hope and love, which are for everyone the permanent path of salvation.'

There are a number of points worth noting here. Firstly, the Church not only acknowledges the existence of private revelation of a personal and ecclesial kind, it says that genuine forms serve a useful purpose. Secondly, private revelation is inauthentic if it is not Christ centered or clashes in any way with public revelation. Thirdly, it seems that Pope Benedict's remarks were mainly about ecclesial forms of private revelation of two kinds, prophetic messages, and ones that give rise to new forms of spirituality. What Pope Benedict has taught illustrates what par. 4 of *Lumen Gentium* had in mind when it said, 'The Spirit guides the Church into the fullness of truth . . . He furnishes and directs her with various gifts, *both hierarchical and charismatic,* and adorns her with the fruits of His grace (cf. Eph 4:11-12; 1 Cor 12:4; and Gal 5:22).'

## Prophetic Messages of a Public-Ecclesial Kind

In this section we can look at two examples of prophetic revelations, one medieval the other contemporary. The first concerns the voices and visions that guided the personal life and military campaigns of St. Joan of Arc (1412-1431). We know a lot about her experiences because she spoke about them in the course of a six month ecclesiastical trial which eventually condemned her to death on spurious charges. Apparently, Joan began to hear three voices speaking to her when she was thirteen. The revelatory words she heard were addressed to her by an angel and saints Margaret and Catherine. They told her how she should live as a Christian woman, and they also instructed her about the way she was to raise the siege of Orleans and to help the dauphin to be crowned king at Rheims. Her voices were clearly prophetic in the sense that she foretold future events and received words of knowledge. For example, her voices told her that she should go to Robert de Beaudricort, captain of Vaucouleurs, and that he would provide her with men. When she obeyed the voices things worked out as predicted. Although she had never met the king, Joan identified him when he was incognito in a crowd.

When Joan was captured by pro-English forces, she was put on trial. It is clear that the judges were preoccupied by her revelations because Joan implied that through them she had direct contact with the divine. As she said herself, 'Whatever I have done that was good, I have done at the bidding of my voices . . . I shall call them to help me as long as I live.' She insisted that, 'they come from God.' The judges felt that, implicitly, Joan undermined the authority of the Church by bypassing the clergy of the Church militant here on earth and communing with saints of the Church triumphant in heaven. During her trial Joan briefly renounced her voices because she was afraid of being tortured and burnt at the stake. But soon afterwards, she retracted her renunciation, and reaffirmed the fact that God had spoken directly to her heart by means of the heavenly voices. As a result, the nineteen year old heroine was executed in a barbaric way by being burnt at the stake. Although the court seemed, not only to deny the fact that Joan had received private revelations, it even seemed to deny the very possibility of such revelations. Subsequently, their legitimacy was vindicated in 1920 when Joan was canonised by the Church.

In 1973 a deaf Japanese nun, named Sr. Agnes Sasagawa claimed that Our Lady had appeared to her on three separate occasions. She had spoken a rather forbidding prophetic message about great sufferings that would afflict the Church and the world at an indeterminate time in the future. The messages were associated with supernatural signs. Light shone from the tabernacle, a statue of Our Lady visibly shed human tears, and in 1982, Sister Agnes was totally cured from her deafness. Her bishop, John Shojiro Ito, went to Rome to consult with the then Cardinal Joseph Ratzinger about the messages. As prefect of the Congregation for the Doctrine of the Faith, he formally approved of them as supernatural in origin and worthy of attention.

## Devotional Messages of an Ecclesial Kind

In 1933 Helena Kowalska (1905-1938), known as Sr. Faustina in religious life, told her confessor Fr. Sopocko in Vilnius, Lithuania, that she was receiving messages from Jesus about a Divine Mercy devotion which he wanted to be promoted in the Church. Fr. Sopocko encouraged her to record the messages in her diary. Sr. Faustina herself predicted that, 'There will come a time when this work, which God is demanding so very much, will be as though utterly undone. And then God will act with great power, which will give evidence of its authenticity. It will be a new splendour for the Church, although it has been dormant in it for some time.' In 1959, some twenty years after Faustina's death, her messages were suppressed by the Vatican, but were accepted again in 1978 as a result of an intervention by Pope John Paul II. Indeed he established the Feast of the Divine Mercy on the first Sunday after Easter as a response to a request of Jesus in one of Faustina's apparitions. Providentially he died on Divine Mercy Sunday 2005 and was canonised on Divine Mercy Sunday 2014.

These developments illustrated what Par. 67 of the *Catechism of the Catholic Church* has stated, 'Throughout the ages, there have been so-called 'private' revelations, some of which have been recognised by the authority of the Church. They do not belong, however, to the deposit of faith. It is not their role to improve or complete Christ's definitive revelation, *but to help live more fully by it in a certain period of history.'* As far as Catholics are concerned they are at liberty either to believe or not believe private revelations even when the Church approves of them. They are received as probable but not as certain.

It is a matter of public record that the Church has withheld its approval from a number of private revelations which have been widely disseminated, such as those of William Kamm, also known as The Little Pebble, who lives in Australia. The Church has also rejected the so called revelations received by prophetess Debra Burslem of the Magnificat Meal Movement which is also based in Australia. In Ireland Christina Gallagher's prophetic messages and activities in the 'House of Prayer' in Achill Island have been a source of controversy. Commenting on them Archbishop Neary wrote in 2008, 'I issued a lengthy public statement to the effect, in essence, that no evidence of supernatural phenomena had been observed but that the persons involved gave every evidence of good faith . . . In summary the 'House of Prayer' has no Church approval and the work does not enjoy the confidence of the diocesan authorities.'

## PRIVATE REVELATION OF THE PERSONAL KIND

A few years ago I published a book entitled, *Gifts of the Spirit and the New Evangelisation*. When I was writing it, it occurred to me that the gifts of the Spirit referred to by St Paul, especially the ones mentioned in 1 Cor 12:8-10, were evangelistic in orientation and could be classified under three headings as gifts of revelation, proclamation, and demonstration. When I read what St. Thomas Aquinas (1225-1274) had to say about those same gifts I was delighted to find that he also understood them within an evangelistic context. He wrote, 'some charisms freely given relate to knowledge [revelation], some to words [proclamation] some to deeds [demonstration].' Thomas's understanding is echoed by Pope Francis in par. 130 of

*Evangelii Gaudium,* where he says that the charisms should be 'channelled into an evangelising impulse.'

The charisms of revelation are wisdom, knowledge, prophecy and discernment of Spirits (Cf. 1 Cor 12:8-10). While it is true that in 1 Cor 12:8, Paul talks about the *utterance* of wisdom and knowledge, both charisms are rooted in the revelatory gifts of wisdom and knowledge mentioned in Is 11:2. Needless to say, they were attributes of Jesus. Writing about him the author of Col 2:3 wrote, 'in Christ are hidden all the treasures of wisdom and knowledge.' Paul Kariuki Njiru says in his book *Charisms and the Holy Spirit's Activity in the Body of Christ* which is based on his doctoral dissertation, 'Both (widsom and knowledge) entail insights granted to the mind. Both of them are revelatory gifts in that they include matter granted in one way or another by direct revelation.' It goes without saying that these gifts informed the public-ecclesial prophecies mentioned already. This is a brief description of the revelatory charisms:

**1.** ***The gift of wisdom*** is firstly a recognition that the message of Christ crucified is God's wisdom. It is also a special ability that enables members of the Christian community to discern the Lord's will and how it may best be applied in a specific situation. St James encouraged believers to ask confidently for this practical gift (cf. Jm 1:5-8). The utterance of wisdom in 1 Cor 12:8 refers to a graced ability to share such insights in a verbal way.

**2.** ***The gift of knowledge*** has more to do with deep, Spirit given insight into the Person and attributes of the Lord together with an ability to understand the meaning of the Scripture and Christian truth. The utterance of knowledge mentioned by Paul in 1 Cor 12:8 refers to a Spirit given ability to teach and preach in an inspired and inspiring way.

**3.** ***The gift of prophecy*** is the special ability that God gives to some members of the community to receive a supernatural message from the Lord. As scripture says, 'For prophecy never had its origin in the will of man, but men spoke from God as they were carried along by the Holy Spirit' (2 Pt 1:21). St Paul added, 'prophecy, however, is for believers, not for unbelievers' (1 Cor 14:22-23), and it affirms people, 'everyone who prophesies speaks to men for their strengthening, encouragement and comfort' (1 Cor 14:3).

**4.** ***The gift of discernment of spirits*** in 1 Cor 12:10 is an ability, given by God to some people, which enables them on their own or the community's behalf, to know whether a prophetic utterance was prompted by God or not. In a wider sense it is an ability to know whether any inspiration, prompting or revelation is from God or not (cf. 1 Thess 5:21).

Over the past forty years or so I have noticed two things about private revelations. Firstly, although they have been associated, down through history, with saintly mystics they are relatively common in Pentecostal and Charismatic circles. Secondly, as was mentioned already, they are not usually concerned with conveying a message to the wider Church or with instigating a new devotion. They are received in more mundane and restricted circumstances such as ministering to a person, or getting a message from the Lord for a group of people, e.g. at a conference.

## PROPHETIC REVELATION

When one reads what St Thomas and Prospero Lambertini (1675 – 1758), who later became Pope Benedict XIV, wrote about the charisms in 1 Cor 12:8-10, a number of points become clear.

Firstly, revelatory gifts are prophetic in nature. Thomas wrote, 'Charisms relating to knowledge can be summed up in the word prophecy. Prophecy consists first and foremost in knowing certain far off things outside the normal knowledge of men. But secondarily it involves speech, since a prophet proclaims to others what God has taught him in order to build them up.' Cardinal Lambertini said that, 'Prophecy is the foreknowledge of future events, but it sometimes extends to past events, of which there is no recollection nor any certain indication; and to present events distant in place and hidden, and to the inward thoughts of the heart; so that a prophet who divinely knows those things which are removed from sense and the natural knowledge of men, and is able to make them known.' It is clear that, among other things, both men thought that prophecy often had to do with intimations of future events. Scripture supports that point of view. In Is 41:22-23 we read, 'Can your idols make such claims as these? Let them come and show what they can do! says God, the King of Israel. Let them try to tell us what occurred in years gone by or what the future holds. Yes, that's it! If you are gods, tell what will happen in the days ahead!.' In this context it is worth noting that in recent years Pope Benedict XVI, like a number of modern writers, shifted the emphasis from foretelling to forth-telling when he wrote, 'The prophet is someone who tells the truth on the strength of his contact with God - the truth for today, which also, naturally sheds light on the future. It is not a question of foretelling the future in detail, but of rendering the truth of God present at this moment in time and of pointing us in the right direction.'

Secondly, St Thomas also believed that although, 'the gratuitous graces are ascribed to the Holy Spirit as their first principle; yet he brings about the works of grace of this kind in men by means of the angels.' (cf Acts 7:53; Gal 3:19) The belief that the angels mediated revelation can be traced back at least to *The Shepherd of Hermas* (c. 150 A.D.). In commandment eleven, on 'True and False Prophets,' the anonymous author wrote, 'the angel of the prophetic spirit that is assigned to him fills the person, and being filled with the Holy Spirit the man speaks to the multitude just as the Lord wills.' Lambertini wrote in similar vein, 'Angels are mediators between God and men, prophetic illuminations are ministered by God through the angelic spirits, who not only enlighten and move the imagination interiorly toward divine appearances, but also they show themselves frequently in human form, foretelling future events, and instructing them in many things to be done.'

Thirdly, Thomas did not believe that a person needed to be in a state of grace in order to receive a prophetic message. Rather than being an inevitable sign of sanctifying grace, prophetic revelation is a gratuitous gift which is given in order to help others to grow in sanctifying grace. Cardinal Lambertini agreed. He wrote, 'We readily admit that a good and modest life is not necessary as an evidence of true prophecy; for there are well known instances of some most wicked men, whom God made use of as instruments to publish his oracles, as we have seen in the case of Balaam and Ciaphas; but these instances are rare.' Benedict XIV also pointed out that, 'In the causes of canonisation and beatification, no account will be made of prophecy,' that is, unless there is firstly proof of virtue. But then he went on to imply that normally holiness was needed when he added, 'Although moral goodness is most profitable to a prophet it is not absolutely necessary. . . It is necessary for prophesying that the mind should be raised to the highest contemplation of spiritual things, this may be prevented through violent passions and inordinate attention to outward things. . . For the most part, therefore, this gift is bestowed by God upon holy men.'

Fourthly, Thomas has very interesting things to say in both of his *Summas* about the way in which revelation is imparted to the human mind, 'This light,' he wrote, 'which inwardly enlightens the mind, is sometimes borne out by other aids to knowledge, both exterior and interior. They may be formed by divine power such as some utterance, or locution, heard by the external senses [ears]. Or it may be an inner locution, caused by God, and perceived by fantasy [image]. Or there may be bodily appearances, external and visible, formed by God [i.e. apparitions]. Or such corporeal appearance may be inwardly depicted in fantasy [e.g. a dream or vision]. By these means, aided by the light inwardly impressed on his mind, man receives a knowledge of divine things; whereas the inner light is sufficient of itself without them.' Echoing the teaching of St. Thomas, Benedict XIV said, that there are three ways in which the prophet receives revelation, firstly, according to the exterior perception of the senses of sight and sound, i.e. external locutions and apparitions; secondly, by the inward senses of sight and sound, i.e., inner locutions, visions, images and dreams; and thirdly, by intellectual representation, i.e. unmediated understanding. Alphonsus Liguori (1696-1787) expressed what Lambertini had in mind when he observed, 'the revelations of hidden or future events to do with certain people, e.g., their death, their promotion to some position, and other similar things, may occur in three ways: by visions, by voices and by the simple apprehension of truth.' In my experience, the most common way in which God communicates in a revelatory way is firstly by means of an inner voice or by an inner vision which is like a video clip that conveys a message and secondly, by a spontaneous and un-thought out awareness or understanding of something, e.g. of a hidden fact about a person's past.

Jack Deere makes a perceptive point where private revelation is concerned. He maintains that it is important to distinguish between

**A.** The revelation itself which is the message from God.
**B.** It's interpretation. Speaking about this point Prospero

Lambertini wrote, 'a revelation could be true and from God, and the human explanation of it false, for man may interpret it otherwise than God understands it.'

**C.** It's application. We can have a true revelation, a correct interpretation and a wrong application., e.g., if a Catholic got a word of knowledge for a Protestant, it doesn't necessarily imply that the Protestant person should become a Catholic.

We have to be right at all three stages if a message from the Lord is going to benefit people. We will have more to say about this and similar topics in other chapters.

## SHOULD CHRISTIANS DESIRE PRIVATE REVELATION?

Should a Christian seek private revelation? Yes and no. It is quite legitimate to expect the Lord to reveal the divine Self, word and will to Christians in prayer, and if needs be, by unusual, charismatic means. That is why St. Paul said such things as, 'we have not stopped praying for you and asking God to fill you with the knowledge of his will through all spiritual wisdom and understanding' (Col 1:9-10), and again in 1 Cor 14:6, 'what good will I be unless I bring you some revelation or knowledge or prophecy.'

When St Paul said in 1 Cor 14:1, 'eagerly desire spiritual gifts, especially the gift of prophecy,' I suspect he was primarily addressing the Christian community rather than individuals. Speaking of the charisms, including that of prophecy, the

*Dogmatic Constitution on The Church* said in par. 12, 'These charisms, whether they be the more outstanding or the more simple and widely diffused, *are to be received with thanksgiving and consolation* for they are perfectly suited to and useful for the needs of the Church. *Extraordinary gifts are not to be rashly sought after.'* It seems to me that the Christian community, as the body of Christ, desires the gifts, but individuals leave it up to God which, if any, of the gifts the Lord wants to bestow upon them for the common good. As John Paul II observed in par. 72 of *Catechesis in Our Time,* 'renewal in the Spirit will be authentic not so much according as it gives rise to extraordinary charisms, but according as it leads the greatest possible number of the faithful, as they travel their daily paths, to make a humble, patient and persevering effort to know the mystery of Christ better and better, and to bear witness to it.'

Not surprisingly, a number of saints have echoed Church teaching in their writings. Although St. Vincent Ferrer believed, as a result of personal experience, that a person could receive a genuine revelation in a gratuitous way from God, he wrote, 'Be thoroughly persuaded, that true revelations, and the extraordinary means by which God's secrets are known, are not the result of the desire, nor of any diligence or effort on the part of the soul itself; but that they are solely the effects of the pure goodness of God communicating itself to a soul filled with humility, who respectfully seeks for Him and sighs after Him with all its strength.' Nevertheless Vincent was wary of private revelation because he was aware that people could be subject to illusions and false inspirations. In his *Treatise on the Spiritual*

*Life,* he wrote, 'The first remedy against spiritual temptation which the devil plants in the hearts of many persons in these unhappy times is to have no desire to procure by prayer, meditation or any other good work, what are called revelations, or spiritual experiences, beyond what happens in the ordinary course of things.'

St John of the Cross agreed with Vincent's caution. He wrote, 'The devil rejoices greatly when a soul seeks after revelations and is ready to accept them; for such conduct furnishes him with many opportunities of insinuating delusions, and derogating from the faith as much as he possibly can; for such a soul becomes rough and rude, and falls frequently into many temptations and unseemly habits.' Finally, St Vincent de Paul seemed to welcome inspirations and revelation in prayer. He wrote, 'The thoughts and considerations which come from our own reflections are feeble lights, showing us only the outside of things and nothing else. The lights of grace which the Sun of Justice shines in our souls penetrate to the innermost depths of our heart, bringing forth marvellous fruits. We must then ask God to enlighten us himself and to inspire in us what pleases him.' But Vincent warned against pride and vanity. 'When people delight themselves in lofty considerations . . . the Holy Spirit is not present. . .but it is the spirit of pride which enlightens the understanding and produces all these fine thoughts. To say it more accurately, in this case the demon himself inspires the person . . . You take up this holy time of prayer to seek your own satisfaction and in taking pleasure in your own thoughts you offer sacrifice to the idol of your own vanity.'

## CONCLUSION

The topics dealt with in this chapter act as an important introduction to what follows. We have noted that while public revelation is complete and sufficient, the Church believes that people can receive private revelation. St Thomas believed that private revelation is virtually synonymous with the charism of prophecy which is informed by the charisms of revelation. It has to be said that this is an area where discernment of spirits is particularly necessary in order to be preserved from illusions and false inspirations. Augustin Poulain (1836–1919), author of *The Graces of Interior Prayer,* thought that at least three quarters of the revelations given to those who have not reached high sanctity are illusions. And there are examples, even in the lives of canonised saints, that even they could be subject to illusions. For instance, in spite of the fact that St. Vincent Ferrer performed countless healings and made many accurate prophetic predictions, he was quite mistaken when he wrote a letter to Pope Benedict XIII in 1412 telling him that the Antichrist had already been born and that the second coming was imminent. Speaking about this kind of phenomenon, Prospero Lambertini wrote, 'It is possible for an otherwise true prophet to foretell what shall not come to pass, that is, to believe himself to be speaking by revelation from God, when in truth he was speaking by the prophetic instinct.' Incidentally, Lambertini also observed possibly in a slightly sexist way: 'The revelations of some holy women canonised by the Apostolic See whose saying and writings in rapture and derived from rapture are filled with errors.' That said, it is good to recall the Latin adage, *abusus non tollit usum,* (abuse of anything does not invalidate its right use).

# CHAPTER ELEVEN

# DREAMS AND VISIONS

In 1982 I was a chaplain in a Dublin hospital. During that time I met the niece of a famous Irish writer. I took the opportunity to talk to her about her uncle. It was fascinating to hear her recount her memories of the well known author. As a result of our conversations a rapport developed between us. Among other things she told me that she was a writer herself but that she, like her uncle, had given up the practice of her faith. Then one day this patient recounted a powerful dream she had recently experienced. When I heard the details it struck me that, in symbolic terms, it was urging her to return to the practice of her faith. But I said nothing. Instead, I asked her what she thought of the dream. She then proceeded to analyse it in a very perceptive way. Eventually she said, 'Father, it seems pretty clear to me that my unconscious mind is urging me to return to the Church and to resume the practice of my Catholic religion. What do you think?' At that point I said that I concurred with her own interpretation. Soon after that conversation the woman made a general confession and began to receive the Eucharist on a regular basis. It was as if the Spirit had helped her to return home to the practice of her Catholic faith by prompting an inspired dream.

In the ancient world people saw dreams as a way of receiving revelation from God. When one reads what the bible has to say about the subject one gets the distinct impression that it expresses two, apparently, contradictory attitudes. Firstly, the bible warns against taking dreams too seriously. For instance, Eccl 5:2, says, 'Dreaming comes from much worrying,' and Sir. 34:5-7 adds, 'dreams are folly, and like a woman in travail the mind has fancies . . . for dreams have deceived many, and those who have put their trust in them have come to grief.' The Prophet Jeremiah was critical of false prophets. He reported that the Lord said, 'I have heard what the prophets say who prophesy lies in my name. They say, 'I had a dream! I had a dream!' How long will this continue in the hearts of these lying prophets, who prophesy the delusions of their own minds?' (Jer 23:25-27). In Zech 10:2 we read that, 'diviners see visions that lie; they tell dreams that are false, they give comfort in vain.'

Secondly, although the scriptures are sceptical at times about the value of dreams, they do accept that God can use them in order to fulfil the divine purposes. 'Unless they are sent from the Most High as a visitation, do not give your mind to them' (Sir 34:6). On the positive side, there is the belief that dreams are the 'dark speech' of the Spirit (cf. Num 12:8 RSV). There are a number of texts that support this point of view. In Job 33:14-15 we read: 'For God does speak—now one way, now another—though man may not perceive it. In a dream, in a vision of the night, when deep sleep falls on men as they slumber in their beds.' In Num 12:6 the Lord says, 'Listen to my words: 'When a prophet of the

Lord is among you, I reveal myself to him in visions, I speak to him in dreams.'

There are many Old Testament examples of people receiving guidance in dreams. The Lord appeared to Jacob in a dream and told him how to outwit Laban (Gen 31:10-13). In 1 King 3:5 we are told that: 'At Gibeon the Lord appeared to Solomon during the night in a dream, and God said, 'Ask for whatever you want me to give you.' In the Greek version of Est 11:2-12, we read of Mordecai's prophetic dream. More often than not, when the chosen people had religious dreams they could interpret them, but when pagans had similar dreams they often needed gifted Jews to discern their meaning on their behalf. For example, early in the Bible two men said, 'We both had dreams....but there is no one to interpret them.' Then Joseph said to them, 'Do not interpretations belong to God? Tell me your dreams' (Gen 40:8). Speaking of Daniel, another Jewish exile, Nebuchadnezzar's daughter in law said of him that he, 'has the spirit of the holy gods in him and . . . a keen mind and knowledge and understanding, and also the ability to interpret dreams, explain riddles and solve difficult problems (Dan 5:11-12).

Dreams played an important role in the New Testament also. In the gospels, Joseph, the husband of Mary repeatedly received guidance in dreams. They concerned his marriage to Mary (Mt 1:20), the exile of the Holy Family in Egypt (Mt 2:13), their return (Mt 2:19) and the decision to settle in Galilee (Mt 2:22). Later in Matthew's gospel we are told how Pilate's wife said to her husband during the trial of Jesus, 'Have nothing to do with that innocent man because in a dream last night I suffered much on account of him' (Mt 27:19). The early Christians also received revelation in dreams. For example, on Pentecost morning St. Peter quoted the words of the prophet Joel, 'I will pour out my Spirit on all flesh, and your sons and daughters shall prophesy, and your young men will see visions and your old men shall dream dreams' (Acts 2:17).

In the scriptures it would seem that dreams and visions are closely related. A vision is a vivid and spontaneous type of daydream, inspired by God when a person is awake. In my experience they come in two main forms, as a picture like a photograph, or as a mental video which might go on for some time. Occasionally they will contain spoken words, at other times nothing is said. St Paul was led to take the momentous step of preaching the gospel to the gentiles in mainland Europe as a result of a vision (cf. Acts 16:6-11). St. Peter was prompted to preach to Cornelius, a gentile, as a result of a dreamlike vision (cf. Acts 10:9-16). Paul and Peter both received verbal messages in their visions.

## Dreams in Christian tradition

Tertullian expressed a common view in the early Church when he wrote, 'Is it not known to all the people that the dream is the most usual way that God reveals himself to man?' Perhaps Tertullian exaggerated a bit when he said that, 'almost the greater part of mankind get their knowledge of God from dreams.' But they were certainly a common way of receiving inspiration. The great St. Thomas Aquinas also wrote about the subject. He said that dreams were caused partly by memories of what we felt and thought while awake, partly by internal and external bodily stimuli occurring while asleep, partly by God or demons influencing our imaginations. So it would be legitimate to consult dreams which are of divine origin. Chapter five recounted a religious dream which exerted a big influence on the life of Bl. Franz Jagerstatter. It is worthwhile to look at a number of other instructive examples.

St. Augustine tells us in his *Confessions* that his mother, St Monica experienced some revelatory dreams and visions, mostly to do with his spiritual destiny. He recounted one in particular, 'In her dream she saw herself standing on a sort of wooden rule, and saw a bright youth approaching her, joyous and smiling at her, while she was grieving and bowed down with sorrow. But when he inquired of her the cause of her sorrow and daily weeping [not to learn from her, but to teach her, as is customary in visions], and when she answered that it was my soul's doom she was lamenting, he bade her rest content and told her to look and see that where she was there I was also. And when she looked she saw me standing near her on the same rule. Where could this dream come from, unless it was that you Lord had listened to the prayer of her heart?' Augustine said that his mother placed a great reliance on dreams of this kind, and that she could discern the difference between natural and inspired dreams. 'She always said, that by some sense, which she could not describe in words, she was able to distinguish between your revelations and her own natural dreams.' Monica's dream literally came true nine years later when

Augustine was converted to Christianity and came to share his mother's Christian faith.

It could be argued that two dreams played an important role in the conversion of the Irish to Christianity. In his *Confessions* St. Patrick (380-462) told us, firstly, how he escaped captivity. 'In my sleep one night I heard a voice saying to me, 'It is well that you fast, soon you will go to your country.' After a short while I again heard a voice saying, 'Look your ship is ready.' It was quite a distance away, about two hundred miles. I had never been to the place, nor did I know anyone there. I ran away and left the man with whom I had spent six years. The power of God directed my way successfully and nothing daunted me until I reached the ship.' When Patrick travelled to mainland Europe he was eventually ordained a priest. Then, when he was on a visit to his relatives in Britain, he had a second dream. 'It was there one night I saw the image of Victor, who appeared to have come from Ireland with an unlimited number of letters. He gave me one of them and I read the opening words which were, 'The voice of the Irish.' As I read the beginning of the letter I seemed at that same moment to hear the voice of those who were by the wood of Vocult, which is near the Western sea. They shouted with one voice, 'young man, we ask you to come and walk once more among us.' I was cut to the very heart and could read no more, and so I woke up. Thank God, after many years the Lord answered their cry.' It is noticeable that this prophetic dream was similar to the one that led St. Paul to come to Europe.

In the more modern era St. John Bosco (1815-1888) was blessed with many charismatic gifts included an ability to predict the future of particular people, to have an accurate knowledge of consciences, and an ability to perform miraculous healings. The Lord often spoke to his heart by means of dreams and visions. The many volumes of the *Biographical Memoirs of Saint John Bosco* report 153 dreams that he wrote down, narrated, or merely mentioned in passing. Most of them were religious in nature and guided his actions. For instance, in his autobiographical, *Memoirs of the Oratory*, John tells us that at the age of nine he dreamed that he, 'saw himself playing with a crowd of neighbourhood boys; many of them were fighting and swearing. He told them to stop, then leapt in with both fists when they did not. Suddenly a stranger, a noble and radiant gentleman, appeared. He told John that he needed to use kindness, not blows, to win over these children. John did not understand. The man said he would give him a teacher, and a majestic Lady showed up. She instructed John to watch, and the boys turned into wild animals - bears, goats, dogs, cats, etc. 'This,' she told him, 'is your field of work. Make yourself humble, strong, and energetic, so that you'll be able to do for my children what you'll see now.' And the beasts turned into gentle lambs. In his confusion, John began to cry. The Lady assured him that in due time he would understand. And he woke up.' In the event, this prophetic dream anticipated John's lifelong work with young people which was characterised by gentleness and patience.

Dreams continued to guide John Bosco's vocation, e.g., during his late teens he was warned against entering a Franciscan monastery and later one of them pinpointed the site of his work in Turin. He also dreamt of future events. For instance, when Piedmont was about to pass a law suppressing monastic orders, late in 1854, Don Bosco predicted 'great funerals at court.' This prophecy was fulfilled a few weeks later. As a result of a vision John not only predicted the unexpected recovery of John Cagliero, who was dying from typhoid fever, he also anticipated that he would be ordained a missionary bishop. Thirty years later that prophecy came true. Is it any wonder then, that John said *apropos* the dreams he had shared, 'let us strive to carry out God's admonitions, no matter what way he may choose to make them known to us.'

## HOW REVELATION IS POSSIBLE IN DREAMS

The psychology of dreams is an interesting and helpful one. Although it is relevant where religious dreams are concerned, it is not my intention to deal with it here. In any case others have done so at length. Suffice it to say that the Bible sees the human person as an inseparable unity of body, mind and spirit. St. Paul adverted to this when he prayed, 'May God . . . keep your whole being, spirit, mind and body, free from all fault' (1 Thess 5:22). What is the difference between the spirit and the mind? The human mind or *psyche* in Greek thought, includes all our conscious and unconscious experiences such as thinking, feeling, memory, and will. The human spirit, *pneuma* in Greek, is that part of a person which can only be satisfied by transcendental relationship with God. It is also capable of receiving revelation from God. When we sleep we can have either natural or religious dreams. The natural kind have their origin in the *psyche*. A genuinely revelatory religious dream has its origin in the human spirit. This is so because the Lord can reveal himself to our spirits by the action of the Holy Spirit, the divine Dreamer within. The Holy One is author of the dream and uses our memories, feelings and imaginations to express the revelation. So a natural dream is a letter from the unconscious, but an inspired dream is a letter written by God, in the chamber of the spirit, upon paper supplied by the psyche, i.e. the unconscious. It is worth noting in passing that some dreams will be wordless while in others we will hear words being spoken.

## Interpreting dreams

Over the years, by the grace of God, I have experienced a number of graphic dreams which revealed something of God's presence and purposes in my life. I value dreams so much that sometimes when I am feeling confused, I pray to the Lord to reveal the divine presence and purposes to me. Before I go to sleep I say a prayer like the following. 'Dear Lord, the psalmist assured us that you bless those you love even while they sleep. Please grant me a revelatory dream tonight which will enable me to experience your loving presence and guidance in my life.' On a number of occasions the Lord has answered my prayer. Let me give an example.

A few years after my ordination the effectiveness of my ministry was being undermined by feelings of unworthiness. Then one night I dreamt that I was standing in the sanctuary of a small church with bare stone walls. Suddenly the door opened, and in came St. Francis of Assisi and some of his companions. I may say in passing that I had taken the name of Francis as my confirmation name. My eyes were riveted on my namesake. To me he was the very epitome of a true man of God. Then out of the corner of my eye I noticed a crippled boy sitting on the floor. Francis moved toward him and gestured to me and his companions to come and join him. Then he asked me to put my hands on the boy's knees and to pray for healing. Francis also prayed. I was overjoyed when I could feel malformed bones moving back into their proper place. Then I glanced upward to look admiringly at Francis only to find that he and his companions had slipped away. Joy turned to dismay. How could the boy's healing be completed without Francis? I thought that I would not be able to finish the healing because of my lack of holiness. Then I woke up.

A number of steps can be taken in order to understand your dreams. If the religious ones are letters written by God, in the chamber of the heart, they need to be opened by recalling them, and read by pondering on them, and accurately interpreted, in order to discover the messages they are trying to deliver.

### 1. *Recall and record your religious dreams*

Researchers have found that if a dream is not recalled within a few minutes after waking up there is a 95% chance that it will slip back into the unconscious and forgotten. As a result it can be helpful to have a note pad or digital recorder beside your bed so that you can write down or record the dream when you wake up.

## 2. *Use the following method of interpretation*

Recognising that dream interpretation is an inexact science, here are four steps which may help you.

1. ***Title.*** If your dream were a short story what title would you give it? For example, if I were to give a title to the dream about St. Francis, I think I would call it, 'The incomplete healing.'
2. ***Theme.*** What was the main gist of the dream, what did it seem to be about? I felt that as long as St Francis the holy man was praying, great things could happen, but as soon as he left nothing much could happen as a result of my inferior prayers.
3. ***Feelings.*** What was the main feeling in your dream? I had a number of feelings, great joy when I felt the boy's legs being straightened and strengthened, but disappointed when Francis disappeared. I also felt powerless to complete the healing because of my unworthiness, although I longed for the boy to be made well. But if I were to pick out the key feeling, it would have been my great joy when I actually felt God's power at work in a healing way.
4. ***Question.*** What was the dream trying to bring to your attention? In my case it dramatised a dilemma I had been aware of for some time. God can only act through very holy people like Francis. He could not act in that way through me a sinner. When I thought about the dream it suddenly struck me that the crippled boy was myself, a man who was bound by many fears, hurts, and a consequent sense of inadequacy. I sensed that God had

healed me to a certain extent, but more inner healing was needed. It would come about as a result of my own prayer and the prayer of others. As I was progressively healed I would learn to exercise my ministry with some of the authority and effectiveness of St. Francis who, in a certain symbolic sense, represented my alter ego.

### 3. *Move from literal to metaphorical interpretations of dreams*

Some dreams can be interpreted in a literal way. But, more often than not, they have a metaphorical meaning. As Freud once observed, 'dreams are the royal road to the unconscious.' They are primarily about inward things rather than external events. Jung was probably correct when he said that usually everyone and everything in a dream is a symbol of different aspects of the self. For instance, a woman might have a disturbing dream about the death of her husband. Interpreted in a literal way, it might be understood as a prediction of his immanent demise or her fear that he might die. Interpreted in a metaphorical way, the dream could be seen as a dramatisation of the woman's feeling of fear e.g. of her alcoholic husband and her repressed anger against him. If that were the case her dream would be saying in effect, 'I wish you were dead.' In the case of my dream of the 'Incomplete healing' I came to see that the crippled boy was a symbol of my own wounded self.

### 4. *Interpret the dream in terms of everyday events*

Usually our dreams are psycho-spiritual responses to the events of the recent and sometimes the distant past. So when you become aware of the main theme and feeling in a dream, ask yourself, 'when did I feel that emotion in the last few days?' It may not be an easy question to answer. Often we fail to acknowledge how we feel as a result of the pace and pressure of everyday living. That is precisely why your unconscious brings neglected feelings to your attention by means of dreams. It is a gentle invitation to acknowledge and, if needs be, to deal with your feelings and the perceptions that evoked them, influenced as they are by your memories, attitudes, values and beliefs. For instance, I felt joy when I heard how people had been healed as a result of the ministry of well known charismatics like the late Kathryn Kulhman (1907-76) and Francis McNutt. But I also felt inadequate to pray in that way myself when I was asked to minister to a sick person two days before having the dream. It was if God was saying, 'if you want to know the joy of seeing people being healed, you will have to deal with your exaggerated feelings of unworthiness by relying solely on the free gift of my transforming grace, which through no merit of yours, makes you a worthy instrument of my power.'

### 5. *Learn to interpret symbols*

Symbols are the language of the dream. Feelings, and ideas which have been repressed during the day may be represented by feeling laden images in the night time videos of the mind. To learn to interpret dreams you would have to become increasingly sensitive to the nuances of symbolism. It takes time and experience because the meaning of symbols is context dependant. For example, water can variously be a symbol of such things as life, death, purification and the unconscious. Over the years I have relied on books such as Tom Chetwynd's *Dictionary for Dreamers*, and *The Penguin Dictionary of Symbols.*

## 6. *Dreams and the future*

While most dreams are not predictive, a small number of religious dreams can have a prophetic dimension and anticipate future events. We noted that fact when we discussed the role of revelatory dreams in the life of St. John Bosco. Christian literature is punctuated by accounts of how devout Christians had intimations of future events in their dreams. For example, when St Catherine Laboure was eighteen she had a religious dream in which she saw an old priest say Mass. Afterwards, the priest turned and beckoned her with his finger, but she drew backwards. Then Catherine found herself in a sick room where she saw the same priest, who said: 'My child, it is a good deed to look after the sick; you run away now, but one day you will be glad to come to me. God has designs on you - do not forget it.' When she awoke Catherine did not appreciate the significance of the dream. A few years later, while visiting a hospital of the Daughters of Charity, she noticed a priest's picture on the wall. She asked one of the sisters who he might be, and was told, 'Our Holy Founder St. Vincent de Paul.' He was the priest Catherine had seen in the dream. Soon after this she joined the Daughters of Charity. This was shortly before Catherine witnessed the apparitions of Our Lady of the Immaculate Conception in the Rue du Bac in Paris.

## Visions in Christian tradition

It is a striking characteristic of Ignatian, as opposed to Benedictine prayer, that it puts a lot of emphasis on the role of the imagination. In his *Spiritual Exercises,* Ignatius of Loyola suggested, that during quiet times Christians would be well advised to imagine an incident which is described in the Bible, e.g., Jesus meeting the Samaritan woman at the well (Jn 4:4-42), as if they were making a video. They could try to *see* the scene and any people who are mentioned in the text. They might choose to see themselves as one of the characters involved. They could also *hear* what is said. They might want to augment the dialogue recorded in the text with words of their own. They could go on to *notice* what the characters do. Finally, they could try to *sense* what the people in the story feel, and what they themselves feel.

On other occasions a facilitator might lead a guided Christian meditation by urging individuals to imagine a scene which might be non-biblical. Or a person might use a book like Anthony de Mello's *Sadhana* to do much the same. I know from personal experience that prayer of an imaginative kind can be very fruitful when it is animated by the Holy Spirit. People who pray in this way often report that they had an inspired sense of the Presence and the guidance of the Lord. However, valuable as it is, this form of openness to the Lord is an example of an ordinary, rather than an unusual charismatic way of tuning in to the Presence and will of God. It is not really what I have in mind when writing about visions. Unlike imaginative exercises, visions are not really in the control of the person's mind and will.

That said there is a clear continuity between the ordinary and unusual forms of imaginative communication from God. From the point of view of this book the point of transition from one to the other is not all that important.

We have already noted the fact that revelatory visions were a common occurrence in the Bible, especially in the New Testament. When one reads the lives of the saints it is obvious that many of them received messages from God in this way, e.g. Sts Vincent Ferrer, Margaret Mary Alacoque, Teresa of Avila, John Bosco, Padre Pio etc. In recent times there have been many reports of visions, some of which have led to new forms of devotion. For instance, in Lent 1936, Sister Maria Pierina De Micheli (1890-1945), who was born near Milan, reported a vision in which Jesus told her: 'I will that My Face, which reflects the intimate pains of My Spirit, the suffering and the love of My Heart, to be more honored. He who meditates upon Me, consoles Me.' In the course of further visions she was urged to have a medal made with the image of the Holy Face upon it. In 1958, Pope Pius XII confirmed that the Feast of the Holy Face of Jesus may be celebrated on Shrove Tuesday for all Roman Catholics. Maria Pierina De Micheli was beatified by Benedict XVI in 2009.

## Three visions that revealed the presence and purposes of God

St Augustine maintained that there were three kinds of visions. He wrote, 'These three modes of seeing – corporeal, spiritual, intellectual – are realised on both natural and a supernatural register. The supernatural mode is when God directly provides new bodily forms, images, or truths to the visionary.' In the Pentecostal and Charismatic Movements, visions of these three kinds are relatively common. They are often experienced following a time when the person has been praying or singing in tongues. It is, as if, this pre-rational form of prayer ploughs the soil of the heart in readiness to receive a revelation from the Lord. In my experience, charismatics tend to have imaginative visions, with or without accompanying words. For instance in 1981, Irish nun, Sr. Briege McKenna attended a charismatic leader's conference in Rome. She recalled how 'a Friar in his Franciscan habit said to me that he was frustrated because he was the youth director for the diocese of Mostar and that the young people were being seduced by the communists.' Sr. Briege prayed for him. She described what happened. In my imagination what, 'I saw was this Croatian priest sitting in the main celebrant's chair in front, and he was looking into the body of the church, and it was packed with young people. And from behind him on the altar there were streams of water, like rivers flowing, and the young people were cupping it and drinking it, and after they would drink it they would go out and bring others others in. I said to him, 'You know Father you don't have to worry, because many young people will come to your church.' Almost immediately, Father Emiliano Tardif (1928-1999), a well known Sacred Heart Priest, walked over and said, 'You know, Father, Our Lady is going to visit your church.' A few weeks later, six young people in Medjugorge claimed that the Madonna had appeared and spoken to them. Since then millions of people have gone to Medjugorge and many conversions have taken place there. It would seem that Sr. Briege's prophetic vision has been fulfilled. The Church has yet to state whether it approves of the apparitions and messages associated with Medjugorje.

## EXAMPLE OF A VISION WITH ACCOMPANYING WORDS

As the years pass I can remember similar revelatory visions. Here are three examples which have had big knock-on effects in my life. Many years ago I visited a woman friend's family. We chatted for a while, had a cup of coffee and listened to Dvorak's *New World Symphony*. At one point my friend went out to the kitchen to prepare a meal. As I listened to the music I had a three part mental vision. In part one I saw gentle peasants dancing joyfully in a field. Suddenly I became apprehensive when I saw sinister looking soldiers marching ominously toward them, with flags waving and drums beating. 'Oh no,' I thought, 'it is always the same. Those with power always oppress the innocent and the vulnerable.'

Then the scene changed. I could see that a lot of the peasants had been killed and others had been wounded. To my surprise, I noticed that, inexplicably, some of the soldiers were also dead or wounded. Spontaneously, some words from Ps 55:6 came to mind, 'O that I had wings like a dove! I would fly away and be at rest.' Then a voice seemed to speak within me, 'If you want Me to take you, I will.' I understood that God the Father was saying that, if I so wished, I could die and that he would take me to himself in heaven. I looked at the dead and the dying, and replied, 'No, I'd better stay for their sake, the dead need to be buried and the wounded need to be comforted.' Then I noticed the cross of Christ from behind. Again I heard the inner voice. It said, 'Now you have learned the meaning of merciful love, it is compassion. My Son also wanted to fly away and be at rest, but he remained for your sake.' I understood that these words referred to his anguish in Gethsemane and his resignation to the will of God, so that we might be saved.

Then suddenly the scene changed again. I could see a great orb of light coming towards the earth. I knew inwardly that it was a symbol of the glory of God. As it drew closer, the soil, rocks, and plants were bleached as they themselves became radiant with light. My body was also transfigured. By now it was rising into the air to meet the approaching orb of light. I looked back toward the earth and I could see peasants ascending, their bodies aglow with light. I also saw that graves were opening and that the dead were rising in light, including deceased soldiers. I was puzzled by this sight. I said to the Lord, 'Why should the soldiers rise, those who oppressed the innocent and the vulnerable?' The inner voice replied, 'Because you didn't presume to judge or to condemn your oppressors, they too will be saved.'

Then the vision ended as suddenly and unexpectedly as it had begun. My heart was racing, my breathing rapid, and my spirit exultant. I felt that the Lord had revealed a wonderful truth to me. God will never be outdone in mercy by his creatures. If believers, who have known the merciful love of God in their own lives, refuse to judge or condemn those who have hurt them, God won't judge them either. They will be saved through no merit of their own. As Jesus said, 'those whose sins you forgive, they are forgiven' (Jn 20:23). Ever since that experience I have tried to abstain, with limited success I must admit, from judging anyone, not even the greatest reprobates and tyrants in history. With God's help I try to identify with sentiments expressed so poignantly in the Ravensbruck prayer. When this notorious concentration camp for women was liberated by Russian soldiers, a scrap of paper was discovered which had been stuffed by a Jewish woman into a crack in the wall behind one of the cots. Written on it were these extraordinary words, 'O Lord, when I shall come with glory into your kingdom, do not remember only the men and women of good will; remember also the men and women of evil. May they be remembered not only for their acts of cruelty in the camp, the evil that they have done to us prisoners, but balance against their cruelty the fruits we have reaped under the stress and in the pain; the comradeship, the courage, the greatness of heart, the humility and patience which have been born in us and become part of our lives, because we have suffered at their hands. May the memory of us not be a nightmare to them when they stand in judgement. May all that we have suffered be acceptable to you as a ransom for them.'

## Example of a sacramental vision

Although I experienced this second vision many years later, I can see in retrospect that it had a good deal of affinity with the first. Some time ago I spent months asking Jesus for a greater sense of his love for me in order that I might love others better. For a while nothing seemed to happen. Then I joined a number of my fellow priests on a retreat. Each evening we had exposition of the Blessed Sacrament for an hour. On one of the evenings I was sitting in my seat contemplating the monstrance. Suddenly in my mind's eye I saw Jesus standing in front of the altar. He wasn't at all like what I expected. He was young and attractive looking. He had short hair and no beard or moustache. He wore a simple off white, one-piece garment and red light was streaming from his right palm and white light from his left palm. At first, His hands were held in a downward position slightly away from his body. Then he slowly raised his palms. There was a momentary flash of light from each. The flashes reminded me of the burst of light that comes from a lighthouse on the sea coast. Then Jesus lowered his extended hands in front of him, in an attitude of blessing, and I found myself sitting in the gentle glow of the converging beams of red and white light. Inwardly I knew that I was sitting in the light of God's mercy and love. My spirit seemed to be illumined. I was immediately reminded of the words, 'We have known and believe the love God has for us' (1 Jn 4:16). It encapsulated my new-found awareness which filled me with peace.

When I reflected in a prayerful way on that experience I could see that the Lord had answered my prayer in a wonderful way. As I meditated, it was if I could hear the Lord say, 'I want you to show to others the merciful love I have shown to you.' Many times I asked the Lord how exactly I should do this. In time he led me to the Golden Rule in Mt 7:12 which says, 'in everything, do to others what you would have them do to you, for this sums up the Law and the Prophets.' When I reflected on that verse I saw that two things would be needed. Firstly, goodwill, a desire to do what is best for the people I meet. Secondly, that it wouldn't be possible without empathy, i.e., an ability to stand in other people's shoes in order to sense, in an understanding way, what they feel and desire in order to respond appropriately in an emotional and practical way.

During my time of reflection I was also reminded of a verse in Hab 3:4 which says, 'Rays came forth from his hands where his power lies hidden.' It struck me that the Lord was urging me to pray with people as an expression of divine love. Nowadays when I talk to people I meet I often end the conversation by asking them whether they would like a prayer for any intention. Experience teaches that even those who are not gospel greedy will often reveal a need. When I'm praying I believe that the invisible light of God's merciful love is flowing through my hands. Indeed, there have been times when I have sensed heat in my palms and a sensation like pins and needles in my arms. I believe that it is caused by the same Holy Spirit that raised Jesus from death to life. I have found that prayers like these can be powerful and effective.

## Example of a Vision with a Prophetic Message

The third vision I'd like to share came to me during a time spent with ecumenical leaders in the North of Ireland long before the Good Friday agreement in 1998. In my mind's eye I could see a number of tall flagpoles with their respective flags flapping in the wind. At the base of each were groups of people. They were shouting and gesticulating in an angry way at the men and women gathered around the other flagpoles. After a time I noticed the cross of Calvary in the middle of the surrounding circle of flagpoles. At first the protesting people didn't even notice it. But as they did, one by one the belligerent people began to be aware of the crucified Lord. Then each one of the groups began to lower its flag, some slowly, others more rapidly. Soon the cross stood higher than all the flags. People began to drift away from their flagpoles to gather around the foot of the cross. Then I heard the Lord say, 'At the moment the flags of your denominational and nationalistic pride are raised higher than the cross. But when you look to me who was lifted up from the earth to draw all people to myself, you will lower the flags of your pride. Then and only then, will you find peace, for in the power of my cross the dividing walls of your divisions will crumble.' Not surprisingly, that vision was an inspiration not only to myself but to those with whom I shared it, in our work for reconciliation. In 1990 Rev. Cecil Kerr included it in his book, *The Way of Peace*.

## Conclusion

I know from talking to Christians in different countries, that many of them hear from the Lord in the ways I have tried to describe in this chapter. It is an aspect of the kind of imaginative faith experience which was referred to in this and a previous chapter. In this area, as in all others, not only is discernment of spirits needed, but it is also important to remember that although a vision may reveal something about the person and purposes of the Lord, one could misinterpret its meaning and as a result go on to misapply it's inherent guidance for practical living. Genuinely religious dreams and visions can have a prophetic dimension. St Thomas Aquinas said as much in his *Commentary on I Corinthians*, chapter fourteen. He wrote, 'For sometimes one is called a prophet, because he . . . sees pictorial visions, and has an understanding of them and he boldly announces to others and he works miracles. Concerning such a one it says in Num 12:6, 'If there is a prophet among you, I, the Lord, will appear to him in a dream, or will speak to him by means of a dream. But sometimes one who has solely pictorial visions is called a prophet, but in an improper sense and very remotely so. Again, one is called a prophet, if he has the intellectual light to explain even pictorial visions made to himself or someone else.'

# CHAPTER TWELVE

# APPARITIONS AND LOCUTIONS

In July 1985, an observer claimed to have seen a statue of the Virgin Mary move in a roadside shrine in Ballinspittle, County Cork, in Ireland. Subsequently many people came to see the phenomenon for themselves. One of my priest friends was adamant that, when he visited the place, he saw Our Lady move and that Padre Pio's image appeared beside her. I can remember that around that time I conducted a mission in the same locality. When I got an opportunity, I went to see the statue for myself. While I was there I didn't see it move in any way. Some time afterwards a similar occurrence was reported in Mount Melleray. Some people even maintained that they saw beams of blue light emanating from the statue of Mary. During a visit to Mount Mellary monastery I took the opportunity to go and visit the leafy grotto which was nearby. Once again nothing happened while I was there. Over the next year or two, other statues of Our Lady were said to have moved in other locations around the country.

About that time Gay Byrne decided to discuss the phenomenon on the Late Late Show, on RTE television. I was invited to participate. Psychologists based in University College Cork explained the phenomenon as an optical illusion caused by staring at objects in the twilight of the evening. Others argued that the moving statues were best explained as unconscious responses to a sense of anxiety that was evoked by the stressful social and religious circumstances prevailing in the country at the time. For my part, I said that I was inclined to interpret such experiences in a Jungian way as day-dreams. I felt that the strange reports could be understood in a symbolic manner as expressions of wishful thinking and projection. For example, if one looks up the entry on 'religious statues' in Tom Chetwynd's insightful and well researched *Dictionary for Dreamers*, it says that when inanimate figures are seen to move in a life-like way it is a sign that, 'what was a dead theoretical concept suddenly has new inner meaning for the dreamer,' and that, 'new potentialities are awakening in the dreamer.' I was of the opinion that a dry doctrinal approach to religion which was prevalent in the years after Vatican II, did very little for people. Evidently, what the faithful were looking for, were doctrines that came alive with religious meaning of an experiential kind. In that context I recalled something Jung wrote: 'Today Christianity is devitalised . . . 'God' has in fact become unconscious to us. This is what always happens when things are interpreted, explained, and dogmatised until they become so encrusted with man-made images and words that they can no longer be seen.' In a sense what people were longing for was a mystical sense of connection with the living God as the One who could communicate with them in word and deed.

## APPARITIONS

In this chapter we will also take a brief look at the phenomenon of apparitions. They are more common than you might think. Scientific research in Iceland discovered that 42% of adults reported having seen an apparition, 31% were of the dead, and 11% of the living. In a Canadian study 32% of the respondents claimed to have seen an apparition. Although religious apparitions are largely visual in nature, often the people who appear in them speak to the visionaries. In that sense the topic is relevant where this book is concerned.

Although there is a psychological continuity between visions and apparitions they are different. A vision is the result of God acting on the inner imagination of the person. An apparition, which seems to be a typically Catholic phenomenon, is a corporeal vision in which the eyes of the body perceive a normally invisible object, such as an angel or a saint, in an external way. It doesn't necessarily mean that the person seen is physically present, but that there is some visible representation of him or her which is made possible by God. Only Christ and Our Lady could actually appear in their bodies, although more often than not, they desist from doing so. It can also be said that an apparition is a charismatic gift granted by God for an edifying purpose. It doesn't necessarily say anything about the sanctity or spiritual maturity of the observer.

There are many examples of apparitions in the Old and New Testaments. The first is recounted in Genesis. God appeared to Adam and Eve in the garden in the cool of the evening (Gen 3:8).

The Lord appeared to Abram and changed his name to Abraham promising to make him a father of many nations (Gen 17:1). Soon afterwards the Lord appeared again to Abraham and promised him a son in his old age (Gen 18:1ff). On this occasion God's presence was symbolised by three angelic men whose appearance seemed to be an intimation of the Blessed Trinity. Jacob had a wrestling match with God (Gen 32:26-29). He was told that because he had 'striven with God and with men and had prevailed' he was to be given a new name and a special blessing that went with it. Moses also had an angel of the Lord appear to him in a burning bush (Ex 3:2). Then in the next verse, the Lord called to him from the bush and revealed to Moses how He planned to use him to deliver his people. Other apparitions of God to Moses are recounted throughout the book of Exodus. Angels or messengers of God also appeared to other people in the Old Testament, e.g. Gabriel appeared to Daniel (Dan 9:21). In the Gospels Moses and Elijah appeared to Jesus at the time of his transfiguration (Mt 17: 1-8; Mk 9: 2-8; Lk 9: 28-36). This apparition on Mount Tabor impressed his disciples. Peter probably thought that Jesus was going to establish an earthly kingdom with the cooperation of Moses and Elijah. However, immediately after this apparition Jesus warned Peter, James and John not to tell anyone about it until after his resurrection from the dead. When Jesus appeared to Saul on the road to Damascus he revealed himself in the form of light and an audible voice (Acts 9:1-19; 22:3-21; 26:9-23). Interestingly, Jesus promised Paul that he would appear to him again in the future. In 1 Cor 15:6-8 St. Paul recounted in an important creedal statement that the risen Jesus, ' appeared to more than five hundred of the brothers at the same time, most of whom are still living, though some have fallen asleep. Then he appeared to James, then to all the apostles, and last of all he appeared to me also, as to one abnormally born.' In Acts 23:1, Jesus appeared to Paul at night.

## APPARITIONS AND THE CHURCH

Over the years there have been a number of notable apparitions in the Catholic Church. For instance, Jesus appeared to St. Margaret Mary Alacoque (1647–1690) on the feast of Corpus Christi 1675 and said, 'Behold the Heart that has so loved men. . . instead of gratitude I receive from the greater part of mankind only ingratitude.' He asked Margaret Mary to initiate a feast of reparation on the Friday after the octave of Corpus Christi. Jesus also appeared to St. Faustina Kowalska (1905-1938). She recounted that on the night of Sunday February 22, 1931, Jesus revealed himself to her in Vilnius as the 'King of Divine Mercy' wearing a white garment, with rays of white and red light emanating from near his heart. In her diary she wrote that she was told: 'Paint an image according to the pattern you see, with the signature: 'Jesus, I trust in You.' I desire that this image be venerated, first in your chapel, and then throughout the world. I promise that the soul that will venerate this image will not perish.'

The Virgin Mary has often appeared to people. St. Marie-Bernarde Soubirous (1844-1879) experienced what is sometimes referred to as 'the great apparition' between 11 February and 16 July 1858 in Lourdes. The lady who appeared to her, identified herself as the Immaculate Conception. She also appeared to

St. Catherine Laboure (1806-1876) in a chapel on the Rue du Bac in Paris. On November 27, 1830 she displayed herself to Catherine inside an oval with rays of light beaming from the precious stones embedded in the many rings she wore on her fingers. Around the margin of the frame appeared the words, 'O Mary, conceived without sin, pray for us who have recourse to thee.' As Catherine watched, the frame seemed to rotate, showing a circle of twelve stars, a large letter M surmounted by a cross, and the stylised Sacred Heart of Jesus and the Immaculate Heart of Mary underneath. Asked why some of the precious stones on her rings did not shed light, Mary replied 'Those are the graces for which people forget to ask.' Catherine then heard Mary request her to take these images to her confessor, and to instruct him that they should be displayed on medals. 'All who wear them,' our Lady promised, 'will receive great graces.'

In 1917 Our Lady appeared to three children in Fatima. On October 13th a large crowd, including newspaper reporters and photographers, gathered at the Cova da Iria. The heavy rain finally ceased and a thin layer of cloud cloaked the sun. Witnesses said later that it could be looked at without hurting their eyes. Lúcia, one of the visionaries, moved by what she said was an interior impulse, called out to the crowd to look at the sun. Witnesses later spoke of the sun appearing to change colors and rotate like a wheel. Not everyone saw the same things, and witnesses gave widely varying descriptions of the 'sun's dance.' The phenomenon is claimed to have been witnessed by most people in the crowd as well as people many miles away.

Apparently the rain drenched ground dried out very quickly.

In all these private revelations, God spoke either directly through Jesus, or indirectly, through his mother Mary. Furthermore, it would probably be true to say that while the visionaries received revelatory messages directly, many people have cultivated devotion to the messages that God was speaking indirectly to their hearts through the visionaries.

## ASSESSMENT OF APPARITIONS

Many apparitions are reported by obscure individuals with little or no public reputation. Their human credibility may rest initially on the attitude of the local clergy and the personal experience of observers. There may, or may not be, phenomena which suggest something out of the ordinary. Often the faithful are left to judge for themselves. If the message seems to be orthodox, the seer has a good reputation, and the signs supportive, then even without an official investigation the faithful can choose to believe that the message/s probably have come from God.

The faithful benefit most when the bishop of the diocese in which the apparition occurred investigates it in order to make a judgment about its authenticity. To do this he will usually appoint a commission of experts to assess the case. Afterwards the decision of the bishop will be one or other of the following.

1. The apparition is judged to be supernatural in origin.
2. The apparition is judged not to have been supernatural in origin.

**3**. The apparition is not yet judged to be supernatural.

Such decisions should be willingly accepted by the faithful. Canon 753 of the *Code of Canon Law* says, 'Although the bishops who are in communion with the head and members of the college, whether individually or joined together in conferences of bishops or in particular councils, do not possess infallibility in teaching, they are authentic teachers and instructors of the faith for the Christian faithful entrusted to their care; *the Christian faithful are bound to adhere with religious submission of mind to the authentic magisterium of their bishops.*' In 1974, the Sacred Congregation for the Doctrine of the Faith issued norms regarding the manner of proceeding with regard to presumed apparitions or revelations. The guidelines were made public in May 2012.

Speaking about apparitions, par. 90 of *The Directory on Popular Piety and the Liturgy: Principles and Guidelines*, says, 'Popular piety has always been interested in extraordinary happenings and events that are not infrequently connected with private revelations. While not confined to Marian piety alone, this phenomenon is particularly involved with 'apparitions' and 'messages.' It then goes on to quote par. 67 of the *Catechism of the Catholic Church* which says, 'Guided by the Magisterium of the Church, the *sensus fidelium* knows how to discern and welcome in these revelations whatever constitutes an authentic call of Christ or his saints to the Church.' Over the years I have often been disappointed when Catholics seemed to put more trust in the messages received by visionaries, some of which were very suspect, than in the scriptures and the teachings of the magisterium of the Church. If a message is not supported by Church authority the followers of popular piety were inclined to say things like, 'The Church will see sense eventually, after all St Faustina's writings were condemned for a time,' or 'the bishop isn't a very spiritual man, he doesn't understand the true meaning of the message the visionary has received.'

Nowadays there are many apparitions competing for the attention of the faithful. A statistical analysis of the Marian apparition directory reveals the following details. During the 20th century there were 386 cases of reported Marian apparitions. The Church made no decision about the supernatural character of 299 of the 386 cases. The Church made a negative decision about the supernatural character in 79 of the 386 cases and said yes to the supernatural character of only 8 cases, Fatima (Portugal), Beauraing (Belgium), Banneux (Belgium), Akita (Japan), Syracuse (Italy), Zeitoun (Egypt), Manila (Philippines) and Betania (Venezuela).

## LOCUTIONS

The word locution in English is derived from the Latin *loqui,* meaning, 'to speak.' A questionnaire responded to by 375 college students found that 71% of them had experienced locutions of some kind or other. Only some of them were religious. Evelyn Underhill suggests that, 'true auditions are usually heard when the mind is in a state of deep absorption without conscious thought: that is to say, at the most favorable of all moments for contact with the transcendental world.'

Spiritual writers, such as St Teresa of Avila, have suggested that there are three kinds of religious locution.

There are auricular locutions whereby the person literally hears someone talking, it could be God, a saint or an angel. For example, St. Luke records that Zachary heard the angel Gabriel speak to him (Lk 1:19). The same angel said to Mary: 'Hail, full of grace' (Lk 1:28). In Jn 12:28 Jesus prayed, 'Father, glorify your name!' Then a voice came from heaven, 'I have glorified it, and will glorify it again.' The crowd that was there and heard it said it had thundered; others said an angel had spoken to him. Jesus said, 'This voice was for your benefit, not mine.' Professor, Tanya Marie Luhrmann of Stanford University tells us that she could still remember, 'how startled I was when a young woman I was interviewing told me God had spoken to her audibly. I was doing ethnographic field work in a quietly charismatic evangelical church in Chicago. This was the kind of church in which people sought an intimate, conversational relationship with God. It was not at all uncommon for people to talk about hearing God. This woman, however, said that she had been to a job interview and that later, while tidying up at home, she had heard God say, 'That's not the one' — and that she had looked around to see where the voice had come from. She told me that she heard from God like that many times. The first time as an adult was when she was driving alone in an unfamiliar part of the city — and God spoke up audibly out of the back seat and told her that he would always be with her.' I must confess that I cannot remember anyone telling me that they had heard God communicate with them in an external, audible voice.

Intellectual locutions involve words which are perceived directly by the intellect without having to be spoken. This gift has its visual parallel in the gift of intellectual pictures. I suspect that many Christians, who are open to the working of the Holy Spirit, hear from God in this way. I can remember a number of occasions when I heard prophetic messages in an intellectual manner either for myself or more commonly for others.

## ASSESSMENT OF LOCUTIONS

Although God can communicate with people by means of locutions of one kind or another, discernment is necessary because the messages could emanate either from the self or the evil one. I must say, I agree with what St. John of the Cross wrote, 'I am appalled at what happens in these days-namely, when some soul with the very smallest experience of meditation, if it be conscious of certain locutions of this kind in some state of recollection, at once christens them all as coming from God, and assumes that this is the case, saying: 'God said to me . . . '; 'God answered me . . . ', whereas it is not so at all, but as we have said, it is for the most part they who are saying it to themselves.' Chapter three of St Teresa of Avila's book *The Interior Castle,* also had very wise things to say about locutions. She was a little more positive in her assessment of them than her fellow Carmelite, John of the Cross. For instance she wrote, 'I caution you on one point--although they may come from God, you must not esteem yourself more highly, for He often spoke to the Pharisees - all the good consists in profiting by His words. Take no more notice of any speeches you hear which disagree with the Holy Scriptures than if you heard them from Satan himself. Though they may only rise from your vivid imagination, look upon them as a temptation against the faith. Always resist them; then they will leave you, and cease, for they have little strength of their own.'

## CONCLUSION

Although God can communicate with people by means of apparitions or locutions it has to be admitted that they are not only unusual charismatic forms of communication, they are relatively uncommon also. There are many followers of popular piety, however, who are given to reading the messages given to visionaries. They regard them as messages from God and feel that they enable them to know the mind of the Lord. We did not look at the psychological dimension of apparitions and locutions because it went beyond the scope of this book. Suffice it to say, that they need to be treated with a degree of caution in order to be preserved from illusion and false inspirations. They should never take precedence over the teachings of the scriptures and the Church in the lives of the faithful.

CHAPTER THIRTEEN

# WORDS OF KNOWLEDGE AND PROPHECY

A number of years ago. I was sitting in my office daydreaming. I recalled in an imaginative way the house where my grandparents used to live on the Howth Road, in Dublin. Then I could see another house right across the road and recalled the name of the English family that used to live there and the names of the two daughters. As I looked at one of the two women, in my mind's eye, I was suddenly aware that her husband had died that very day. Needless to say I prayed for the repose of the man's soul and for the comfort of his wife in her loss and grief. I had no way of checking out the veracity of that intuition because I didn't know her married name or where she lived. A few weeks later I happened to meet my sister Marie. To my utter surprise she said she had been talking to one of the two sisters from the Howth Road, and that she had mentioned in passing that her brother in law had died a few weeks before. I asked my sister if she could remember the date. When we checked it on a calendar, it was the same day that I had experienced the intuition that he had just died. Coincidence or a prophetic revelation from God? I suspect that it was the latter.

This chapter will deal with unusual forms of guidance; words of knowledge and prophecy. We begin by looking at the former. In *The New International Dictionary of the Pentecostal and Charismatic Movements*, Francis Martin wrote, 'We may define the gift of the 'word of knowledge' as being the charismatically endowed capacity to express some aspect of God's plan as it is at work in creation here and now, revealing something of God.' Anglican bishop, David Pytches, said in a more comprehensive way in his book *Come, Holy Spirit* that the word of knowledge is a, 'supernatural revelation of facts about a person or situation, which is not learned through the efforts of the natural mind, but is a fragment of knowledge freely given by God, disclosing the truth which the Spirit wishes to be made known concerning a particular person or situation.' Because many Christians are unfamiliar with this unusual phenomenon, we will examine it briefly from a scriptural, theological and experiential point of view.

## The Word of Knowledge in the Old and New Testaments

There are many instances of the word of knowledge in the Old Testament. We will advert to just three of many possible examples. The prophet Nathan knew about David's sin of adultery with Bathsheba, and he used the parable about the poor man and the lamb before confronting him by saying, 'You are that man' (2 Sam 12:1-12). Daniel had an inspired sense that Susanna was innocent of the accusations made by two lustful old men. He devised a test which exposed their guilt and the woman's innocence (Dan 13:44-49). When Saul was chosen as king, he hid himself. We are told, however, that the people ' inquired further of the Lord, 'Has the man come here yet?' And the Lord said, possibly through someone in the gathering uttering a prophetic word of knowledge, 'Yes, he has hidden himself among the baggage' (1 Sam 10:22).

In the New Testament we are told that Jesus was able to read people's hearts and to predict future events. For instance, he appeared to know all about Nathaniel although he had never met him before (Jn 1:48), and he was able to tell the Samaritan woman at the well that she hadn't one husband, but five (Jn 4:18). When asked to pay the tax, Jesus knew about the shekel in the fish's mouth, which Peter would later retrieve (Mt 17:27). On another occasion, Jesus told the disciples that they would find a donkey in a certain place (Mk 11:2) and that they would meet a man carrying a pitcher of water (Mk 14:13). During his scourging at the pillar the Roman soldiers taunted the blindfolded Jesus, by saying: 'Prophesy, who hit you?' This indicated that Jesus was known to have an ability to speak words of knowledge.

In the New Testament Church some of the believers were granted the word of knowledge. For example, in Acts 5:1-11 St. Peter seemed to get such a word about the misdeeds of Ananias and Sapphira. Another man named Ananias in Damascus met Saul as a result of a word of knowledge, 'The Lord told him, 'Go to the house of Judas on Straight Street and ask for a man from Tarsus named Saul, for he is praying. In a vision he has seen a man named Ananias come and place his hands on him to restore his sight' (Acts 9:11-12). St. Peter met with Cornelius, in much the same way when he and the centurion received words of knowledge (Acts 10:17-23).

It has to be said that there is a disagreement among scripture scholars when it comes to the charism of the word of knowledge. Some maintain that it is implicit in 1 Cor 12:8 where St. Paul refers to the 'utterance of knowledge.' Commenting on these words, Gordon Fee has written in his *Commentary on 1 Corinthians*, 'Some have suggested that Paul here has in mind a supernatural endowment of knowledge, factual information that could not otherwise have been known without the Spirit's aid.' He reiterated that point in his book, *God's Empowering Presence*. George Montague seems to espouse the same point of view in his book *The Holy Spirit: Growth of a Biblical Tradition.* He says that the utterance of knowledge may refer to 'an inspired knowledge of a fact.' By way of example he refers to an incident already adverted to, namely the way in which the prophet Nathan knew about David's sin with Bathsheba (2 Sam 12:1-12).

Other scholars understand the word of knowledge as an aspect of the gift of prophecy which is mentioned in 1 Cor 12:10. It is clear that this is Jack Deere's understanding, particularly in chapter five of his book, *The Beginner's Guide to the Gift of Prophecy*. It seems to me that St. Thomas Aquinas also saw words of knowledge as an exercise of the prophetic gift. In par 728 of his commentary on *First Corinthians* he said, 'to another is given prophecy, which is divine revelation declaring with unchangeable truth among events . . . Another is knowledge of the human heart, as in Jer (17:9).' Although it is not really important how one categorises the word of knowledge, I am of the opinion that it is an aspect of the gift of prophecy. In terms of the subject matter of this book, it is an unusual, charismatic way of hearing God speak to the heart.

## PENTECOSTAL AND CHARISMATIC EXAMPLES OF WORDS OF KNOWLEDGE

In the 20th century a number of well known Pentecostals and charismatics exercised the charismatic gift of words of knowledge. I suppose the person who was best known for this activity was the late Kathryn Kuhlman (1907-1976). She exercised a healing ministry for many years in the U.S.A. What made her unusual was the fact that she didn't pray for healing with the laying on of hands. Instead she would talk and pray until she received an anointing of the Holy Spirit. Then inspired by words of knowledge she would say who was being healed of what ailment in a specific area of the auditorium. The following words are taken from a transcript of one of her miracle services. 'There is a heart condition disappearing. Wonderful Jesus, I give you praise and glory..... There is a case of sugar diabetes....the sugar is draining from your body....an ear has been opened completely. Someone hears me perfectly. In the balcony. Check on that someone. Up there in the top left balcony is a man with a hearing aid. Check that ear sir. Hold your good ear closed tight; you hear me perfectly.' Speaking about her exercise of this remarkable gift Kathryn said: 'My mind is so surrendered to the Spirit, that I know the exact body being healed; the sickness, the affliction, and in some instances the very sin in their lives. And yet I do not pretend to tell you *why* or *how*.'

Former scripture Professor Jack Deere has recounted a fascinating encounter that took place at a time when he was utterly sceptical about all the charisms, including the word of knowledge. He arranged to meet a man called Eddie Bauer in Kansas City. When he visited, Bauer told him that eight nights before he had a dream about Jack. As soon as he recalled it, he had written it down. Then in a succession of stages Eddie proceeded to tell Jack one thing after another about his life, e.g., what he had prayed for in his hotel that morning, about his father's suicide when he was twelve, and about the hurt and bitterness he felt about the way he had given up his sporting activities in order to focus on intellectual pursuits which failed to bring him fulfilment. Then he said, 'The Lord is going to make up for the loss of your father to you. He will send you new fathers. You won't learn from just one man. You will have the father you need for each new stage of your life.' Deere says that the man who spoke the prophetic word of knowledge was uncannily correct in all that he said. Apparently his words marked the beginning of a new beginning in Deere's life. His attitude to the charisms changed. Instead of opposing them he began to exercise them in his ministry, especially the word of knowledge. He gives many examples of words he himself has received over the years. Prescinding from questions to do with the psycho-spiritual dimension of words of knowledge, they can be invaluable in different ministry situations. I would like to advert to four kinds that I have been aware of in my own life and the lives of others.

## Reading of Hearts

There is a type of word of knowledge which is sometimes referred to as the reading of hearts *(kardiagnosis)*. It consists of a knowledge of the secrets of hearts which is not the result of empathy or an ability to read body language. Rather it is a supernatural ability communicated by God. When one reads the biographies of saintly people like the Cure of Ars and Padre Pio, there is evidence that they received this gift on numerous occasions. As someone who is far from being saintly there have been a couple of occasions when I have known the sins of others. For instance, years ago I helped to conduct a parish mission in Ireland. While a colleague was preaching, during the men's week, I got an inward sense that there was a man present who had committed five very serious crimes. I won't mention them here, but I knew what they were. I was also convinced that this was the first time he had been in a church for fifteen years. Furthermore, I felt that that God was more than willing to forgive him if he was sorry for what he had done. When I finished giving the announcements that evening, I referred in a general way to what the Lord had revealed to me. Not surprisingly, there was an atmosphere of great silence as I spoke. Afterwards I told my colleague that if the word of knowledge was genuine the man in question would end up in his confession room or mine. Two days later, when one particular man came into the confession room, I knew immediately, when I saw his silhouette, that he was the one that the Lord had told me about.

Suffice it to say that when we spoke together it became clear that the word of knowledge was completely accurate. The man repented in a flood of tears and was reconciled with God.

## Guidance in intercessory prayer

Nowadays there are many charismatic individuals and groups that engage in intercession for others. They can be guided in their prayer by means of a 'word of knowledge.' The first time I experienced the guidance of the Spirit in this way was in Oct 1977. I was a teacher in a boy's boarding school at the time. One day as I was going from one class room to another I received a very unexpected word of knowledge that enabled me to know that the actor Charlie Chaplin would die on Christmas day of that year. As I walked up the corridor I met a priest colleague and told him about my word of knowledge. I said, 'We often hear people say that they had an anticipatory premonition about an event *after* it has happened. I want to tell you today, months before it happens, that Sir Charlie Chaplin will die on Christmas day this year.' He gave me a puzzled look but said very little. I used to attend a weekly prayer meeting in those days and I informed the members about the word of knowledge and asked them to pray for Charlie that he would have a peaceful death and that God would have mercy on his soul. Occasionally I'd look at the paper to see if he was ailing, but there was no news.

Shortly before Christmas I bought a stereo radio. When I woke up on Christmas morning I turned it on in order to admire its more fulsome sound. When I did, the very first words I heard were, 'Sir Charles Chaplin died in Switzerland early this morning.' When I went to breakfast, the colleague I had informed about Chaplin's impending death said, 'My God Pat, you were right about Charlie Chaplin. Do you find it scary to know something like that?' 'No,' I replied, 'I would have been scared if he didn't die, because I was as sure of that fact as I am of my own existence.' Soon after that I conducted a retreat in England. While I was there I saw a movie called *City Lights* in which Charlie Chaplin was a poor man who gave all that he could to help a blind girl to get an operation to restore her sight. As I watched, I felt that God was saying, 'In real life, Charlie Chaplin grew up in poverty in London. As an actor he depicted the lot of the poor in a sympathetic and compassionate way. That is why I wanted you to pray for him.'

I have described that kind of prayer for others in chapters entitled, 'Prayer as Intercession,' in *Prayer in Practice* (2000); and 'Group Intercessory Prayer,' in *Word and Spirit* (2011). Both of them explain how prophetic words of knowledge can guide intercessory prayers offered in faith to God. I should acknowledge in passing that my understanding of this important form of prayer was greatly helped by the teaching of the Lydia Fellowship International which is an organisation for women intercessors. Cindy Jacobs talks about the role of charismatic guidance in intercessory prayer in her book, *The Voice of God: How God Speaks Personally and Corporately to his Children Today* as does Arthur Wallis in his excellent book, *Pray in the Spirit.*

## Guidance in prayer for inner healing

Those who pray for inner healing are sometimes led by a 'word of knowledge' to focus on a repressed memory. I must say that I have found this gift can be a great help when ministering to the needs of others. Let me give a few examples. Recently I attended a prayer meeting. During a quiet time I focused on God the Father and asked him if he wanted to reveal anything to me. At one point I felt he was saying that a woman in her late forties was present who had suffered a sexual assault in a hotel room many years before. I also had a feeling that God was saying that the devil had prompted the attack. A little later I mentioned that a woman was present who had suffered a traumatic event in a hotel many years before, without saying anything about the sexual attack or the role of the evil one. Immediately a woman at the back of the room put up her hand to indicate that she was the person in question. When I got a chance to speak to her privately, she explained that she had been given a date rape drug and assaulted by a number of men in a hotel bedroom where they tried to recruit her as a prostitute some twenty six years before. Not surprisingly she felt traumatised by her experience and suffered from a lot of fear and anxiety as a result. I prayed that her fear would be healed and that she would be delivered from any spiritual oppression that might have resulted from that terrible incident.

About two years ago I conducted a retreat in England. I was there for eight days. Each afternoon I was available so that retreatants could come to see me for a chat, prayer, or the sacrament of reconciliation. On one of the days a women who was working in the retreat house asked if she could talk with me. I said it was okay. She had a tale of woe to tell which among other things included a serious addiction. We talked for about an hour and at the end I offered to say a brief prayer with her. As she was leaving the room, I was surprised to hear an inner voice saying, 'I want you to ask her about the disaster which befell her when she was twelve years of age.' My initial reaction was one of resistance, I wasn't sure if the question was coming from my own overblown imagination or from the Lord. However, after a few seconds I said spontaneously, 'By the way, before you leave can I ask you a question, what disaster befell you when you were twelve years of age?' The woman stopped and looked at me with a mixture of surprise and dismay. 'How did you know that?' she asked. I said, 'because God asked me to ask you that question. Would you like to talk about it?' 'I didn't tell you about the incident,' the woman replied, 'but a disaster did befall me when I was twelve.' When she recounted what had happened it was quite obvious that it was the likely cause of her addiction and other problems. I prayed again for inner healing, but this time in a much more focused, expectant way, believing that I was doing so in accordance with God's will. Two or three days later the woman asked to see me again. She looked and sounded more positive. 'Father,' she said, 'I want to thank you for the chat and the prayer you said for me the other day. Now I really feel that I can overcome my addiction with God's help.' 'What made the difference?' I asked. She responded, 'for a long time I didn't feel that God cared about me, because I had prayed for help many times but none seemed to be forthcoming. But when you said that God had prompted you to ask me about the disaster that had befallen me, I knew that God knew all about me and also cared about me. That has made a big difference. Now I feel that with God's help I will be able to cope.'

More recently I was asked to conduct a healing service in Leeds Cathedral in England. Before the service was due to begin I prayed that the Lord might help me to know who or what was going to be healed. As I did so, I felt that God the Father was enabling me to understand that a man would come to the healing service who had been haunted for many years by dark, disturbing dreams. I also had a sense that they were being caused in some way by an evil spirit. During the service I administered the sacrament of the anointing of the sick to many people. When I was doing so, I stopped when I came to one particular man and asked him why he had come forward for the anointing. 'I need inner healing,' he responded. 'For about twenty years now I have been afflicted by nightmares, really upsetting and scary dreams. I have prayed many times that the Lord would relieve me of them, but so far nothing has happened.' I was really surprised. The man was telling me exactly what the Lord had told me when I was praying. I said to him, 'you are a fortunate man indeed, because the Lord told me you would come forward for healing. A bad spirit has been oppressing you. I will pray now because it is the Lord's will that you be healed.' As I began to anoint him my body literally shuddered as I sensed the presence of the Lord's Holy Spirit. Although I have no way of knowing whether the man was actually healed, I'd presume that he was.

## GUIDANCE AT HEALING SERVICES

As the ministry of people like Kathryn Kuhlman and John Wimber have shown, words of knowledge are sometimes granted to those praying for physical cures, particularly at healing services. Here are a few personal examples that I can recall. In 2010 I was in London to speak at a conference. On the Saturday night I conducted a healing service. It was one of those blessed occasions when lots of words of knowledge came to me. One of them was about a woman's eyelid which had turned inward so that her eye lashes were irritating and infecting her eye in a painful way. When I got that word it confused me. I had never heard of anyone suffering from that particular complaint. But I decided to take courage by mentioning it. When I asked if anyone was present who was suffering from a turned in eyelid, I was surprised and a bit relieved to see a woman's hand being raised. I asked her neighbours to put a hand gently on her and to pray. The next morning the woman asked to speak. She told us about her eyelid and how she had been due to have surgery to rectify the problem. 'I won't need it now' she announced, 'my eye has been completely healed!'

In March of 2012 I was in the Czech Republic to speak at two venues. While I was visiting a monastery in Zeliv I conducted a healing service during which I received a number of words of knowledge and prayed for people. When I returned in early 2013 I was told about three interrelated healings. A woman said that she, her husband and daughter had attended the healing service a few months beforehand. Apparently I had said during the service that a man was being healed of brucellosis, a woman of cystitis and another woman of heart disease. The woman said that her husband had been suffering from brucellosis for some time, that her daughter had been treated with antibiotics to clear up cystitis but without success, and that she herself had suffered from heart disease. 'I am glad to tell you,' she said, 'that thanks to the grace of God, all three of us have been healed.'

Sometime in 2012 I celebrated an outdoor Mass in Valetta, Malta. When Holy Communion had been distributed I asked the Father in heaven if there was anyone he wanted to heal. I felt that he was saying to me that there was a man present who had a diseased and painful hip. When I described the symptoms, a man of about sixty put up his hand. I got his neighbours to pray for him. The next day I met him and he said that he had no pain in his hip. Fearing that it might be an instance of a temporary placebo effect, I asked him to contact me a month later to confirm whether he was truly healed or not. In due course I received an email which said, 'I am writing to confirm that my hip has 'remained healed' and your word of knowledge just after Mass (You had declared 'A hip is being healed') was very true. On hearing your words I remember saying to myself 'Could it be mine? If so , thank you Jesus.' I did not feel anything physical but when we got up I realised that the dull pain in my left hip, that I had learnt to live with over the years, was not there. Well, I can now say 'Praise you, Lord Jesus, and thank you for healing my hip.'

It is not too hard to know whether words of knowledge are from God or not. Did they prove to be accurate and did they lead to blessing of one kind or another? But with Sts Peter and John I would want to say, 'why does this surprise you? Why do you stare at us as if by our own power or godliness' (Acts 3:12) we did any of these things. It was as the result of faith and the free gift of God's unmerited and undeserved grace.

## PROPHETIC GUIDANCE

As Anthony Thiselton points out in his book, *The Holy Spirit in Biblical Teaching through the Centuries and Today,* the words 'prophet' and 'prophecy' are derived from the Greek *prophetes,* meaning 'interpreter', or 'spokesman,' i.e. the one who proclaims inspired revelation. The noun *propheteia* relates to interpreting the will of God (Romans 12:6; 1 Cor 12:10) and is the main focus of this chapter. The verb *propheteuo* relates especially to proclaiming the revealed word, and sometimes to prediction, e.g., when Agabus predicted a famine which would effect the entire Roman world in Acts 11:28. Prophecy could be defined as an ability which is granted to a believer, by the Spirit, to speak forth words from God that do not come from the person's natural intelligence or knowledge. St Thomas Aquinas said in his *Summa Theologica*: 'In a broad sense the subject of prophecy is whatever man knows by God's revelation. It differs from other charisms such as wisdom and knowledge and understanding of speech, the subjects of which man can know by natural reason, though not as perfectly as by God's light....*Prophecy is knowledge imprinted on the prophet's mind by the teaching of God's revelation.*' Thomas added that prophecy is primarily a 'divine revelation, announcing future events with unshakeable truth.' He believed that all things pertaining to revealed knowledge could be gathered under the umbrella of prophecy. As such it was the key to a proper understanding of all the charisms in 1 Cor 12:8-10. St. Paul expressed the triple purpose of prophecy when he said in 1 Cor 14:3: 'everyone who prophesies speaks to men for their edification, exhortation and comfort.' There are a number of ways in which this can occur.

## Prophetic messages addressed by God to oneself

On a small number of occasions I have felt that God was addressing a prophetic message to myself. In 1982 the Lord spoke such a message to me as I travelled by train in Boston, Massachusetts. It went as follows,

> 'Leave the city with its proud flags and go to the breach in the wall. Go and stand in the breach the place of insecurity. Stand in the breach where the wind blows, where the jackal cries and where the enemy enters under the cloak of darkness. Stand in the breach and listen to my word. Stand in the breach and pray for yourself and the people. Then call my people to the breach to rebuild the walls of Jerusalem.'

I can remember saying to the Lord that I would close my eyes, open the Bible at random, place my finger on the page, and if it was on the words, 'rebuild the walls of Jerusalem' I'd believe that the prophecy was from God. When I cut the Bible and looked at the verse my finger was resting on, I found that it was Ps 51:18 which reads, 'rebuild the walls of Jerusalem.' As I have written about that prophecy in the first chapter of *Word and Spirit* I will say nothing about it here. As I look back, however, I can see that it has had a big impact on my life and has guided me ever since.

On another occasion I heard these prophetic words being addressed to my heart.

> 'I do not despise your imperfection. I live in it. When you see the flaws in your brothers and sisters, and the wounds in your own heart, do not feel that they will separate you from me. I live in those wounds. I reveal myself through your brokenness. When you look at the cross you do not see a perfect Lord, but a broken one. You do not see light, but darkness. You do not see joy, but anguish and pain. My child I have descended into the depths of your vulnerability, there to reveal the glory of my Father. For I love you in your brokenness, and you run away from it, as if it were not acceptable to me, as if I would despise it. It is my treasure. My light shines forth in all that you fear. So look to it. Accept it, in the knowledge that I am within it, and that you will learn to see me in places you have never seen me before and in a world that frightens you today. You will see my face shining through tomorrow, for you will have changed, you will see as I see, my glory is everywhere.'

## Prophetic messages addressed to others

Between the years 2006-2008 I lived in a parish in Detroit, Michigan. Each Sunday I would preach at Mass. One particular weekend while I was preparing my homily I can remember hearing the following words within. They were so clear and memorable I was able to write them down. They read as follows:

> 'I am the Lord your God the holy one. My people, do not compromise with sin. If there is mortal sin in your life, do not deny or excuse it. Repent, receive my forgiveness, avoid the first stirrings of temptation and believe that I will deliver you from the web of evil that holds you captive. If there is venial sin in your life, do not tolerate it. Be aware that secret and un-repented sin in the lives of those who believe in me is the greatest single obstacle to the work of my Spirit.
>
> I want you to be holy, I want you to turn away from the ways of the world. I call on you to root out your sins, great and small alike. Be assured that I will not only enlighten your heart to know your sins I will enable you to turn away from them by a great and liberating outpouring of my grace. Be holy as I am holy. There is no substitute for this holiness. There is no plan, effort, or activity, no matter how well intentioned, which will accomplish my purposes if you are not holy like Me. When your heart is cleansed, my Spirit will pray ardently within you, it will guide you in ways you have not known, it will empower and protect you from the deceptions of the evil one. It will fill you with my joy.

> I weep for the world and my Church. There are many, who because of their great and repeated sins, are travelling the wide road that leads to perdition. Call them to repentance, before it is too late, so that they may come back to me. I promise you that many of them will heed your words when they see my holiness shining forth in your lives. My people, the time of breach-mending is at hand. I will enable you to re-build the walls of Jerusalem. I am about to accomplish a great work of restoration, but woe to those who do not heed my voice.'

I can remember incorporating that prophecy into my sermon. I can't say that it had a dramatic effect. That said, a number of people talked to me about it's contents and one or two asked for a printed copy. Over the years I have heard a number of genuine prophecies being spoken at Charismatic Renewal gatherings. When one hears a genuine *rhema* word, it is like the two edged sword mentioned in Heb 4:12 13 which, 'penetrates even to dividing soul and spirit, joints and marrow; it judges the thoughts and attitudes of the heart' and evokes an answering amen within.

Myles Dempsey, a leader of the Charismatic Renewal in Britain, has been receiving prophetic messages for years. In an article in *Goodnews* magazine he wrote, 'Just before the New Dawn conference in 2001, I received a word of warning which I shared briefly at the time. The following month I was reminded about that word and repeated it in greater detail at a prayer meeting on the evening of 10th September 2001. The words I used were,

> 'An event of worldwide significance is soon to take place and when it does it will have two main consequences : it will result in consternation for the nations but will lead to a time of glory for the Church.'

After speaking these words I told the people,

> 'It could be in the nature of a massive financial collapse like what occurred in 1929, only on a much larger scale. After all the economic structure of the world is so brittle that it could suddenly come down like a house of cards and you might see people jumping from the windows of the skyscrapers of New York.'

The following morning I received a phone call from Lisbon. I was told, 'Turn on your television, turn on your television!' I immediately tuned in. I thought I had the wrong programme and was seeing a horror movie. Then I realised that what I was watching was live from New York and I remembered the words I had spoken the previous night. There, before my eyes, the twin towers, a symbol of the world's financial system, were falling down like a pack of cards while people were jumping out of skyscrapers. My words had proved prophetic without my realising it.'

Prophecy can also be delivered in the form of an utterance in tongues. Because it is unintelligible the leader of a prayer meeting will ask the members to pray for an interpretation as opposed to a translation. It will usually come in the form of a prophecy in the language of those present, or a scripture text. I can remember a woman giving a strong utterance in tongues at a prayer meeting I attended many years ago. Then we waited for an interpretation. It came in the form of a prophecy for a particular woman who had come to request prayer for her daughter who was very ill in hospital with a mysterious ailment. One of those present said that the baby would be healed but that it would take time. In the interim the mother would have something difficult to contend with. Afterwards we found out that things worked out much as the prophecy had indicated. The baby recovered rapidly two weeks later when her doctors discovered that she was allergic to milk. But before that happened, the mother was involved in a car crash when her leg was slightly injured.

Anyone who reads Smith Wigglesworth's book, *Greater Works,* will see that he often interrupted his talks by giving an utterance in tongues which he himself went on to interpret straightaway. Occasionally, a person will give a prophecy in tongues which is literally translated by somebody present. I have only come across that phenomenon on one occasion. A woman gave an utterance in tongues and a missionary nun who was present was able to translate what had been said in Swahili. The message was mainly about Mary being the queen of peace. What was remarkable about it was the fact that, a month or so later, there was a reported apparition of Our Lady in Medjugorge in Yugoslavia where she declared that she was queen of peace.

## PROPHETIC PREACHING

Prophetic revelation from the Lord can take the form of inspired and inspiring preaching. In 2002 a controversial abortion referendum was held in Ireland. At the time I was contacted by NBC. The American network asked if they could interview me and film me giving a sermon on the divisive topic. Following the recordings, I found that sixteen hours of material were in the can. Afterwards it was condensed to six minutes in Dublin and further reduced to two and a half minutes by editors in New York. To my surprise I found that twenty five seconds of my contribution was included. I asked the American crew, 'what part did you use?' One of them replied, 'actually we included some spontaneous, but passionate remarks that you made when you had completed your sermon. You sounded as if you were inspired so we included them.' Perhaps, those unpremeditated words were prophetic because they had been revealed to me on the spur of the moment. I know that there have been occasions when I was listening to a very good homily or talk when I suspected the speaker had reached a purple patch that was prophetic rather than didactic. For example, when Pope John Paul II spoke in Limerick in October 1979, I felt that the following words were truly prophetic, 'Your country seems in a sense to be living again the temptations of Christ: Ireland is being asked to prefer the 'kingdoms of the world and their splendour' to the Kingdom of God (cf. Mt 4:8). Satan, the Tempter, the Adversary of Christ, will use all his might and all his deceptions to win Ireland for the way of the world. What a victory he would gain, what a blow he would inflict on the Body of Christ in the world, if he could seduce Irish men and women away from Christ. Now is the time of testing for Ireland. This generation is once more a generation of decision.' Events in church and state have since proven just how prescient the Holy Father happened to be.

## Conclusion

The discernment of sprits, which is mentioned in 1 Cor 12:10, is not so much about a generalised ability to distinguish inspirations that come from God from those which do not, as a God-given charism to identify which prophecies are prompted by the Spirit from those which are not. Instead of testing the authenticity of a word of knowledge or prophecy oneself, Christians often have to rely on the judgement of a member of the community who has the charism of discernment of spirits. Even the best intentioned people can, on occasion, be subject to illusions or false inspirations. Even though he was aware of this, St. Paul wished that everyone could prophecy. He wrote, 'brothers, be eager to prophesy' (1 Cor 14:39). He also wrote. 'Follow the way of love and eagerly desire spiritual gifts, *especially the gift of prophecy*' (1 Cor 14:1). Again in 1 Thess 5: 19-21 he wrote, 'Do not put out the Spirit's fire; do not treat prophecies with contempt.' It seems to me that the Church in every country and community, needs God's vision for the future, and one of the main ways in which that vision will be given to us is by means of the prophetic gift.

# Section Four

## Some Practical Implications

## CHAPTER FOURTEEN

# LET THE HAND BE CONFORMED TO THE HEART

During the troubles in Northern Ireland many men were incarcerated in Magilligan prison, near Limavady. A number of people in Derry City volunteered to transport relatives who wished to make prison visits. Most of the prisoners were Catholic Republicans. So imagine the surprise of one group of Catholic women when they were told that the lady who repeatedly drove them to and from the prison camp was not only a Protestant, but the widow of a policemen who had been murdered by the IRA. So they asked their driver if the rumour was true. She said that it was. Then the women asked her why on earth she had volunteered to bring them to see men, one of whom who might have murdered her husband. The woman admitted that she didn't find it easy. Then she went on to explain that she knew only too well that she was a sinner and that, through no merit or good work of her own, Jesus had forgiven all her sins. Afterwards she realised in her heart of hearts that Jesus was saying to her, 'though they do not deserve it, forgive those who have sinned against you, just as I have forgiven you.' Then the Protestant woman explained, 'by volunteering to bring you to the prison I am responding as best I can to the teaching of my merciful Lord.' That Protestant woman's willingness to live out the Gospel message, to such an heroic degree, has inspired me ever since.

In Exodus 24:3 we read, 'When Moses went and told the people all the Lord's words and laws, they responded with one voice, 'Everything the Lord has said we will do'.' Jesus echoed those sentiments when he said: 'Everyone who hears these words of mine and puts them into practice is like a wise man who built his house on the rock' (Mt. 7:24), and again, 'Blessed rather are those who hear the word of God and obey it' (Lk 11:28). The last recorded words of Mary at the marriage feast of Cana were, '*Do* whatever he tells you' (Jn 2:5). It is not surprising, therefore, that James taught, 'be doers of the word, and not hearers only, deceiving yourselves. For if anyone is a hearer of the word and not a doer, he is like a man who observes his natural face in a mirror; for he observes himself and goes away and at once forgets what he was like' (Jm 1:22-24). While the reference to hearing is about attention to the scriptures in particular, it can be extended to include all the forms of hearing, ordinary and unusual which have been explored in the previous chapters. It is not enough to hear God's word, one must act on it. The saints were well aware of this.

## FROM HEARING TO DOING

St Vincent de Paul, appreciated the importance of union with Christ and openness to the word and guidance of God. In 1656 he said to a young priest, called Antoine Durand, C.M., who he had appointed as superior of a seminary, 'Establish a close union between yourself and our Lord in prayer.' He counselled, 'That is the reservoir in which you will receive the guidance you will need to fulfil the duties on which you are now about to enter. When in doubt, have recourse to God the Father and say to him, 'O Lord, you are the Father of light, teach me what I ought to do in these circumstances ... Whenever there is a question of doing a good work, say to the Son of God, 'O Lord, if you were in my place, what would you do? . . . I give you this advice not only for those difficulties which will cause you stress, but also *that you may learn directly from God what you shall have to preach and teach* following the example of Moses who proclaimed to the people of Israel only that which God had inspired, so that he could declare, 'The Lord says this.' Vincent warned, 'Sentiments of love of God, of kindness, of good will, praiseworthy as these may be, are often suspect if they do not result in good deeds. Our Saviour said that his Father is glorified in our bearing much fruit. We should be on our guard, for it is possible to be well mannered exteriorly and filled with noble sentiments toward the Almighty in our minds and stop there. When the occasion for action arises such people fall short.'

This is typical of Vincent's practical, down to earth approach to the Christian life. The person listens to God in order to express what he or she has heard in the form of loving acts of evangelisation and service. Not surprisingly, he stressed the importance of making practical resolutions at the end of one's prayer time. They flow from one's contemplation of the presence and purposes of the Lord. He said, 'Making resolutions is one of *the* most important parts of our prayer, and perhaps the most important . . . The main fruit of prayer consists of personal resolutions strongly and firmly made. They should be resolutions which you are convinced of and which you are prepared to undertake, taking into account the obstacles to be overcome.' When God the Father asks us to say or do something, he will always give us the power to do so. In chapter four I shared how a verse in Phil 2:13 became a *rhema* word for me many years ago. It says, 'God is at work in you, both to will and to work for his good pleasure.' It makes three interrelated assertions which are well worth reflecting on.

Firstly, St. Paul says 'God is at work in you.' Not everyone is consciously aware of this wonderful truth. That is why Paul asked the Corinthian Christians the rhetorical question, 'Do you not realise that Christ Jesus is *in you*' (2 Cor 13:5). In Romans 8:9 he asserted, 'the Spirit of God *lives in you*.' Paul also said, that God the Father, 'is over all and through all and *in all*' (Eph 4:6). The three Persons of the Blessed Trinity are present, therefore, in the human heart, and they are active in their different ways within the personality.

Secondly, St. Paul says that the Lord is at work within enabling us to know and embrace the divine will. This book has been a commentary on how exactly the Lord reveals the divine purposes in ordinary and more unusual revelatory ways. As Paul said in Rm 12:2, 'be transformed by the renewal of your mind that you may discern what is the will of God.' Not only does the Lord reveal the divine will, the Spirit urges the person to embrace it no matter what the cost.

Thirdly, once the person intends to carry out God's will, he or she will be given the power in their weakness to do so. St. Paul asserted that point repeatedly in his own life. When he asked the Lord on three occasions to remove a mysterious thorn from his flesh, God replied, 'My grace is sufficient for you, for my power is made perfect in weakness' (2 Cor 12:9). Paul endorsed the truth of that promise when he said, 'I can do everything through him who gives me strength' (Phil 4:13). These important points are relevant in every aspect of daily Christian living. Once we hear the voice of the Lord, the Spirit will not only enable us to want to do God's will, no matter how difficult it might seem, it will also give us the power to do so. As 1 Peter 4:11 urged, 'If anyone serves, he should do it *with the strength God provides,* so that in all things God may be praised through Jesus Christ.'

## POWER IN POWERLESSNESS

Anyone who tries to live the Christian life in a conscientious way knows that what God asks us to do, such as avoiding temptation, overcoming an addiction, loving others unconditionally, and forgiving those who have hurt us repeatedly, is impossible from a human perspective. To help me to appreciate the implications of that point, I sometimes engage in what I refer to as my Holy Saturday meditation. I imagine that I approach the tomb of Jesus and ease myself past the stone at the entrance. Given my girth, that takes some doing! Anyway, when I get inside the tomb I find that it is very dark. But after a while my eyes get accustomed to the gloom and I can dimly see the embalmed body of Jesus lying on a shelf of rock. I go over and lie down beside him because there is enough room to do so.

I turn on my side and look at the blood stained outline of his body beneath the burial cloths. I ask myself, 'who is this lying beside me?' I am amazed as I find myself replying, 'this is Jesus Christ, the Son of God, and here he is lying beside me devoid of breath, pulse or life. The all powerful One has become utterly powerless.' Then I say to the inanimate corpse of Jesus, 'I experience lots of weakness in different areas of my life such as, overcoming sin, escaping self-absorption, having the unhesitating faith that is needed to pray effectively for others, etc.' Sometime later, I imagine that I see a blazing light illumine the tomb. I know that it is the light of the Holy Spirit, the Lord and giver of life. It invades the lifeless body of Jesus and raises it to glorious and everlasting, new life. As he ascends, I cry out to him and say, 'Lord Jesus don't forget about me, I need to experience the same power of the Holy Spirit in my weakness.'

Sometime ago I read of an extraordinary phenomenon which I hadn't heard of before. It is described by Niels Christian Hvidt in a Danish book with the lovely title, *Miracles - Meetings Between Heaven and Earth*. It contains one fascinating chapter entitled, 'The Miracle of the Holy Fire in Jerusalem' which describes an extraordinary phenomenon. With good reason Orthodox Christians regard it as perhaps the greatest of miracles and see it as a continuous reminder of the Lord's resurrection.

Apparently, for fifteen hundred years or more the 'miracle of fire' has occurred annually on Easter Saturday night in the Holy Sepulchre, in Jerusalem. Constantine the Great built the tomb in the middle of the fourth century. Since then it has been destroyed many times. The Crusaders constructed the building we see today. Around Jesus' tomb they erected a little chapel with two rooms, one in front of the tomb and then the tomb itself, which holds no more than four people. This room is the location of the miracle of fire. It has been described by a number of pilgrims over the centuries. For instance, in 1106-07 Daniel, a Russian abbot, wrote a detailed description of the holy fire which he witnessed in the course of a pilgrimage to the Holy Places.

Each year large crowds gather around the tomb. They include Christian Arabs, Greeks, and in recent years people who come from Eastern Europe and Russia. Nowadays the ceremony is broadcast live in many Christian Orthodox countries. Beginning at around 11:00 in the morning Christian Arabs chant traditional hymns in loud voices accompanied by the sound of drums and dancing. But at 1:00 p.m., the chants fade out, and there is silence. Then the Patriarch of Jerusalem enters the sepulchre. Between 1981-2000 that role was fulfilled by Archbishop Diodorus Karivalis. Before his death in 2000, which was caused by diabetes, he described what he had experienced on many occasions.

'After all the lights are extinguished, I bow down and enter the first chamber of the tomb. From here I find my way through the darkness to the inner room of the tomb where Christ was buried. Here, I kneel in holy fear in front of the place where our Lord lay after his death and where he rose again from the dead.

Praying in the Holy Sepulchre in itself for me is always a very holy moment in a very holy place. It is from here that he rose again in glory and spread his light to the world. John the Evangelist writes in the first chapter of his gospel that Jesus is the light of the World. Kneeling in front of the place where he rose from the dead, we are brought within the immediate closeness of his glorious resurrection. Catholics and Protestants call this church 'The Church of the Holy Sepulchre.' We call it 'The Church of the Resurrection.' The resurrection of Christ for us Orthodox is the centre of our faith, as Christ has gained the final victory over death, not just his own death but the death of all those who will stay close to him.

I believe it to be no coincidence that the Holy Fire comes in exactly this spot. In Matthew 28:3, the Gospel says that when Christ rose from the dead, an angel came, dressed in a fearful light. I believe that the intense light that enveloped the angel at the Lord's resurrection is the same light that appears miraculously every Easter Saturday. Christ wants to remind us that his resurrection is a reality and not just a myth; he really came to the world in order to offer the necessary sacrifice through his death and resurrection so that man could be reunited with his creator. In the tomb, I say particular prayers that have been handed down to us through the centuries and, having said them, I wait. Sometimes I may wait a few minutes, but normally the miracle happens immediately after I have said the prayers. From the core of the very stone on which Jesus lay an indefinable light pours forth. It usually has a blue tint, but the colour may change and take on many different hues. It cannot be described in human terms. The light rises out of the stone as mist may rise out of a lake - it almost looks as if the stone is covered by a moist cloud, but it is light.

This light behaves differently each year. Sometimes it covers just the stone, while other times it gives light to the whole sepulchre, so that people who are standing outside the tomb and look into it see the tomb filled with light. The light does not burn - I have never had my beard singed in all the sixteen years I have been Patriarch in Jerusalem and have received the Holy Fire. The light is of a different consistency than the normal fire that burns in an oil-lamp. 'At a certain point the light rises and forms a flame in which the fire is of a different nature, so that I am able to light my candles from it. When I thus have received the flame on my candles, I go out and give the fire first to the Armenian Patriarch and then to the Coptic Patriarch. Thereafter I give the flame to all people present in the Church.'

I find that story awe inspiring. In my Holy Saturday meditation I imagine that the blue light of the Spirit also enters me. Then I recall the following glorious words of St. Paul in Eph 1:18-20, 'I pray also that the eyes of your heart may be enlightened in order that you may know . . . his incomparably great power for us who believe. *That power is like the working of his mighty strength, which he exerted in Christ when he raised him from the dead* and seated him at his right hand in the heavenly realms.' Isn't it wonderful. God, by his Spirit, is at work within our powerlessness to give us power to live in accord with the words that God has spoken to our hearts.

Earlier in the book I quoted some words from par. 521 of the *Catechism of the Catholic Church*. They are worth recalling in this context, 'Christ [by his Spirit at work in our human weakness] enables us to live in him *all* that he himself lived, and he lives it in us.' The word 'all' in this quotation is significant because it implies that not only can we do ordinary things; if God so wills it, we will also be empowered in our weakness to do extraordinary things, even to the point of healings and miracles. At this juncture we will turn our attention to the working of what Pentecostals and Charismatics refer to as deeds of power, or signs and wonders (cf. Acts 4:30).

## DEEDS OF POWER

The Second Vatican council taught that there were two universal calls in the Christian life, the call to be holy and the call to evangelise. Pope John Paul II brought them together when he wrote in par. 90 of *Redemptoris Missio*, 'The universal call to holiness is closely linked to the universal call to evangelisation.' There is a reciprocal relationship between the two. We cannot grow in holiness without evangelising, and we cannot evangelise effectively unless we are holy. As was mentioned in another chapter, the charisms in 1 Cor 12:8-10 can be divided into three groups. Firstly there are charisms of revelation such as wisdom, knowledge, and discernment of spirits. Then there are gifts of proclamation such as the utterance of wisdom, knowledge and prophecy. Finally there are gifts of demonstration, such as faith, healings and miracle working. According to St. Thomas Aquinas the groups are interdependent. When we proclaim the Gospel, our words should be the fruit of inspirations, promptings and revelations. But those words need to be backed up by deeds. They can take many forms. Here are some examples.

Firstly, there are the seven corporal works of mercy, i.e., to feed the hungry; give drink to the thirsty; clothe the naked; shelter the homeless; visit the sick; visit the imprisoned and bury the dead. Added to these are the seven spiritual works of mercy, i.e., to instruct the ignorant; counsel the doubtful; admonish sinners; bear wrongs patiently; forgive offences willingly; comfort the afflicted; and pray for the living and the dead. Surely, Bl. Frédéric Ozanam (1813-1853) was an outstanding example of a Christian who practiced and promoted the corporal and spiritual works of mercy.

Secondly, there is action for justice, i.e., seeking out and rectifying the systemic causes of people's oppression and suffering, such as unfair and inequitable laws. Speaking about this, Pope Francis says in par. 188 of his Apostolic exhortation, *Evangelii Gaudium,* 'The Church, guided by the Gospel of mercy and by love of mankind, hears the cry for justice . . . it means working to eliminate the structural causes of poverty and to promote the integral development of the poor, as well as small daily acts of solidarity in meeting the real needs which we encounter.' William Wilberforce (1759–1833) was an outstanding example of what the Pope had in mind. He engaged in a life long campaign to abolish the grossly unjust practice of slavery in the British Empire. As members of the Society of St Vincent de Paul and others have shown, one doesn't necessarily have to be a politician like Wilberforce in order to identify and tackle the systemic causes of injustice and oppression in contemporary society.

Thirdly, there are supernatural deeds of power. St. Thomas Aquinas stated that the proof of the message shared by Christians is authenticated, among other things by, 'the evidence of works done by them such as none other than God could do, such as healing the sick and other miracles.' A number of contemporary Christians perform deeds of power such as the late Emiliano Tardif in Canada, Sr. Briege McKenna and Eddie Stones in Ireland, Damian Stayne in England and Francis McNutt and Fr. Peter Rookey in the USA. The key to performing signs and wonders is the charism of faith.

## The Charism of faith

In his catechetical lectures St. Cyril of Jerusalem (313-386) talked about this kind of faith. 'The one word faith,' he explained, can have two meanings. 'One kind of faith concerns doctrines. It involves the soul's ascent to and acceptance of some particular matter. . . The other kind of faith is given by Christ by means of a special grace ... Now this kind of faith, given by the Spirit as a special favour, is not confined to doctrinal matters, for it produces effects beyond any human capability. If a man who has this faith says to this mountain move from here to there, it will move. For when anybody says this in faith, believing it will happen and having no doubt in his heart, he then receives that grace. It is of this kind of faith, moreover, that it is said: If you have faith like a grain of mustard seed. The mustard seed is small in size but it holds an explosive force; although it is sown in a small hole, it produces great branches, and when it is grown birds can nest there. In the same way faith produces great effects . . . you may receive from him that faith too which transcends man's capacity.' It is this kind of faith that enables believers to carry out the injunction of Jesus to, 'Put out into the deep' (Lk 5:4).

As I explained in my book *Expectant Faith*, the charism of faith refers to a special grace, given to some believers, by the Holy Spirit, which enables them in particular situations, to discern with convinced and expectant faith of a heartfelt kind, that God will manifest his unconditional mercy and love as a sign of the coming of the Kingdom, through a deed of power, such as a healing, exorcism or miracle. The charism of faith can be expressed analytically by means of the following points.

1. It is a special grace, that is given to *some* by the Spirit, in order to perform an act of service.
2. It is not a gift for all situations in general, it operates in *particular* situations.
3. It is rooted in the discernment of God's, *here and now will*, by means of the gifts of revelation.
4. Knowledge of God and God's will leads to the heartfelt conviction, and trustful *expectation* that God is beginning to act in the present and will continue to act in the future.
5. God's mercy and love are manifested by a *deed of power* such as a healing, exorcism or miracle.

6. Such deeds of power *demonstrate* that the Kingdom of God has already begun to be present and is an anticipation of the end times.

## JESUS' ATTITUDE TO FAITH

It has often occurred to me when reading the gospels, that it was usually the charism of expectant faith that Jesus commended in the lives of the people he met. For example, when the Roman centurion asked Jesus to help his dying servant, he showed remarkable faith when he said, 'Lord I am not worthy to have you come under my roof, but only say the word and my servant will be healed.' Jesus was so impressed by the soldier's unquestioning confidence in his ability to heal, that he exclaimed: 'Truly, I tell you, in no one in Israel have I found such faith' (Mt 10:8;10).

On more than one occasion, Jesus admonished the apostles for their lack of this kind of expectant faith. For example, when the storm blew up on the lake, the apostles were scared of sinking. They roused their sleeping companion, 'Lord, save us!' they cried, 'we are perishing!' (Mt 8:25). With magisterial authority, Jesus calmed the sea with a word, and turning to the apostles he said, 'Why are you afraid, you of little faith?' Clearly, he was not content with the trusting faith they had exercised. Evidently he either expected them to have such confidence in God that they themselves would have been able to say to the wind and the waves, 'In the name of God, be still, be calm' (cf. Ps 107:25-30) or that they would have felt confident that they would survive the storm because Jesus was in the boat .

Jesus also spoke about the nature and need of charismatic faith. For example, when the apostles failed to exorcise a young boy, they asked: 'Why could we not cast it out?' to which Jesus replied, 'Because of your little faith. For truly, I tell you, if you have faith the size of a mustard seed, you will say to this mountain, 'Move from here to there,' and it will move; and nothing will be impossible for you' (Mt 17:19-22). On another occasion Jesus cursed a fig tree which had failed to bear fruit. The following morning when Peter drew his attention to the fact that the tree had withered overnight, the Lord replied, 'Have faith in God.' Then he went on to say, 'Truly, I tell you, if you say to this mountain, 'Be taken up and thrown into the sea,' and do not doubt in your heart, but believe that what you say will come to pass, it will be done for you. So I tell you, whatever you ask for in prayer, believe that you have received it, and it will be yours' (Mk 11:22-25). It is a remarkable promise.

## FAITH AND HEARING GOD'S *RHEMA* WORD

The gift of expectant faith, described by Jesus, is evoked by a conscious awareness of God and God's will which can be revealed in one or other of the many ways described in this book, but especially by the charisms of revelation, e.g. a word of knowledge. Writing about this important point Christopher Marshall has observed in *Faith as a Theme in Mark's Narrative,* 'The exertion of God's transcendent power, which faith seeks, is always subject to the constraint of God's will. The certainty of faith, in other words, presupposes *revelatory insight* into the divine intention, though this must be actualised by the believer's volitional commitment to refuse doubt and seek undivided faith (cf. Mk 5:36; 9:22-24).' Writing about the kind of faith Jesus advocated, Edward O' Connor observed in *Faith in the Synoptic Gospels,* 'Evidently, the faith which He is speaking of is not belief in the strict sense of assent to a truth, but the *confident expectation,* based on trust in God, which should animate our prayer. Future events, *without a special revelation about them,* can only be the object of hope and not faith.' Whatever way it comes, the revelation of God's will evokes the mustard seed of inner certainty that is characteristic of expectant faith. As St. Paul pointed out in Rm 10:17, 'faith comes from hearing the message *[rhema],* and the message is heard through the word of Christ.'

Once a person knows God's existential will for the here and now, he or she also knows that it contains the power to accomplish what it says (cf. Is 55:11). There is an example of such an revelatory word in Matthew's account of how Peter walked on water. At first the apostles were terrified when they saw Jesus coming toward them across the waves. 'Take courage!' he said, 'It is I. Do not be afraid.' Then Peter, who instinctively realised that trusting faith of the hesitant kind would not be enough in the circumstances, replied, 'Lord, if it is you, tell me to come to You.' Then Jesus spoke only one word. He said to Peter, '*Come.*' When Peter heard that revelatory *rhema* word, it was enough to remove his fear and to evoke the gift of unhesitating, expectant faith. As long as Peter relied solely on it and the One who uttered it, he could walk on water. But as soon as he adverted to gravity, wind and wave, his fear returned. He began to sink as he lapsed from expectant to hesitant faith. He cried out: 'Lord save me!' Having reached out to rescue him Jesus admonished him, 'You of little faith,' he exclaimed, 'why did you doubt?' (Mt 14:22-34).

Heartfelt faith of the expectant kind, is so sure of God's will that it acts and prays with the *conviction* that the Lord is doing something in the *present*. This kind of faith is mentioned in 1 Jn 5:14, 'This is the confidence we have in God, that if we ask anything according to his will, he hears us. And if we know he hears us in whatever we ask, we know *we have obtained* the requests made of him.' As the Letter to the Hebrews puts it: 'Faith is the assurance [in the present] of the things hoped for [in the future], the conviction [in the present] of things not seen [in the future]' (Heb 11:1). The late Derek Prince pointed out in *Faith to Live By*, 'hopes that are based on true faith in the heart will not be disappointed. But without this basis there is no assurance that our hopes will be fulfilled.'

## Praying within one's measure of faith

One way of exercising faith is by offering to pray with people who have needs of any kind. The disclosure of any need indicates a certain openness to the grace and power of God. Remember the beatitude, 'blessed are those who are poor in spirit, [i.e. who know their need of God], the kingdom of heaven is theirs' (cf. Mt 5:3). The person who is ministering can go on to ask, 'would you mind if I said that prayer for you right now?' The person being asked this question will usually say that it is okay. Then the Christian evangeliser can say, 'do you mind if I place my fingers on your forehead or shoulder?' Again, the response will usually be, 'That's okay'. The person who is offering a prayer of intercession or command could use this little formula of words to begin with. 'God is love. God loves you. Because he loves you he wants what is best for you. His love is the answer to your deepest need and the needs of the people you care about. He is beginning to respond to those needs even now as I pray.' Then you pray about the issue that the person has raised. If you receive a word of knowledge either before or during the prayer you can pray in the present rather than the future tense, with great confidence. Here is a contemporary example:

In November of 1999 I spoke at a day of renewal in the University of Nagoya, Japan. I met my interpreter Kaoru before the people arrived. She mentioned that there was a very attractive chapel nearby and added, 'you should go there, Father, to pray.' I decided to follow her advice. I asked God for guidance for the day. As I prayed to God the Father I got the impression that a middle aged woman, dressed in dark clothes, would attend the talks. She would be suffering from a painful hip, and would walk with a limp because one leg was shorter than the other. I thought to myself, I must mention that disability when we have the healing service later in the day.

The day of renewal ended with Mass. When communion had been distributed, I began to pray healing prayers. During that time of ministry I recalled the word I had received earlier in the day. I mentioned the lady with the bad hip who walked with a limp, and asked if there was anyone present who suffered from that ailment. Two hands went up. I looked at the two women and got the distinct impression that I was only authorised to pray for the woman who was directly in front of me. I left the sanctuary and walked down to where she was seated. She described her symptoms. I asked her to sit up straight with her back against the seat. Then I suggested that she raise her legs a little in front of her while keeping them together. When she did so, it was quite obvious that one leg was about two inches longer than the other. Then I asked her permission to put my hands on her bad leg in order to pray for her. She consented, and so I began to pray a prayer of command. In my mind's eye I imagined the leg stretching like rubber while thanking God that, by divine power, what we desired was happening. When the prayer was complete it occurred to me to ask the woman to again raise her legs a little in order to see if there had been any change. For a moment I hesitated. I thought to myself, what will the people think if the prayer has made no difference? Then I thought, no!, I must live by faith. So I asked the woman to raise her legs. When she did, there was an audible gasp from the many onlookers and then a spontaneous burst of applause. Thank God, the two legs were exactly the same length. When I returned to Japan two years later I made enquiries about the woman. I was told that in fact she was Korean, and a member of a prayer group in Nagoya and that her healing was complete and permanent.

When praying with someone it is important to do so within 'the measure of faith' (Rm 12:3), one has received. If one has not heard a word from the Lord one has to avoid saying a presumptuous prayer of command. For example, if I had prayed for the woman with the bad leg without having received a word of knowledge, I might have said something like this. 'Lord, nothing is impossible to you. In your Name I say to this disability, yield to the healing power of God at work within you. May the Holy Spirit, the Lord and giver of life, hasten to accomplish God's loving and life giving purposes within you. And I thank you Lord, that even now you are breathing your peace into this situation. Amen.' Notice that such a prayer is slightly agnostic and non-specific. While affirming in a *general* sense that God is at work, it does not directly address a *particular* disability e.g. arthritis, by telling it to be healed. The beauty of a prayer like this is twofold. Firstly, it allows one to go to the limit of the measure of faith one currently experiences. Secondly, it disposes the heart to receive a revelation of God's will even as one is praying. I have known a number of occasions when I started praying for someone with hesitation, but as a result of a touch of the Holy Spirit during the prayer, my faith became expectant and therefore more specific and authoritative.

## Conclusion

John Paul II said in par. 20 of *Redemptoris Missio*, 'Preaching constitutes the church's first and fundamental way of serving the coming of the kingdom.' Speaking about the importance of one-to-one evangelisation, Paul VI said in par. 46 of *Evangelii Nuntiandi* 'Side by side with the collective proclamation of the gospel, the other form of evangelisation, the person-to-person one, remains valid and important.' Pope Francis has a lot to say about that specific point in pars. 127-129 of *Evangelii Gaudium*. If these two forms of verbal evangelisation are to be authoritative and effective they will need to be rooted in an experiential awareness of the person and word of God. As Pope Paul VI said in par. 76 of *Evangelii Nuntiandi*, 'This world is looking for preachers of the gospel to speak to it of God whom they know as being close to them, *as though seeing him who is invisible.*'

In contemporary secular culture many people wonder whether God exists. Christian believers, on the other hand, take God's existence for granted and ask instead, 'what on earth is God *doing* for heaven's sake?' Their God is not a static One who exists in lonely isolation, but rather a Trinitarian God who is always active in a benevolent and dynamic way in the world. As Jesus testified, 'My Father is always at his work to this very day, and I, too, am working' (Jn 5:17-18). Whereas God once achieved the divine purposes through the life and labours of Jesus Christ, now they are achieved in and through the efforts of the members of his mystical body, the Church. Over the years I have come to appreciate the fact that God reveals the divine presence, attributes and purposes by communicating them to believers. When we sense the numinous, and hear what God the Father has to say, it is important to have that word inform and guide our actions. Having told the parable of The Sower, Jesus explained, 'As for what was sown on good soil, this is he who hears the word and understands it; *he indeed bears fruit,* [as a result of acting accordingly] and yields, in one case a hundredfold, in another sixty, and in another thirty' (Mt 13:23).

# CHAPTER FIFTEEN

# EPILOGUE

Marriage Encounter was popular in many countries, including Great Britain and Ireland, especially in the 1970s and 80s. One of the influential priests in the movement was an American Jesuit named Chuck Gallagher. I can remember how, in one of his books, he asked the important question, is love primarily a matter of relationship, or a form of service? He answered by saying that, first and foremost, it is a relationship. Service should be the expression of that relationship rather than a substitute for it, as it often is. Arguably that was the point which Luke was making in his story about Jesus' visit to the home of Mary and Martha in Lk 10:38-42. He wrote, 'he came to a village where a woman named Martha opened her home to him. She had a sister called Mary, who sat at the Lord's feet listening to what he said. But Martha was distracted by all the preparations that had to be made. She came to him and asked, 'Lord, don't you care that my sister has left me to do the work by myself? Tell her to help me!' 'Martha, Martha,' the Lord answered, 'you are worried and upset about many things, but only one thing is needed. Mary has chosen what is better, and it will not be taken away from her.'

In the 19th century, Polish artist, Henryk Siemiradzki painted a beautiful picture of this incident. Instead of being set indoors Jesus and the two sisters are depicted outdoors in the bright sunlight. Jesus is sitting on a low wall in a sort of terrace or patio. His hands are gesticulating as he talks in an animated way. Mary is sitting at his feet listening attentively. On the left hand side of the painting Martha is approaching on a short path that leads to the patio. She has a pitcher in her hand. Presumably it contains water she has just taken from an adjacent well. A number of points can be made about the incident. Firstly, as dear friends, the desire of the two women was to do what they could to make Jesus feel welcomed and appreciated. Secondly, in Luke's mind Mary represented love as relationship, and Martha represented it as service. When Martha complained that Mary was not contributing to the preparation of the meal, Jesus gently pointed out that, whereas she was anxiously preoccupied with service, Mary had chosen the better part in wanting to relate to him, and to listen to what he had to say. Mary was contemplative. Instead of talking a lot, or getting involved in many activities, she served Jesus by affording him an opportunity to speak from his heart. She paid sustained, empathic and loving attention to what he had to say. Because of her performance anxiety, Martha was mainly focused on *her role* as hospitable hostess.

Nowadays many Christians are more like Martha than Mary. Often they know about the person of Jesus while neglecting to get to know him in person. Popes John Paul II and Benedict XVI spoke a good deal about the advent of a new Springtime for Christianity. They also suggested that it would be inaugurated by a new evangelisation, one that would enkindle the fires of Pentecostal revival and renewal. However they warned that this act of service would only be effective to the extent that it was rooted in an experiential relationship with the Lord. In par. 91 of *Redemptoris Missio,* John Paul II linked contemplation and evangelisation when he wrote, 'Unless the evangelist is a contemplative he cannot proclaim Christ in a credible way. He is a witness to the experience of God, and must be able to say with the apostles: 'that which we have looked upon...concerning the word of life...we proclaim also to you' (1 Jn 1:1-3).' In 2010 Benedict XVI said something similar in his letter, *Ubicumque et Semper* (par.10), 'To proclaim fruitfully the Word of the Gospel one is first asked to have a profound experience of God.'

## Discipleship, Holiness and Divine Providence

In the introduction I said that this book was going to be a study, albeit in an implicit way, of discipleship, holiness, and the belief that God has a plan for the universe (cf Col 1:15-20) and for our collective and individual lives. God provides us with the means of carrying it out. We follow God's plan by discovering our vocation. To begin with, there is our basic calling in life, whether married or single. Then within the context of that calling, there is what could be referred to as a vocation within a vocation. For example, a lay man could feel attracted to marriage and sometime later called to become a deacon. A woman could feel called to the single life and later to a life of caring for handicapped children. Furthermore, all of us are encouraged, as John Paul pointed out in par. 85 of *Mission of the Redeemer,* to live 'a life of complete docility to the Spirit' in order to do those things which enable us to fulfil the small print of our vocational calling. It is not too surprising, therefore, to find that St. Faustina Kowalska (1905-38) wrote in section 291 of her *Diary* that faithfulness to the inspirations of the Holy Spirit is the shortcut to holiness.

The foregoing chapters have described how a person can be guided by God's Spirit, in ordinary and unusual ways, in the circumstances of everyday life. Those who know and follow the will of God are the true disciples of the Lord. As Pope Francis said to catechists at the end of September 2013, 'The first thing, for a disciple, is to be with the Teacher, to listen to him, to learn from him ... it is a journey that lasts the whole of life!' The Greek words for disciple and discipleship are the noun *mathetes*, meaning 'one who learns,' and the verb *akolouthein*, meaning 'to follow after.' Christian disciples are those who, when they learn what God wants, faithfully follow the divine will with the help of the Holy Spirit. Understood in that way, they live lives of obedience. It is worth noting that the English word obedience is derived from the Latin, *oboedire*, from *ob* 'towards,' and *audire* 'to hear.' The obedient disciple is the one who hears the word of God and lives accordingly (cf. Lk 11:28). In this way, he or she grows in the holiness of life spoken about in chapter twelve. In words that are reminiscent of those of St Faustina, St. Therese of Lisieux (1873-97) explained, 'Holiness consists simply in doing God's will, and being just what God wants us to be.'

## Conclusion

If I were asked to identify the greatest single cause of the current crisis in the Church I would reply that it is due to the fact that so many of its leaders and members are guided by human thinking rather than the mind and will of God. If we desire to see revival and renewal, e.g., by means of the new evangelisation, it will only come about when people are docile to the guidance of the Spirit in the ordinary and unusual ways which I have tried to describe in this book.

I want to conclude with some well known words of Cardinal Mercier (1851-1926) which have meant a lot to me since boyhood. 'I am going to reveal to you,' he wrote, 'the secret of sanctity and happiness. Every day for five minutes control your imagination and close your eyes to all the noises of the world in order to enter into yourself. Then, in the sanctuary of your baptised soul, which is the temple of the Holy Spirit, speak to that Divine Spirit, saying to Him:

> *O Holy Spirit, beloved of my soul, I adore you. Enlighten me, guide me, strengthen me, console me. Tell me what I should do; give me your orders. I promise to submit myself to all that you desire of me and to accept all that you permit to happen to me. Let me only know your will.*

If you do this, your life will flow along happily, serenely, and full of consolation, even in the midst of trials. Grace will be proportioned to the trial, giving you the strength to carry it and you will arrive at the Gate of Paradise, laden with merit. This submission to the Holy Spirit is the secret of sanctity. As the psalmist says, 'Show me your ways, O Lord, teach me your paths; guide me in your truth' (Ps 25:4-5). What Mercier said about individuals, applies in equal measure to Christian groups and indeed to the whole Church.

# SOME USEFUL BOOKS


### GENERAL BOOKS

Burgess, Stanley M., Eduard van der Maas,, eds. *The New International Dictionary of the Pentecostal and Charismatic Movements*. Grand Rapids, MI: Zondervan, 2002.

Doyle, David Paul. *When God Spoke to Me: The Inspiring Stories of Ordinary People Who Have Received Divine Guidance and Wisdom*. Franklin Lakes: The Career Press, 2010.

Groeschel, Benedict J. *A Still, Small Voice: A Practical Guide on Reported Revelations*. San Francisco: Ignatius, 1993.

Hvidt, Niels Christian. *Christian Prophecy: The Post-Biblical Tradition*. Oxford: Oxford University Press, 2007.

Lambertini, Prospero (Benedict XIV). *Heroic Virtues, vol., 3*. London: Richardson & Son, 1852.

Poulain, S.J., R. P. Aug. *The Graces of Interior Prayer: A Treatise on Mystical Theology*. London: Kegan Paul, Trench, Trubner & Co. Ltd., 1910.

Rahner, Karl, S.J. *Visions and Prophecies*. London: Burns & Oats, 1963.

Schwebel, Lisa J. *Apparitions, Healings & Weeping Madonnas: Christianity and the Paranormal*. New York: Paulist Press, 2004.

### Ordinary forms of guidance

De Sales, Francis. *Finding God's Will for You.* Bedford NH: Sophia Institute Press, 1998.

Green, S.J., Thomas. *Weeds Among the Wheat*. Notre Dame: Ave Maria Press, 1984.

Pacwa, S.J., Mitch. *How to Listen When God Is Speaking: A Guide for Modern-Day Catholics*. Frederick, MD: The Word Among Us Press, 2011.

Toner, S.J., Jules. *Discerning God's Will: Ignatius of Loyola's Teaching on Christian Decision Making*. St Louis: The Institute of Jesuit Sources, 1991.

### Unusual charismatic forms of guidance

Bockmuehl, Klaus. *Listening to the God Who Speaks: Reflections on God's Guidance from Scripture and the Lives of God's People.* Colorado Springs: Helmers & Howard Publishers, 1990.

Clark, Steve. *Knowing God's Will.* Ann Arbor: Servant, 1974.

Deere, Jack. *The Beginner's Guide to the Gift of Prophecy.* Ventura: Regal, 2008.

*Surprised by the Voice of God.* Grand Rapids: Zondervan, 1998.

Goll, Jim. *The Seer: The Prophetic Power of Visions, Dreams, and Open Heavens.* Shippensburg: Destiny Image, 2004.

Jacobs, Cindy. *The Voice of God: How God Speaks Personally and Corporately to his Children Today*. Ventura: Regal, 2004.

Yocum, Bruce. *Prophecy*. Ann Arbor: Servant Books, 1976.

*Further copies of this book can be obtained from*

**Goodnews Books**
*Upper level*
*St. John's Church Complex*
*296 Sundon Park Road*
*Luton, Beds. LU3 3AL*

*www.goodnewsbooks.net*
*orders@goodnewsbooks.net*
*01582 571011*

*other books by*
*by Pat Collins C.M.*
*also available*

The Gifts of the Spirit and the New Evangelisation
He Has Anointed Me
Basic Evangelisation
Gifted and Sent
Mind and Spirit
Word and Spirit